Help Yl

For Noah and Evie

Teach Yourself®

Help Your Child Succeed at School

Jonathan Hancock

For UK order enquiries: please contact Bookpoint Ltd,
130 Milton Park, Abingdon, Oxon OX14 4SB.
Telephone: +44 (0) 1235 827720. *Fax:* +44 (0) 1235 400454.
Lines are open 09.00–17.00, Monday to Saturday, with a 24-hour
message answering service. Details about our titles and how to
order are available at www.teachyourself.com

For USA order enquiries: please contact McGraw-Hill Customer
Services, PO Box 545, Blacklick, OH 43004-0545, USA.
Telephone: 1-800-722-4726. *Fax:* 1-614-755-5645.

For Canada order enquiries: please contact
McGraw-Hill Ryerson Ltd, 300 Water St, Whitby, Ontario L1N 9B6,
Canada. *Telephone:* 905 430 5000. *Fax:* 905 430 5020.

Long renowned as the authoritative source for self-guided
learning – with more than 50 million copies sold worldwide –
the *Teach Yourself* series includes over 500 titles in the fields of
languages, crafts, hobbies, business, computing and education.

British Library Cataloguing in Publication Data: a catalogue record
for this title is available from the British Library.

Library of Congress Catalog Card Number: on file.

First published in UK 2010 by Hodder Education, part of
Hachette UK, 338 Euston Road, London NW1 3BH.

First published in US 2010 by The McGraw-Hill Companies, Inc.

This edition published 2010.

The **Teach Yourself** name is a registered trade mark of Hodder
Headline.

Typeset by MPS Limited, a Macmillan Company.

Printed in Great Britain for Hodder Education, an Hachette UK
Company, 338 Euston Road, London NW1 3BH, by CPI Cox &
Wyman, Reading, Berkshire RG1 8EX.

The publisher has used its best endeavours to ensure that the URLs
for external websites referred to in this book are correct and active
at the time of going to press. However, the publisher and the author
have no responsibility for the websites and can make no guarantee
that a site will remain live or that the content will remain relevant,
decent or appropriate.

Hachette UK's policy is to use papers that are natural, renewable
and recyclable products and made from wood grown in sustainable
forests. The logging and manufacturing processes are expected to
conform to the environmental regulations of the country of origin.

Impression number   10 9 8 7 6 5 4 3 2 1
Year   2014 2013 2012 2011 2010

Acknowledgements

I owe my parents a huge debt of gratitude for the rich and happy childhood they gave me, and for the love and support they continue to show.

Thank you to everyone involved in making this book happen, especially Victoria Roddam and her team at Hodder Education; my agent, Martin Toseland and Caroline Shott, inspirational CEO of The Learning Skills Foundation.

Many teachers offered their advice and guidance at different stages of this project. I would like to thank them all, particularly Sharon Harris and Kevin Fossey at the University of Brighton. I'm very lucky to teach in a supportive and forward-thinking school; my thanks go to Joyce Jones and to all the staff, children and parents at St Mary's Primary, Portslade.

My own amazing children, Noah and Evie, supplied many of the examples in this book and helped me test all the activities and games. They inspire me every day with their delight for learning.

And to my wife, Lucy: thank you for your unwavering love, your insights and ideas, and for sharing the adventure of parenthood with me.

Image credits

Contents

Meet the author

Welcome to *Help Your Child Succeed at School*!

I was one of the lucky ones. My parents supported my learning
in countless ways: taking me to the library to find topic books;
testing me on my weekly spellings; keeping an eye on my
homework. They took an interest in what I was doing in school,
and they made it very clear that they were always there to help.

But when I look back at my childhood, I realize that my parents
did so much more for me. From the day I was born they were
boosting my chances of success, in school and beyond, by the
fundamental ways in which they shaped our family life. They
weren't pushy, 'hothouse' parents – far from it. They didn't
overburden me with their aspirations or pressurize me to
succeed. They just did what parents of successful and happy
children have always done. They gave me the core skills to be
a confident, happy learner, and made learning a completely
natural part of life at home. In the way they talked to me,
the day trips we took, the games we played, they helped me
develop the skills and attitudes that would be most useful to
me in school. Yes, they showed me flashcards and practised
times tables and bought me chemistry sets, but I'm sure it was the
everyday activities that had the greatest impact on my learning;
in particular, on the way I *felt* about myself as a learner.

To be successful in school, children need many things – and
ultimately, just one thing: the support of the people who care
the most.

My aim in writing this book is to give parents a range of
strategies to help them help their children. It explores tactics
that have worked for other parents, explains techniques that
teachers use productively in school, and reveals what the latest

research says about how we can boost our children's chances of success. It considers questions such as, which parenting styles have the biggest impact on learning? What are the key characteristics of a supportive family life? When children do really well in school, how have the adults in their lives helped them to thrive?

Every child is unique, but they all have the right to be brilliant in their own way. I hope this book reveals just how many practical things we can do to help to support their progress, enrich every aspect of their development, and nurture a love of learning that will last a lifetime.

Jonathan Hancock, Brighton 2010

Only got a minute?

Primary school offers wonderful opportunities and serious challenges. Children survive and succeed by working creatively and flexibly in a range of subject areas, completing tasks alone and with others, organizing their time and energy, performing, competing and tackling a variety of assessments and tests. To achieve their full potential, they need to be prepared for success – by you.

Children need a repertoire of thinking and learning skills. They must use their whole brain to maximum effect, combining logic and creativity, learning by seeing, hearing and doing, and playing a key role in making every lesson a rich and memorable experience. They need strategies for remembering information and for using it in new and interesting ways. As well as gaining knowledge, understanding and skills, their work in school has to shape their brain for the challenges ahead.

Your child's approach to school should be confident and excited but also respectful and calm. They must be able to motivate themselves, to listen carefully and follow instructions, and to concentrate for long enough to complete quality pieces of work. It's vital that they use their particular talents and natural styles of learning, but also that they develop the other areas of their intelligence. Strong communication skills are vital.

Children who do well at school are helped by a good diet, healthy exercise, and the right amount of rest and sleep. Your child's home life can give them everything they need to feel happy and safe, developing the ways in which they think, talk and act, and preparing them to get the very best out of every minute of every day they spend in school.

5 Only got five minutes?

Brain-building

Learning skills develop in the womb and you can take an active role in building your child's brainpower as soon as they're born. By stimulating their senses, activating their communication skills and providing a safe and secure environment for them to explore, you're helping them shape their brain for the challenges ahead. There are many different aspects of intelligence. Children need the chance to develop their full range of abilities. Your child may have a preferred learning style, but you can train them to use a wide variety of strategies for gathering, exploring and remembering information.

Learning styles

Find ways of stimulating children's visual learning, helping them to get maximum benefit from the images they see and the words they read. Train children's listening skills to help them take in all the information they hear. Children also learn by doing, so encourage them to explore by touching, holding and feeling.

Communication

Working with others in school brings opportunities and challenges. Children need to be willing to experiment, eager to embrace new experiences and ready to cope with all the complexities of joining a community of learners. Communication skills are key. Children need to be able to understand instructions, discuss activities with adults and classmates and convey their knowledge and skill in a variety of ways.

The media

Television, films, games and the internet all have a big impact on children's learning – both positive and negative. Monitor and restrict your child's access to the media, but also maximize its benefits. It can excite their imagination and help to train their memory, concentration and problem-solving skills.

Words and numbers

Parents' support is vital as children grow their core literacy and numeracy skills. Conversations, games, experiences and activities help to nurture each stage of development.

In literacy, children need to be confident with speaking and listening, reading and writing. A literate household values language, has fun with it, and seizes every opportunity to use it well. To be good at maths, children need to develop a core understanding of numbers, patterns, shapes and measures. You can help to make maths exciting and fun and use it to stimulate your child's thinking skills.

Social life

The modern primary curriculum is rich and varied. Your child needs flexible skills to do well in each area and to find ways of connecting different strands of learning. They also need to have the right attitude to school, and you play a huge role in shaping their respect for teachers and the patterns of behaviour they have to adopt. Children need to be confident and communicative, but also to know their place in school; their responsibilities as well as their rights.

Healthy childhood

Diet has a major impact on children's success in school. The brain needs key nutrients to develop properly and to work at its best. Physical activity boosts mental success, and sports and games teach children about themselves as well as how to work well with others. Good sleep is also crucial, so parents need to establish bedtime routines that give bodies and brains all the rest they need.

The family

Family life can reflect all that's best about thinking and learning. Take every chance you get to stimulate children's interests and to excite them about developing new areas of knowledge and skill. Talk to them about their thoughts and feelings and encourage them to reflect on what their brain can do – and how they can use it better.

Tests

Children are assessed and tested more than ever before. With a strategic and organized approach and practical support from home, it's possible to take the stress out of tests. Make sure you know what they're doing and how well they're getting on, and use results and reports to help them plan their next steps forward.

New challenges

Moving on to secondary school can be a daunting prospect, but there are many ways to ease the transition. You child's thinking skills will help them to gather information, access support, and make positive moves to control their emotions. Help them to reflect on the balance of their day and to take responsibility for their own achievement and happiness.

Succeeding together

Brilliant children work in partnerships: with their parents, their friends, their schools, and with all the communities of learners they join. This book is about providing sensitive guidance, practical support, rich opportunities, and the love and security that children need more than anything to achieve their full potential in school.

10 Only got ten minutes?

Brilliant brains

As a teacher, it's easy to spot the children who've been equipped for brilliance. They come from varied backgrounds and different sorts of families; they have their own personalities, interests and skills; but in everything they say and do, they provide evidence of the support they've received at home.

Brilliant children have strong communication skills. Their particular talents may lie in talking, writing, using sign language or drawing pictures, but the important thing is that they can communicate clearly and appropriately and change their style to suit different situations and audiences.

Successful children tend to have very powerful imaginations. They use their keen senses to activate their creativity and they seize every opportunity for make-believe. They borrow from books, films, theatre shows and computer games to inspire their own imaginative ideas.

But these children can also think logically. They use their understanding of structure and order to organize their thinking, prioritize their ideas, and make clear connections. They're used to explaining themselves and arguing their point of view.

Their crucial skill lies in using both sides of their brain at once. They can combine unstructured, creative thinking with detailed analysis and logical thought.

Learning skills

Successful children have favourite ways to learn, but they're not limited by them. They strengthen their visual learning by creating their own memorable images. They extend auditory learning by writing rhymes and songs and adding sound clues to their memories. They take every opportunity to learn physically, touching objects and constructing models.

The children that do really well in school know how to switch on their learning. Their family life involves traditions that help to structure memory and celebrate it. In school, they use their memory skills to follow instructions and look after their property as well as to boost every area of their learning.

Brilliant children work well with others. They can make the most of their personality and they know how to find a clear role; but they're also developing other aspects of their character and trying out new positions on the team. Sometimes they're the leader: directing the group, assigning jobs, planning the project.

Different thinkers and learners

Natural puzzle solvers are highly motivated to find answers and achieve results. They pursue definitive answers and keep the team going when others want to give up.

Some children are eager investigators. They have a wide variety of interests outside school and they adore sharing their passions with others.

Many brilliant children have visionary ideas, and they've come to expect adults to value them. They formulate big theories and give their teams ambitious plans to pursue.

Natural builders love construction projects and often take the lead in hands-on tasks. They've been given many opportunities to make things at home and picked up some useful craft skills.

For other brilliant children, writing is their first love. The story tellers in class have been brought up with books, love reading and having stories read to them, and can use their understanding of sequences and patterns to organize their thinking and direct group tasks.

It's possible to be a rebel and achieve great things in school. Rebellious thinkers tackle problems in imaginative ways and bring excitement and humour to teamwork.

Some children's genius lies in their ability to perform and entertain. They've usually been given generous opportunities to sing, dance and act at home, and they love having an audience in school.

Brilliant talkers love sharing their ideas, asking and answering questions and discussing the best ways to approach every piece of work.

Some children are born entrepreneurs. They've always been rewarded for their hard work and they respond well to incentive-schemes in school. Their competitive spirit drives their achievement in a range of tasks.

Whether working alone or with others, children's brilliance comes out in many different forms. Their talents may be musical, sporting or artistic. To achieve their full potential they need to tap into their gifts to help them cope with the many and varied challenges of school.

Success in school

Brilliant children have strong literacy skills before they even get to school. They have access to a wide selection of books at home. Their parents have nurtured their reading skills, encouraging them to use all the clues available as they learn to decode text. They also have plenty of opportunities to write: diaries, postcards, shopping lists, emails. They use their imagination to write creative stories of their own.

Successful children have also been brought up to be confident with maths. Their homes value numeracy, helping them to build up a core vocabulary of mathematical words by discussing numbers, shapes and measures as part of their everyday life.

In fact, their life outside school prepares them for every aspect of their education. They've become scientists by discussing their ideas about the world around them. Their families have helped them to discover answers for themselves and to explore all their ideas about science.

They're already confident with ICT (Information and Communication Technology), able to experiment with a range of equipment. They've been trusted to use computers, cameras and other electronic gadgets around the home.

Successful children have developed an interest in geography and a core level of understanding about places and people. They have a strong sense of where they live, and ideas about where they'd like to go.

Their home life has also prepared them to study history. They're used to talking about the past, present and future. They've had opportunities to visit historic buildings and to see, hear and touch evidence from the past.

Artistic children have been encouraged to experiment with different materials and styles. They come from families that value art, displaying pictures and photographs and choosing objects for their form as well as their function.

They also know how to design and build. They come to school with good craft skills and advanced fine motor control. They've talked about how things work, discussed their design ideas, and now they're ready to show off all their practical skills in school.

Family life must also nurture children's musical interests and talents. When a child has been sung to, given simple instruments to bang and shake, played a wide range of musical styles, and encouraged to discuss their likes and dislikes, they're ready to be brilliant in Music lessons at school.

Sporting achievements in school also depend heavily on activities at home. Children need opportunities to play the sports and games they love, and to try completely new ones. Children who talk about health and fitness at home are ready to make the most of all the physical opportunities in school.

Some children speak different languages at home, or have had the chance to develop their foreign language skills abroad. Learning a new language in school requires children to be flexible thinkers and confident communicators, able to use their imagination and to relish new challenges.

Brilliant children can apply their talents to exploring religion, faith and philosophy. They've been given access to other communities and encouraged to respect everyone's ideas and beliefs. The empathy and understanding they experience at home rubs off on all their relationships in school, helping them to develop secure friendships.

Heading for success

Brilliant children apply themselves to every task they face. They use all their thinking and learning skills in lessons, homework, and in tests and exams. They've been prepared to try their best without worry or stress, given the time and space to revise, helped with organization and planning, and equipped with strong study skills to make every part of the learning process easy and fun.

High achievers benefit from a healthy lifestyle. The quality of their diet is clear in the packed lunches they bring in and the school meals they choose. They know why breakfast is so important and remember to drink water throughout the day, maintaining their concentration and focus. They enjoy exercise: for the way it makes them feel, the chance it gives them to achieve and shine, and the opportunities it provides to learn about themselves and others.

Successful children get good sleep. They arrive at school rested and alert. They've been brought up to have regular bedtimes and relaxing evening routines, and they expect to feel tired at the end of a busy day.

It's no accident that some children do really well in school. Whatever their family circumstances, however much money or time or space they have, their families make sure that they're stimulated and entertained in a variety of positive ways. The love and support of others merges into their own desire to be brilliant, making primary school the launch pad for their long-term happiness and success.

Introduction

The single most important factor in your child's success is you. More sensitive about their needs and more concerned about their future than anyone else, you are best placed to help them achieve their full potential. Babies are born with an automatic desire to become learners, to explore the world around them, to develop all the knowledge and skills they need to thrive. How they progress in that quest is very much down to the adults close by.

The scientific proof has been there for decades. A research study in the 1960s tested 5,000 children at ages 8, 11 and 15. It looked at school results alongside evidence about family background and parenting, and its conclusions were very clear. The most significant influences on a child's achievement were the level of interest they received from their parents; their parents' hopes and aspirations; and the kind of lives their parents led themselves.

A recent project in the UK, 'Numbers Count', gave an insight into why parents can make all the difference. This 12-week project was designed to support children who were falling behind in maths. Although the one-to-one tuition the children received was delivered by teachers, the approach they took was much more like that of a concerned parent:

▶ *working with just one child, not a class of 32*
▶ *discussing maths and sharing personal ideas*
▶ *playing fun games with numbers*
▶ *using props that the children could touch and hold*
▶ *singing counting songs*
▶ *finding real, practical uses for maths, like saving and spending money.*

The results were remarkable and made national news. Thirty-two per cent of the children added between 6 and 11 months to their 'mathematical age', and both teachers and parents reported striking changes in the children's abilities, interest and confidence in maths.

For many of the children, 12 weeks of personal tuition was all it took to bring them back in line with their peers and equip them with the learning skills to keep up. The long-term benefits of the project will now be evaluated, but the early results are impressive enough for it to be rolled out nationwide along with several other similar schemes. What they have all shown is the impact of close, practical, fun teaching – which is just the sort of support that parents are best placed to give.

Your child is in school for only 15 per cent of their time. Teachers do their best to give them the education they deserve, but what they deserve even more is interest, direction and practical help from the people that mean the most to them; the people who were there from the word go.

New research shows just how significant that support can be. Children from caring, nurturing backgrounds consistently perform better in school. So what is it about these families that help their youngest members to succeed?

Since before they were born, your child has been learning how to learn. Their brain has developed into an astonishingly complex mechanism, where electrical impulses and chemical reactions work together to perform miraculous feats of information-management and data-handling. Nature, nurture and each new learning challenge have combined in a process of physical brain-building and mental habit-forming. Your child has developed a personal approach to exploring, testing, remembering and applying knowledge and skills. They have designed the way their unique brain learns, and that process will continue for the rest of their life.

But these early years are the vital ones. This is when the most significant developments in learning skills occur; when life at home and experiences in school have the potential to make every child a confident, creative and committed lifelong learner.

This book has been written to help children and their families make the most of this rich and exciting time. The modern primary school offers wonderful opportunities for learning. Supported and strengthened by life outside the classroom, children can build firm foundations in all school subjects and master the really important social and personal skills. At the same time they can develop a way of thinking that helps them cope with all the challenges still to come.

Although they might not always admit it, children love learning. From day one they're investigating the world around them to collect information about surviving, thriving and having fun. They even choose to test themselves. What child can resist walking along a wall – just to see if they can; pushing themselves to balance the highest tower of bricks; or giving themselves a score out of ten in their own personal test of goal shooting, car-spotting or pavement-crack dodging? With the right kind of help, your child can be proud of their knowledge and skills, set the highest targets for themselves, and begin to take responsibility for their continuing success.

Learning needs to be a partnership: between children, schools, families and the wider community. There are some very famous examples of this working to achieve brilliance.

Wolfgang Amadeus Mozart had an extremely supportive father, who transported him around the courts of Europe and provided him with the emotional and practical backing to make the most of his talents. Leonardo da Vinci relied on the support of patrons and mentors to bring his remarkable ideas to life. Marie Curie's father encouraged her early interest in science by showing her the equipment he'd used in his own experiments. Albert Einstein's parents spotted his talents early and helped him cope with setbacks at school. Just like you, these parents knew that their child was unique and wanted to help them find their best path to achievement and fulfilment.

Our views on success and the things we value in children's learning may have changed over the centuries, but these famous names still shine out as valuable examples of brilliance, and how to nurture it. Their creative, flexible, ambitious minds were given the practical and emotional conditions to thrive, just as your child's natural talents can be discovered, supported and maximized today.

There are plenty of benefits for all involved in the 'team', not least the wonderful sense of shared pride in a child's success. There are also potential barriers – particularly time, with teachers negotiating a crowded curriculum, and family life feeling ever more hectic and full. With this firmly in mind, the research findings, advice and activities in these pages are all focused on making the most of every learning experience, rather than adding more pressure. The book is designed to be a practical guide, helping parents of primary age children understand what goes on in schools today and what they can do to support and enrich it. In the car, around the meal table, at bedtime, on holiday: there are endless opportunities to activate and enrich those essential learning skills.

Even young children are challenged to use their brains in many different ways. As soon as they start primary school, they're likely to be taking charge of their uniform, equipment, lunchbox, sports gear and club money before they even leave the house. At breakfast club they could be relating to older children and unfamiliar adults. Arriving in the classroom, there are letters to be handed in and property to be organized before the school day even begins. And once it does, your child will be learning in a variety of subject areas, some taught discretely, others combined or overlapped. Sometimes they'll work independently; on other occasions in pairs, small groups or as a whole class. Their lessons will challenge them to investigate, solve puzzles, discuss, debate, plan, draft, improve, assess... They'll need to make choices about what they do and how they do it. Their work will have to be presented in a number of different written and spoken forms, sometimes in front of an audience, sometimes as part of assessments and tests. Their day may even involve a rehearsal for the school play, trips out or visitors in school, responsibilities as a monitor or prefect, activities in the lunchtime maths club, after-school football practice, homework to complete, consent forms to be signed and money collected – before the whole process starts again tomorrow.

There are so many different areas of knowledge and skills being stimulated and tested every day, so there's no shortage of areas in which parents can help.

The 'core' subjects in primary school are Literacy, Numeracy and Science, with ICT (Information and Communication Technology) now also receiving special recognition. There are clear guidelines for how much time is devoted to these subjects, along with PE (Physical Education) and RE (Religious Education) – although the precise details of this are agreed locally. The remaining areas of study, the 'foundation' subjects, are Art, Design and Technology (DT), Music, History, Geography and PSHE (Personal, Social and Health Education and Citizenship).

Schools may be 'faith schools' of different types, aided and influenced by religious organizations and denominations. Clearly this affects the character and ethos of the school, but so too does the school's history; its head teacher, staff and governing body; the wider community around it, and of course the particular children and families linked to it at any one time.

While schools are dynamic organizations, education policies are also in a continual state of flux. The rules and guidelines governing what schools teach and how they teach it are always changing, as is the process by which they are monitored and assessed. Schools are under constant pressure to survive inspections, meet government targets and do well in league tables. At the same time, successful schools are being given more freedom to adapt their curriculum and to try out new ideas. There's a growing emphasis on flexibility as schools regain the power to choose how they want to teach the particular children sitting in front of them. In many primary schools this involves a return to something like the 'topic' teaching of old. Themes are chosen, lasting half or even a whole term, and individual school subjects are taught in more creative and connected ways. A topic lesson on 'The Romans', 'Chocolate' or 'Africa' might involve literacy, science, history, art, music and more, all interwoven and taught in context as a way of exciting children and deepening their understanding.

Some schools have removed the subject labels altogether. Others are experimenting with just a few subjects or in particular age groups, and there are still those who teach all the subjects discretely and follow nationally designed units of work. Primary schools are more varied and different than they've ever been.

The need for parents to understand what's going on in school has never been greater. And for children, a robust and flexible approach is vital if they're going to cope with changing demands and make the most of the exciting opportunities that come their way.

At its best, learning is exciting and absorbing, teaching your child meaningful knowledge and skills in ways that they can remember and apply. It also demonstrates how to learn, continuing the delicate process of self-programming that began in the womb.

To be a confident and successful learner, your child will need to develop their own repertoire of effective thinking skills. High on the list are organization, creativity and communication. Even young children are called on to:

▶ *make subtle decisions*
▶ *assess their own work, and their friends'*
▶ *discuss complex ethical, moral and philosophical questions.*

The sooner they can engage confidently with these varied challenges, the better they are at shaping their thinking – and the more motivated and ambitious their learning development will be.

Effective learners are happy and fulfilled. They share their knowledge with family and friends and give back to their communities. They make the most of all the opportunities their school has to offer, and every success propels their next step forward.

Even before your child starts school you can be preparing them for the challenges ahead. Once they reach the classroom, every part of family life can be shaped to support their school career. And it really doesn't have to feel like hard work. I know from experience how tiring parenting can be; but as a teacher I'm also aware of the huge difference it makes when a child's home life nurtures their learning. The games and activities in this book are designed to be interesting and fun for everyone involved, developing thinking and learning skills as part of everyday family life. There are many practical and satisfying ways to achieve a strong home/school partnership, with your child at the very centre.

Part one of this book is about switching on your child's learning skills to help get them ready for school. A warm-up of the whole brain and its full range of thinking skills, it explains how to discover your child's natural talents, along with the areas that need more development. It explores the latest theories about learning styles, outlining powerful techniques to shape children into fully rounded learners. There are strategies for developing your child's concentration and focus, including ideas to help even the youngest children start to take charge of their learning.

Part two gives detailed guidance about every subject in school. It offers ideas for complementary activities to try at home and a range of quick and easy strategies for supporting and deepening learning. There are techniques for managing behaviour, boosting confidence, and supporting children as they take on new roles and responsibilities.

Part three explores the overall impact of family life on success in school. It presents the latest research into nutrition and mental performance, along with activities to promote physical health and good sleep. The exercises here involve the whole family in a child's learning life, as well as making powerful connections with the wider community. There's advice on tackling the final challenges of primary school, including tests and exams, and ideas to ease the transition from primary to secondary education.

Throughout the book there are activities, experiments and games to try with your child. Some of them are designed with a particular age group in mind, but most of them are for you to use as and when you think they might help. You know your child best, and the collaborative nature of this book offers you many opportunities to get to know them even better, especially the ways in which they think and learn. The more closely you engage with their thought processes, the more you'll find out about key aspects of their character. You'll recognize areas they need to work on, as well as particular talents that can be tapped into, in and out of school.

Try any of the activities you think could help your child and tailor them to suit their age and ability. Playing a seemingly childish game can be a great way of encouraging older children to discuss their learning and explore refreshing new angles of thought. Younger children often find it exciting and enriching to be pushed beyond their comfort zone. Encourage your child to discuss the activities with you: what works, what doesn't, what they enjoy, and any ideas they have for getting even more out of your time together.

To be successful in school, children need to be flexible, confident learners, able to motivate themselves, pursue their own interests, and apply their skills and knowledge to a wide range of challenges and opportunities – many of which are still unimagined.

The internet has changed they way we view knowledge. Accessing facts and figures is now the easy bit. The rote learning prized by the Victorians simply no longer matches the subtle skills required to evaluate, manipulate and apply the infinite information at our fingertips.

Family structures have also changed. Homes and families come in all shapes and sizes, just as every child is unique. Many key principles apply to everyone, but there's certainly no 'one size fits all' approach. Use the advice and exercises offered by this book to discover what works best for your child and your family. Remember, parenting is a two-way process. Watch and listen carefully, give them the time and attention they need and your child will teach you many of the most important lessons about parenting.

Keeping a diary can help practically, as well as leaving you with a fascinating record of their childhood. Make notes about your child, and about you. Record the way their learning develops; the activities that seem to have most impact on them; the moments when they show you new skills or make breakthrough discoveries; and all your observations and feelings along the way.

With understanding and practical support from the people around them, every child can enjoy a happy, rich and fulfilling primary school career. They can teach their parents a thing or two along the way and emerge with the confident and flexible brain skills necessary for an exciting life of learning.

Part one

Getting ready for school: preparing children to be brilliant

1

Your child's brainpower: how to activate it

In this chapter you will learn:
- *how children's brains develop*
- *the importance of stimulating your child's senses*
- *strategies for developing key thinking skills*
- *ways of activating your child's memory*
- *how to interest children in their own learning.*

Building your child's brain is a joint operation. The genes they've inherited provide foundations and set up some aspects of thinking and learning skills; but even before birth, parents are working with their children to design and construct their brain, to 'hardwire' it for the challenges to come. It's both a huge responsibility and an opportunity to be seized and celebrated.

Learning begins

Research has proved that babies can learn in the womb. One study involved parents playing particular tunes repeatedly to their unborn babies. After birth, scientists found that the babies responded differently to the music they'd heard before.

It seems that, to survive, our children are born ready to learn, searching for details about their environment and the people around them.

At just one month old, babies can sort faces, holding their gaze longer when looking at people they've seen before. As they process this information, they're shaping their brains and dictating how their mental structures develop. They're learning how to learn.

The experiences children have at the very start of their lives have a big impact on the thinking skills they develop. It's a wonderful time for parents to get involved and help.

Insight

We learn at a faster rate and in a more intense way during our first three years than at any other time in our lives. What we learn and how we learn it is fundamental to our development. Although active from the start, our memory skills quickly strengthen as we grow.

At two months old, babies can remember an event – but for no more than two or three days.

By one year they can remember an important person or notable event for several months. They're able to copy something that they've seen only once.

At two years, children have the capacity to recall more details of an event: who did what, when and where. Depending on their language skills they can often describe a variety of things that have happened during the day.

Three-year-olds use language as a key tool for remembering and learning – a hugely significant step forward. Flexibility with words gives them the ability to store information in much more subtle ways, organizing memories to make accessing and using them easier.

By the age of four, our children are aware of themselves as learners. They can direct their brains specifically to learn new things, and they can say what they know – and what they've forgotten. But short-term memory storage is still limited, the systems still being built. It seems that the emphasis in these early years is on gaining the most useful long-term knowledge and skills to survive.

Five-year-olds' brains are much better at connecting new learning with stored knowledge and linking different memories together. They show more of the flexibility that we take for granted as adults, but which has only come through the process of brain-building that's been going on since birth.

At six years, children know that memories are strengthened by rehearsal and repetition. They can learn consciously, test themselves, and find clever ways to boost their memory.

A seven-year-old who has progressed safely through all these stages of mental development is able to remember in a way that's both organized and creative. Their memories are stored in complex ways, sorted into interconnected categories. They can use the things they know to write imaginative stories, solve problems and make decisions – including about where to take their learning next.

So the journey a child takes to being a conscious and confident learner begins with their DNA, but is then affected – for good and bad – by everything and everyone they encounter in those early years; and, crucially, by the way in which they use their brain. Helping them to use it well, to build a brain that's ready for all the challenges ahead, is what this book is all about.

The first few months: stimulating the senses

The emphasis in the early weeks and months should be on activating the senses and providing a safe and secure environment in which to start learning. Your young baby is eager to know about the world into which they've arrived, but they've got limited ways of exploring it. Helping them to make the most of their senses stimulates their thinking and brain-building.

A baby's vision focuses at around 20 cm – just right for seeing the face of the person holding them – and parents quickly learn to place objects in the right place to be seen.

Insight

Contrasts and clear shapes are vital for a baby to see well. Scientists have discovered that babies need to see their parents' hairlines – that is, where their face 'ends' – to be able to process the face and remember it.

There are some great black-and-white shape books on the market for babies. A simple mobile strung with clear shapes in contrasting colours will keep a baby entertained and engaged. As they watch it sway and turn just above them, they're strengthening their eyesight as well as boosting their brain's ability to process shapes and patterns.

Most parents naturally talk and sing to their babies in a higher pitch than normal – and there's good reason for this. Babies find it easiest to hear sounds in the high frequency range. They're missing a small bone in their inner ear which carries low sounds to the brain, protecting them from being deafened by their mother's heartbeat. In fact, their hearing is weaker in general to guard them from their own crying! So stimulate your baby's developing sense of hearing with a range of different sounds: rattles, toys, music boxes; natural sounds like wind, water and birdsong; and a variety of voices. If they can remember music from when they were still in the womb, they can certainly build their brain's memory structures by listening to tunes and songs in the first months after birth.

Touch is also important from day one. Babies need physical contact for reassurance and they enjoy stroking and massage. At birth they tend not to respond to gentle touch, but their sensitivity quickly improves along with their ability to reach out and grasp, prodding and feeling the things around them. Giving them a range of textures to explore nurtures their ability to feel differences and to start sorting the sensations they receive in subtle ways.

As babies become more co-ordinated and more mobile, they quickly progress to tasting and smelling the things around them. Provide them with safe things to put in their mouth and encourage this vital stage of their development.

Sensory overload is easy, so look for signs that your baby is being over-stimulated. But take your lead from them and you'll see how keen they are to study faces and clear shapes, to listen to gentle sounds and to connect with their world through touch, smell and taste – all within an environment that's calm and safe. By activating your child's senses from day one you're helping them to build a personal database of sense information. They're learning to separate and sort the information they receive, to make decisions about the bits they prefer, and to remember some of the details of their experiences. They're building their capacity to learn, and developing an appreciation of senses that will be vital to their learning in the long run.

LANGUAGE AND LEARNING

Equally important is their ability and confidence with language. By three months, babies are becoming conversationalists, babbling and cooing and exchanging sounds with the people close to them. To develop into confident thinkers and learners, children need excellent skills of communication, both with others and with themselves. Parents have a crucial role to play from the very start.

Well before word skills develop, children are building the key language structures in their brain, laying the foundations for talking, reading and thinking in words and clear ideas. When you talk and sing to your baby you teach them about the rhythms and sounds of language and help them to hear differences in tone and pitch. You also encourage them to talk and sing back to you, shaping and strengthening their own language systems.

Successful children chat with their parents. They use language to express themselves, to explore their thoughts and ideas and to help them learn. The earlier you start the better, talking to your child in a way that's appropriate to their age and ability and a completely natural part of family life.

As young children experience new things, give them the words to describe what's going on. Repeat the words, making clear links with whatever senses might help them to understand and remember the word, for example: 'What a beautiful banana. Such a yellow banana (lick your lips). I bet it's going to taste *so* sweet and delicious. It smells so fresh. Listen to how squashy this banana is as I mash it up. Do you love banana? Can you say "banana"?'

Obviously you won't be talking like this all the time! Being a parent is exhausting enough, and you need time and space for your own thoughts and conversations. Besides, it's good for children to hear a range of speech styles. But when you do engage with them in this close, structured way, they'll feel particularly special, and you can be confident that you're helping them develop their interconnected language and learning skills.

When your child says something particularly valuable, echo it back to them: 'Yes you're right, it *is* sunny today!' As well as reinforcing their thoughts, extend their ideas: 'It's *so* sunny, I think we need to put our hats on, don't you?' Encourage their brains to go further and to see both logical and creative connections: 'We need hats to keep us safe; but what colour hat do you feel like today?'

As your child's speech develops, occasionally rephrase their words, improving their accuracy in a way that breeds confidence, for example:

> **Child:** *'Tommy be's hot.'*

> **Adult:** *'Yes, Tommy is hot. Tommy is so hot he needs to take off his jacket.'*

Child: *'We done that the day after yesterday Mummy.'*

Adult: *'You're right! We did do that the day before yesterday; that was Wednesday…'*

RHYMES AND SONGS

Classic action rhymes like 'This little piggy' are a great way to teach babies and young children about language. Steady rhythms, memorable rhymes and all the accompanying touching and tickling make for delightful and powerful learning experiences. These mini works of art are deceptively complex and rich in meaning.

A clapping song like 'Pat-a-cake, Pat-a-cake, baker's man' helps children to explore the way sounds make up words which then become phrases with meaning. The claps show that some words are more important than others. Your child's brain sorts the words by rhyme ('man/can') and alliteration ('pat it and prick it'), making subtle observations and distinctions. They're practising their memory skills, tuning in their brains to rhythms and patterns, developing physical co-ordination (even if you're patting your baby's hands for them) and experiencing the fun of learning with someone they love.

These rhymes are treasures of shared memory that have been passed down through countless generations. Their familiarity can be as comforting to adults as to children, and they remind us that repetition – of words, events, traditions – is an important part of feeling safe and secure. Children love discussing routines and rituals, whether they're mundane chores like washing the clothes or rare and special moments like Christmas morning. It's an extremely important part of their mental development.

Discuss jobs with children while you're doing them. For babies and toddlers, make the most of bath time, table setting or the regular weekly shopping trip. Chat about the order in which things happen and the logic of organizing it this way. Recall the last time you did it together and look ahead to the next. Use conversation to help your child build the mental structures they'll need to become organized and confident thinkers and learners.

Talking is also vital for stretching children's abilities. Through clever questions, parents can learn about their child's thinking and challenge it to go further, at the same time as introducing the language of thinking itself. For example:

'Remember when...?'
'What's your best idea for...?'
'How did you work out...?'
'Is that how you imagined...?'

This process is called 'metacognition' or 'thinking about thinking': describing, discussing and evaluating what's going on in your own head. Metacognition plays a key role in your child's success in school. Primary teaching increasingly involves children in the learning process, challenging them to work on specific thinking skills, to make decisions about how to use their brain to tackle particular challenges, and to assess and discuss their success. The more aware they become of their thinking skills, the better equipped they are to develop and use a range of effective strategies to calculate, imagine, remember and learn.

By stimulating their senses, developing their language skills and providing them with opportunities to explore their own thinking, you're shaping the way your child's brain grows. These are themes that will reappear many times throughout this book, just as they're vital to children throughout their lives.

Your seven-year-old will probably not need to be given safe plastic toys to put into their mouth, but they will need to experience a range of tastes. Your nine-year-old may not jump at the chance to sing 'One, two, buckle my shoe' with you, but they'll certainly welcome help to organize mathematical concepts in creative and memorable ways. Your 11-year-old should be able to use a range of strategies to prepare for tests and exams – but only because they've been thinking about thinking for as long as they can remember.

The following activities are labelled for particular ages purely as starting points. They can all be returned to at different stages and reframed to match your child's needs. Older children will often enjoy revisiting activities they remember from the past, and you can become more and more explicit about the thinking that's going on.

From one year: make problem-solving fun

Questions play such an important role in learning. They're prompts to think and respond in certain ways – and invitations to be brilliant. As a teacher, I'm very aware of children's differing ability to understand and tackle questions. Some are scared by them, immediately confused, powerless to imagine where they might go in their mind to find answers. They're often the children who struggle with behaviour and friendships, unable to question themselves about what's going on or to look for the answers that might just make things better.

But other children have been brought up to enjoy the challenge of questions, their brains built to help them explore all the possibilities. They feel confident that pursuing answers can be enjoyable and helpful in many different situations.

So, when you and your one-year-old are faced with a question, use it as an opportunity to solve it together. Show your child some of the techniques you use when you're looking for answers, modelling strategies that they can try themselves.

Start with an exaggerated expression of puzzlement. Widen your eyes, open your mouth, raise your shoulders and open out your hands to mime, 'There's a problem, oh dear, what are we going to do?' Your child responds quickly to your facial clues so they're likely to engage with this mood of questioning straight away. Make sure they can tell – from a smile, a glint in the eye – that this problem is going to be fun to solve. Look around you for a moment, emphasizing that you'll need to search for help from different directions. Scratch your head to tell your child that answers can sometimes be found in there.

Next, you need to say exactly what the question is. This is such an important habit for children to get into, and one that will pay dividends in a wide range of situations: emotional problems, exams, key life decisions. For young children, speak slowly and clearly and give your words dramatic impact: 'Teddy has gone missing.' Say it a few times, and rephrase it to help build understanding of the dilemma: 'Teddy has gone missing, he's not here. Where is he? We need to find Teddy!'

Then, ask the most important question in any problematic situation: 'What are we going to do?' There's a lovely rhythm to this phrase. Say it a few times and it becomes almost a mantra with a rhythmical quality that's warm and reassuring. Think of Dorothy and her friends in *The Wizard of Oz*, chanting as they enter the forest: 'Lions and tigers and bears, Oh my! Lions and tigers and bears, Oh my!' Michael Rosen's classic picture book *We're Going on a Bear Hunt* reflects the way that rhythm and repetition, in words and ideas, help to set up our brains to look for answers. The family members in this book overcome a series of obstacles on their way to the bear's cave, always confident that they'll be able to solve every problem. With your own child, approach questions with exaggerated confidence. After all, even if you don't find Teddy right away, you know there'll be other things you can try. You're not scared to pursue the answer until you find the solution – which is such a wonderful attitude to encourage as you prepare your child for all the challenges of school.

So, where *is* Teddy? As you lead this particular bear hunt you can model so many useful problem-solving strategies for your child:

> You say: *'Can we remember what Teddy looks like and smells like? Can we spot him or sniff him out now?'*

> You demonstrate: *that all our senses can be used to help us remember, think creatively and explore our ideas.*

You say: *'Let's have a look in every room in the house, one by one.'*

You demonstrate: *that being systematic is important in solving problems.*

You say: *'Let's stop and relax for a moment. Maybe we can just guess where Teddy has gone?'*

You demonstrate: *that sometimes answers are found by using intuition, gut instinct or good old-fashioned common sense.*

However you find Teddy – and even if you don't get to him straight away – you're showing your young child a range of effective problem-solving strategies. By modelling them through a relaxed, enjoyable, shared experience, you're helping to embed them as very attractive thinking habits for the future.

From two years: collect treasure

A small wicker basket is already an enjoyable object for your child to touch and carry. But fill it with some special treasures and it becomes something to excite their senses, boost their memory and engage them in inquisitive exploration.

Treasures can be found anywhere. Look for items that are safe and interesting to touch, smell, and probably taste. Include a range of colours and make sure a few of the objects make a sound. Natural and man-made, hard and soft, rough and smooth; the collection should be as varied as possible. Pine cones, shells, a wooden ball, an oddly shaped stone, Russian dolls, castanets, a football medal... It's not hard to gather together a personal collection of treasures which your child will love to test, explore, sort, hide and 'discuss' with you as you share in a variety of learning games. It's a great way to develop a subtle awareness of senses, along with a bank of words to go with them. It gives a fantastic early boost to your child's scientific interest, knowledge and skill.

You can use treasure baskets to test and enhance memory: Can your child work out which object has been removed? When you put the items in pairs, can they remember which went with which? Over time, as you make small changes to the collection of objects, does your child notice the items you've added?

Insight

Use objects that activate shared memories: a pebble from a trip to the beach, for example, or a tree decoration from their first Christmas. Challenge your child to put them in order and talk to them about all the feelings attached to these special souvenirs. Your treasure basket can grow along with your child, opening up new dialogues about learning and becoming a treasured family record.

From three years: help them to pretend

Your child will love to play make-believe games. Tapping into their imagination at any stage in their childhood is a great way to support their learning. Make sure they get plenty of unstructured time to have fun in their own imaginary worlds, alone and with friends, but occasionally take a role yourself. You'll find it can be a rich learning experience for you both.

By watching closely you can find out a great deal about your child's imagination. What sort of stories do they tell, which scenes do they enjoy acting out? We learn best when we're happy, interested and engaged, so it's important to know what subjects and scenarios excite your child. Look for clues about where they might like to develop their knowledge, and about the particular ways in which they use their creative imagination. The fantasy structures young children build in their minds can become the foundations of their learning in school.

BE THE COSTUME SUPPLIER

Help your child explore a range of different roles. You can give them suggestions for their games by supplying interesting hats or shoes, coats or bags. You can also support their own ideas by digging out bits and pieces to match whatever game they've chosen to play. Costumes help children of all ages to get into character and to experiment with the ways in which people move and talk and think. This ability to see different perspectives and to imagine other people's emotions is absolutely vital when children go to school – so get your child doing it early and give them a real head start.

BE THE PROP MASTER

Encourage your child's creativity and lateral thinking. How many different uses can they come up with for a colander or a walking stick? What can household objects like cushions and boxes turn into, with a bit of imagination? Model the creative process yourself: 'I'm going to look closely at this bath sponge and squeeze it to see what different shapes it can make. Let me think... what does it look like now? I know, how about I bend it this way, into a mouth, and use it as a puppet. What voice should I give it...?'

You're developing your child's confidence to find inspiration in everyday places and to let one idea spark another. You're showing them that there's no 'right' answer when the imagination is in full flow, just great ideas. Far too many children I meet in schools have no such sense of freedom, no confidence to see where their ideas might take them.

To start building memory skills, use props in pairs and groups. Challenge your child to find a way of using two or more items at once. Ask:

▶ *How are they similar?*
▶ *Who would use them both?*
▶ *Can you imagine a way to put them together?*

A child might use a wooden spoon to fix imaginary screws into an old radio, turn a bowl and silk scarf into a cosy home for a pet, or put a whisk and a shoe box together to make a laser-shooting robot. And when they're good at that, try playing imagination games with larger sets of objects. Can your child tell you a story or act out a scene using a group of items, one after another? An orange, an old watch, a plastic bottle, a torch...?

Have a go yourself to demonstrate: the orange is a planet in space, high above your head, the final destination for your space mission; use the watch as a countdown timer: '3, 2, 1... blast off'; the bottle becomes the rocket, zooming around the room; when you land, the torch can be your laser, protecting you from any unfriendly aliens as you walk across the strange new world...

Props can inspire adventures, but they can also help children develop the key skills they need to learn and remember. When they take everyday items, bring them to life in their imagination and link them into memorable scenes and stories, they're sampling learning at its exciting, imaginative best. You'll find that they can recall all the props they used and remember every detail of what happened. They're building a brain perfectly suited to learning anything and everything in school.

BE AN AUDIENCE MEMBER

Show children that you value their imagination, and that it can produce 'real' results to be shared and enjoyed. As well as being generally supportive of their performance, choose some specific aspects to praise. Show them how imaginative games can spark off ideas and memories.

For a three-year-old, you might simply bring them a book, photograph or souvenir that connects with what they've shown you. With older children you can explain your thinking more clearly, for example: 'Setting up that shop on your bed reminded me that we have to go and buy some groceries,' or, 'You firefighters have got me really interested in what a real fire-station must be like.' Teach your child that imagination can light a fire under many different kinds of thinking.

BE A REVIEWER

Help your child to develop a vocabulary to support their imagination. After a game or mini-show, reflect aloud on what you saw them do with their amazing brain, choosing vocabulary to suit their understanding:

'You *played rockets.*'
'You *made up a rocket ship.*'
'You *imagined a rocket, with all the whizzes and bangs.*'
'You *used your imagination so well to turn our sofa into a rocket ship.*'
'You *forgot about moving like a spaceman for a moment, didn't you? But then I loved the bit where you remembered to dodge those imaginary asteroids! I could tell you were seeing them in your mind.*'

At each stage of their development you can prompt your child to reflect on their creativity, supplying words and phrases – 'played', 'made up', 'imagined', 'forgot', 'remembered', 'mind' – that help to get them thinking about thinking.

From four years: have fun with fingers

As children's interest in counting and ordering develops, they naturally use their fingers to help them. We have a base ten, decimal system *because* we have ten fingers (and thumbs), so it makes good sense to get children practising on their hands and building useful physical and visual frameworks for maths.

Encourage your child to see their fingers as a line of ten. In school they'll be shown number lines to help them increase and decrease numbers, moving along the line in jumps of different sizes. If they're already confident with their own personal number line of ten fingers, they'll be ahead of the game.

Try it yourself. With your hands in front of you and your palms towards you, start with the thumb of the left hand – one, two, three, four, five – and then continue with the little finger of your right – six, seven, eight, nine, ten. (There's a natural tendency to start with the thumb on both hands, but this means that the 'number line' goes in two directions!) Another way is to have one palm facing you and one turned away, so that you can start with the same finger on both hands. Go with what your child prefers, and get them practising the 'ripple' of fingers as they move from one to ten – then back again.

With your number line in place you can play games like 'One, two, three, four, five, once I caught a fish alive', touching each of your child's fingers in turn or getting them to move the right one at the right point in the song. Talk to them about where they can find the biggest and smallest numbers, and what happens when they move in one direction or the other along the line.

COUNTING, ADDING AND SUBTRACTING

Start with your 'digital' number line in front of you, your hands held in whichever way works best for you.

Next, close both fists so that you start with 'nothing', no fingers held up. Add two: in other words, extend the first two fingers on the left – the start of the number line. Then add three, so that all five fingers of your left hand are unfolded.

Without support, young children almost always use two hands to answer this question, making it much harder to see the logical increase along the number line.

They're likely to count the final total of fingers – one, two, three, four, five – rather than simply spotting that a whole handful of fingers has been raised: five. So using the 'finger line' technique consistently helps children to use known facts to speed up their calculations.

When you help your child to add three more, make sure they raise the next three fingers along the line. And to work out the new total, prompt them to start with five (since they don't need to count that whole hand again) and 'count on' the extra three: six, seven, eight. Again, this structured approach to finger counting helps to establish core numeracy skills, giving your child clear and effective visual models for maths.

When they start subtracting, children notice a big difference: that the last finger still extended – the one that tells them the answer – is now getting closer to the left. They can see that adding goes one way, subtracting the other. Rather than ending up with a few fingers on one hand and some more on the other, which then have to be counted to get to the solution, they're left with a single recognizable group of items, growing or shrinking in a visually logical way. Adding clearly increases the previous total; subtracting decreases it.

As your child's numeracy skills develop and they extend their line of manageable numbers way beyond ten (and, later, beyond zero in the other direction), they'll always have this core structure of understanding built into their brain.

See if your child can cross their hands, swapping left and right, and still count along their line of fingers in both directions. How quickly can they find and wiggle finger four or finger eight? This is a great way to energize children's thinking, challenging the two hemispheres of their brain to co-operate in different ways.

THE TWO SIDES OF THE BRAIN

The left side of the brain controls the right side of the body, and vice versa. We know that the two hemispheres have particular characteristics: the left is dominant in the more logical thought processes, the right side biased towards more creative and imaginative thinking. And although maths is traditionally considered a left-brained, logical discipline, neuroscientist Norbert Jausovec showed that children with the strongest maths skills tended to be those who could use the right and left sides of their brains in combination.

> ## Insight
>
> Get your child to draw consecutive numbers in the air using their left hand, right foot, right hand, left foot... Challenge them to touch their opposite shoulders and tap out alternate numbers. Occasionally ask them to use their non-dominant hand to draw or write numbers and shapes. Physical cross-over exercises like these are great for developing 'whole-brain thinking': an approach which will become increasingly important in your child's learning journey.

From five years: explore the past, present and future

This is another exercise which involves both sides of the brain: the logical left to put events in order, and the more random right to explore events in creative ways. It's also a powerful way of developing your child's awareness of their mind at work.

Start by choosing a theme to think about. It could be something you happen to be discussing, like friends or animals or food; or it could be a topic you've specifically chosen to explore: holidays, kindness, Grandma. The exercise splits into three clear parts.

▶ **Past:** *how far back can you go to think about the theme you've picked? Talk to your child about shared memories, and about the different things you recall. Who were your earliest friends? Who remembers most about that day at the zoo? Which foods did you enjoy as babies? Try to include as much detail as possible, and tap into as many different senses and emotions as you can.*

▶ **Present:** *next, consider your theme as it affects life now. What did you do with your friends today? Did you see any animals on your journey to school or work? How many different foods have you eaten today? Keep using your 'mind's eye' to picture events that should still be particularly vivid.*

▶ **Future:** *finally, think and talk about experiences still to come. What do you hope you will do with your friends tomorrow, next week, in ten years' time? What animals would you like to have as pets? For your next birthday, what sort of cake would you like? Use your imagination and really try to 'see' into the future.*

This activity is a lovely way to discuss details of your shared life as well as your individual experiences. It has huge value, simply as a way of chatting and bonding – more of that quality talk time that plays such a huge part in children's growth and success. But is also stimulates some key thinking skills and helps to build important structures in the brain.

CONNECTED THINKING

You'll find that memories spark other memories. Some memories will 'agree', giving more details about shared moments. Others may not quite correspond and you'll have to investigate further to see if you can get any closer to the truth.

Thoughts about the future may remind you of extra information from the past. Talking about something that happened today might suddenly remind you of an important thought about tomorrow. You're helping your child to see that memories connect and weave together in complex networks, and that these networks can be tapped into from different points.

Ordering memories helps to build skills of organized thinking and mental 'housekeeping'. To be a successful learner, your child needs to think clearly and logically, understand processes, causes and effects, and work through tasks in order. But it's vital that they're also a creative thinker, able to use their instincts, senses, imagination, and to develop fluid connections and combinations. In this activity, exploring memories through images and feelings activates the creative right side of the brain, which in turn injects vibrancy into the logical, left-sided sequences and structures. It's a wonderful way of encouraging your child to use their brilliant brain to the full.

From six years: play Pelmanism

This is the classic 'pairs' memory game played with a set of picture cards. You can buy ready-made sets, adapt other card games, or make cards of your own. Older children will enjoy helping you make a set featuring their favourite animals, vehicles or comic-book characters. Make sure that the cards can be divided into matching pairs, and that they're all identical from the back.

Get ready by shuffling the cards and laying them out face down in a grid pattern to fit the space you've got. The players then take it in turns to search for pairs, using memory skills to match new cards with ones that have already appeared.

When it's your go, you turn over any two cards of your choice. If they match, you keep them and take another turn. If they're different, make sure the other players have seen both cards and then turn them back over, ready for the next person to have a try.

As you play Pelmanism with your child, make the most of the opportunity to talk about memory. What strategies are they using to remember where the cards were last seen? Which cards are most memorable – and why are some cards in the set always the last to be found?

You can suggest ways of 'tagging' the cards you see; for example, linking them to nearby pieces of furniture, or even the players they're closest to: 'The rabbit card is in the corner of the grid pointing towards the door. Why don't I imagine a giant rabbit has just walked into the room?'; 'This cowboy card is near Ellie, so I'm going to imagine she's wearing a big cowboy hat today.'

Use Pelmanism to practise children's natural learning skills, their powers of observation and their spatial awareness, and to prove that memory skills can be improved. Celebrate every time someone uses a memory trick to win a pair. And whenever you take time to play the game, feel confident that you're helping your child to build a flexible, connected brain; the left-brained logic of the grid working in tandem with the right-brained creativity of imaginative memory clues.

From seven years: write strange stories

I've never met a child who doesn't love stories. The stories we tell and are told keep changing as we grow, just as our culture of story-telling has changed over time, from cave paintings to Twitter updates. But all stories have key features in common and tap into some deep-rooted aspects of human thought.

Once again, stories involve the key combination of the right and left brain: colourful creativity held together by pattern and logic. A story excites us and fires our imagination, but we can only follow and remember it because it has shape and structure.

Sharing stories with children is essential to their healthy mental and emotional growth. Stories simultaneously reassure and challenge. We know their shapes but we're constantly surprised by their contents. They strengthen our memories, give us frameworks to construct and communicate our own thoughts, and supply the images and ideas that will help to push our thinking further.

But when children are old enough to take control of the story-writing process themselves, there are wonderful opportunities for maximizing the power of a story.

Find some old magazines – ones with lots of glossy photographs, illustrations, adverts. Using scissors and glue, show your child how to cut out a collection of images and then stick them onto paper, ending up with some truly surreal and memorable stories.

We know the sort of things stories need: characters, settings, props. The fun in this game is choosing pictures that rarely go together, then combining them to powerful effect. You stick them – in weird and wonderful combinations – onto a piece of blank paper, then either add a few written clues about what's happening, or simply talk through the picture sequence between yourselves.

So if you find a footballer, a toaster, a fish and a supermarket, your story might start with a footballer kicking the toaster through the supermarket window. You could use a felt pen to draw in some movement lines and 'special effects' as the ball crashes through the glass – where it's caught by a fish. Madonna then appears, carrying a tin of cat food and an aeroplane...

This fun activity teaches children many things about creative, confident thinking skills. It shows them that inspiration can be found anywhere, and that 'old' ideas can be reorganized into new and exciting material. It demonstrates that the most memorable information is funny and strange and colourful – *and* connected and structured in some way. It lets them practise their creativity with no 'right' or 'wrong' answers to worry about, but encourages them to think and talk about the end results.

Telling sophisticated stories is such a clear sign of well-developed thinking skills. By the time your child can work with you on an activity like this, exploring their imagination, choosing resources to inspire ideas, organizing information in clever and memorable ways – and discussing their thought processes as they go – you'll know that they're on the right track. They'll be ready to extend their brains in ever more exciting directions, developing learning skills such as lateral thinking and philosophical enquiry. With your continuing support they'll be ready to make the most of their mind and seize every new opportunity to learn.

10 THINGS TO REMEMBER

1 *Support all the key stages of your child's mental development, helping them to build a strong and flexible brain by using it well.*

2 *Seize every opportunity to strengthen all their senses.*

3 *Talk to children, extending their thinking and building their powers of communication.*

4 *Sing action rhymes to activate key literacy and numeracy skills.*

5 *Nurture children's imagination by taking a range of supportive roles in their make-believe games.*

6 *Use finger counting to help children structure their thinking about maths.*

7 *Introduce children to both sides of their brain, stimulating creative and logical thinking skills.*

8 *Use puzzles and projects to train children in problem-solving strategies.*

9 *Develop children's story-telling skills to prepare them to explore and remember many different types of information.*

10 *Children of all ages can discuss their thinking, reflect on their developing understanding and skills and take a real and active interest in their learning.*

2

Engaging with learning

In this chapter you will learn:
- *the truth about intelligence testing*
- *how different forms of intelligence can be recognized, nurtured and developed*
- *techniques for strengthening visual, auditory and kinaesthetic learning styles*
- *the links between emotional wellbeing and learning success.*

While Chapter 1 explored the important areas of every child's brainpower, this chapter concentrates on *your* child. You want them to be successful in relation to others, because that's one way that success can be seen and measured. But mostly you want them to achieve their individual potential, developing in ways that make them happy and fulfilled.

The thinking skills discussed in the previous chapter are the foundations of a brilliant brain, essential for success in school. When using these powerful strategies, your child is building and strengthening their brain, rehearsing the most effective approaches to a range of different tasks.

So how do we measure a child's brilliance? Clearly each and every challenge they face reveals something about their ability, whether it's a spelling test, a karate exam, an art competition, or simply the quality of a conversation or their success in making new friends. You can watch your child and gauge their success at problem-solving, generating ideas, learning from their mistakes, understanding their own mind. But other people will be testing them in different ways. Assessments, tests and exams, from early primary onwards, will attempt to pin down your child's success in individual areas of thinking and learning. Many will give a precise score for their performance and compare them with their peers.

Are any of these methods more important or more accurate than the others? Is there one method of revealing your child's brilliance, their 'intelligence', their potential for success?

Testing for brilliance

The key thing to understand is what any test does and does not reveal. Typically, the result will show how well a child does on that particular test on that particular day. It's likely to reflect how well they were prepared for the test in question, whether through natural ability or careful support and training, and how much they wanted to do well; how much energy and commitment they brought to the task. Their success will depend on so many things, including: how they felt physically and emotionally on the day; how many times they'd faced a similar challenge before; how well they understood what they were being asked to do; and, of course, how the person setting the test chose to mark it.

An important question to ask is what exactly is a test assessing and valuing when it delivers its result? Keep that in mind, remember all the possible factors affecting success, and then you can reach a decision about what the test score or verdict really means for your child.

With this sort of perspective, many tests can be extremely useful. They can give your child a chance to perfect particular skills, reveal areas where they can improve, and provide a chance for you to celebrate their success. Tests can be enjoyable challenges, encouraging children to direct their own learning and to do their very best.

But of course that's not always the case. Think of your own experiences; of the times when tests felt like demonstrations of failure, pointing out all the things you couldn't do and revealing how much better other people had performed. How many tests actually ruined your confidence and prevented you from trying to improve? How often were you led to believe that a test or round of assessments delivered a damning overall verdict on your ability and your chances of success?

Be particularly suspicious of people trying to pin down your child's brainpower. Since Alfred Binet first set 'intelligence tests' for French schoolchildren at the start of the twentieth century, a number of different attempts have been made to achieve a single measure of ability, accompanied by a great deal of controversy along the way.

Insight

It's important to know that Binet warned against trying to score ability as if it was fixed. He designed his tests to highlight children who needed special help with their learning, not to give every child a particular rating. He focused on aspects of reasoning and short-term memory, providing a very limited snapshot of thinking skills; but nevertheless his work became the leading influence on intelligence testing around the world.

The concept of an intelligence quotient or IQ was devised by researchers assessing conscripts to the American military in 1917. They calculated IQ by deciding on a person's 'mental age', dividing it by their age in years, then multiplying by one hundred. So a 20-year-old mind in a 20-year-old body scored 100, the 'normal' result, and a simple-looking scale was created on which everyone could be compared with the norm. Again, intelligence was assumed to remain fixed for life, and an IQ score was seen as a useful fact upon which any number of attitudes and decisions could be based.

By the mid 1950s the military felt that more sophisticated tests needed to be developed. David Wechsler published his Adult Intelligence Scale in 1955, measuring verbal comprehension, working memory and reasoning. He described intelligence as the '...capacity of a person to act purposefully, to think rationally, and to deal effectively with their environment.' This test was clearly looking for very practical, logical ways of thinking – perhaps useful in the military, but only part of what it takes to be brilliant in the real world.

WHAT DO INTELLIGENCE TESTS REALLY TELL US?

So, your child has achieved a high IQ score, which proves that they have good reasoning skills, a strong working memory, probably a large vocabulary and confidence with words. It shows most of all that they are good at taking intelligence tests. Maybe they're just naturally good at answering questions like these. Maybe they've been specifically trained to take the tests. What is clear is that they are focused, fast workers, with efficient test-taking abilities – so of course they're likely to keep doing well in all the assessments that come their way.

They may be able to turn their talents to other areas of achievement, but not necessarily. These tests say nothing about creating thought-provoking paintings or writing powerful poetry; performing the perfect pirouette or scoring a breathtaking goal; maintaining strong friendships; solving problems in the real world; understanding patterns of emotion and thought.

IQ tests analyse and reward very specific types of thinking, and they should be valued in those terms: no more, no less. What really matters is how your child combines their many different thinking skills and applies them to achieve real results. They also need to reflect on their own thinking, direct their development, and stay interested and motivated to achieve satisfying lifelong learning. IQ tests don't really scratch the surface of any of that.

If your child needs to take an IQ test, all the skills developed throughout this book will help. Their test result may open doors, change other people's opinions about them, or help you and others to give them support. But it must not be used to define their 'intelligence'. There are simply too many other areas of ability that need to be valued and supported. The activities in this book will help you to see how well your own child's skills, knowledge and key personal qualities are developing. You can make sure they're being supported to achieve their own brand of brilliance.

Multiple intelligences

There are so many different types of intelligent children, so many different ways of being successful, happy and fulfilled. Getting to know your unique child is essential to helping them achieve their full potential.

The American psychologist Howard Gardner was very keen to challenge the traditional views on intelligence and IQ. His work on 'multiple intelligences' has been extremely influential in widening our understanding of what it means to be clever.

Gardner developed his theories from the simple observation that there are many different sorts of brilliant people: Albert Einstein, Tiger Woods, Picasso, Madonna, Barack Obama, Gandhi – they've all achieved outstanding results in their own field – but although they share certain key traits, their types of achievement and the thinking skills involved are clearly very different. How could a single view of intelligence ever hope to understand them all?

The traditional IQ test simply doesn't inform us about artistic intelligence, philosophical skill, brilliance as a singer or athlete or chef – or so many of the other really interesting and significant ways of achieving success. So Howard Gardner mapped out seven different 'intelligences'. The first two were the ones most often analysed in intelligence tests: linguistic intelligence and logical-mathematical intelligence, traditionally taught in schools as Literacy and Numeracy. They're the two key thinking skills measured in IQ and other classic intelligence tests.

LINGUISTIC INTELLIGENCE

Children who have strong skills in this area are sensitive to language, both written and spoken. They can learn languages quickly and use them in subtle ways: to communicate effectively, to express themselves creatively and persuasively and to structure their thoughts and activate their memory.

LOGICAL-MATHEMATICAL INTELLIGENCE

This type of thinking involves analysing logically, calculating and investigating accurately. A key factor is a child's ability to find patterns and draw conclusions.

Children who do well in these two areas are the ones most easily identified as 'clever'. Their abilities can be tested and quantified. Their skills give them a strong foundation on which to build their confident, flexible brains, and they can operate well in the world because they're able to do what's required of them: understanding instructions, finishing written work, solving maths questions, carrying out effective science experiments.

But Howard Gardner recognized that these skills are not the sum of intelligence. Traditionally 'clever' children also show off their abilities in many other ways; and other children, while not so clearly skilled in language or logic, can also demonstrate remarkable achievements. He knew that a wider range of intelligences had to be recognized, to help us extend our children in many more directions and to celebrate the full range of their abilities and talents.

So, to the first two he added five more:

▶ **Musical intelligence:** *hearing, comparing and patterning sounds; appreciating pitch, tone and rhythm. There are clear parallels with linguistic intelligence, but also with*

logical-mathematical intelligence, since children with strong
musical skills are good at detecting patterns in music.

▶ **Bodily-kinaesthetic intelligence:** *using the brain to control
the body to help solve problems and achieve physical results.
Children who shine in this area are dancers, athletes, physical
game-players, and they also use their bodies – gestures,
actions, physical experiments – to help them think and learn.*

▶ **Spatial intelligence:** *seeing patterns in spaces of different sizes.
Again there are clear overlaps with other intelligences, since
thinking like this influences physical movement and mental
calculation. It can help to solve engineering problems, plan
sports tactics and compose powerful works of visual art.*

▶ **Interpersonal intelligence:** *understanding other people's
thoughts and feelings, their motivations and their needs. This is
a crucial ability for living and working with others and it plays
an important role in children's success and happiness in school.*

▶ **Intrapersonal intelligence:** *understanding oneself, and acting
upon that knowledge. This is a measure of how well you can
recognize and reflect upon your own thought processes and
emotional experiences: your fears, passions, worries, attitudes.
It also involves the ability to make changes in your behaviour
and your life.*

Which of these descriptions remind you of your child? Are there
areas where they clearly shine or struggle?

Howard Gardner's 'seven intelligences' had a major impact,
mainly because the idea rang so true. When David Beckham
bends the ball into the top corner of the net, there are elements
of linguistic intelligence, because he's talked and planned with
his team-mates, and logical-mathematical intelligence, because
he's followed that plan and made some very accurate calculations
to strike the ball perfectly. But clearly the dominant intelligence
is bodily-kinaesthetic, with a fair amount of spatial intelligence
included – along with enough intrapersonal intelligence to control
his thoughts and feelings to help him achieve brilliance under
intense pressure. You could even argue that he's fuelled by an
understanding of other people's needs and emotions (interpersonal

intelligence) and driven on by the rhythmical chants and emotive songs of the crowd (musical intelligence). What is certainly clear is that his ability is spread across a wide range of intelligences, and could never be truly captured by a typical intelligence test.

In the years that followed, Gardner explored more areas of intelligence and added 'naturalist intelligence' to his original seven. This sort of ability is evident in children who can glean information from nature, analysing and classifying as they develop their understanding of the living world.

He also provoked a great deal of debate by considering spiritual intelligence, moral intelligence and existential intelligence: the ability to grapple with the very biggest issues of life, the universe and everything. Discussions about these ideas are obviously complicated by people's own spiritual and moral views, and there are disagreements about what exactly can be measured and what should be valued. But there is something very valuable in celebrating ever more areas in which children can be developed and ways in which their brilliance can shine.

Your child can be helped to develop all these forms of intelligence. Howard Gardner was very keen to prevent them from becoming limiting definitions, labelling children in ways that might stop them extending themselves in all areas. The activities in this book are designed to enrich children's natural talents – supporting the born athlete, the talented philosopher – but they're also there to develop the intelligences that come less readily to your child.

Learning styles: visual, auditory and kinaesthetic

The same attitude is very important when it comes to learning 'styles'. As with Gardner's multiple intelligences, we know that there are different approaches to learning, and that they need to be measured, developed and celebrated in different ways. Your child may well have a leaning towards one way of learning, which needs to be recognized and used, but they have to develop the full range of learning styles if they're going to achieve their full potential:

- ▶ **Visual learning:** *by looking, reading and watching. Children inclined to visual learning enjoy books and magazines, follow instructions carefully in words and pictures, and may find it harder to understand and remember information that does not come with visual prompts.*
- ▶ **Auditory learning:** *by hearing and listening. If your child responds best when you read aloud, and follows instructions most accurately when they're delivered audibly rather than written down, then this is probably their 'go to' learning style. Their mind may tend to wander when all they have is written text.*
- ▶ **Kinaesthetic learning:** *by touching, moving and doing. Some children prefer to learn by diving straight in and experimenting, taking a hands-on approach to learning. Holding and playing with things can help them concentrate on other forms of information, and they can get frustrated when they're told to sit down and keep their hands still.*

Insight

It's important not to give your child labels like 'visual learner' or 'kinaesthetic learner'. Unfortunately, when learning skills first filtered into classrooms, many teachers did just that, defining each child with a single learning style, encouraging them to use that strategy whenever and wherever they could – and, in the process, dramatically limiting their chances of success.

A good teacher presents lessons involving all three learning styles, allowing children to access the full range of strategies. Children can certainly work with thinking skills that suit them and make the most of what comes naturally. But they must also be helped to develop a rounded approach to learning.

A crucial benefit of spending time with your child and sharing their learning is that you get to see their natural learning style. It will actually be a complex mix of the three main categories, and may well change from task to task; but understanding their preferred approach helps you to support them well. It lets you give them activities they enjoy, but also directs you to extend them into other approaches. It helps them build the full repertoire of thinking skills into their brain.

STRENGTHENING VISUAL LEARNING SKILLS

Provide your child with a range of writing and drawing materials, including pens, pencils and crayons in different colours, and a ruler, rubber and pencil sharpener. Find opportunities for your child to paint. Give them access to plenty of different things to write and draw *on*. They'll love to have a ready supply of scrap paper – like documents that have only been printed on one side – plus a little fresh paper for their best work. Find them old diaries to write in, notebooks with just a few pages written on that can be removed to make a new start, and more unusual materials like the backs of cereal packets or unfolded shoe-boxes. Make sure there's a place where they can go to explore their writing and drawing, set up with all the equipment they need.

Encourage your child to describe what they can see around them, using as many different descriptive words as possible. Talk about the films and TV programmes they've watched, in terms of what they looked like – the colours, the backgrounds, the special effects – as well as what happened. Use visual skills through questioning to explore the past and the future:

'When you close your eyes and think of Grandpa's garden, what
    does it look like?'
'If you took a photograph of your group of best friends, what
    would you see?'
'What do you think the holiday caravan is going to look like?'

Play 'I spy' games with your child, changing the rules slightly so that a different detail has to be used every round: 'I spy with my little eye something that's... blue/curved/see-through/shiny...'

When they're exploring and learning new information, make sure they have something to look at to make the most of their visual strength. Find books with great pictures. Search the internet for images that will back up the more abstract ideas they might be studying, like 'friendships', 'percentages' or 'slavery'.

Celebrate the power and impact of all things visual with trips to cinemas, art galleries and countryside viewpoints.

STRENGTHENING AUDITORY LEARNING SKILLS

Ensure your child has access to a variety of recorded and broadcast music. On CDs and MP3s, on the car radio or digital TV, there's no shortage of music from every style and genre. Talk about their likes and dislikes and get into the details of *why*: is it the instruments, the rhythms, the tunes? Find somewhere at home which can become their 'listening place' – perhaps a cosy corner of their bedroom – and equip it with a CD player, headphones, and recordings of speech as well as music.

Describe the world through sound. Ask your child to close their eyes and name every different sound they can hear. Help them to widen their vocabulary for sound, using words like 'pitch', 'tone' and 'volume'.

Explore memories and imagined ideas through the sense of hearing. Ask your child what sounds they can remember from a holiday, a party or a trip to the zoo. What do particular people's voices sound like? Move forward in time to imagine sounds that *might* be there: at their new school; when you all go to the bowling alley; if a dinosaur landed on the roof of the car.

Insight

Play a version of 'I spy' called 'I hear': 'I hear with my little ear something that sounds... high and chirpy/electronic/ rhythmic and thumpy'. Encourage children to invent new adjectives to match the sounds around them.

Find ways to add sound to the information your child is learning. Search the internet for sound effect files to add to projects. Use household props to recreate the sounds of Roman swords clashing, pyramid stones being dragged, a T-Rex stalking its prey. Encourage them to include descriptions of sounds in the notes they make.

Celebrate your child's abilities with sound by watching live performances, visiting echoey rooms and valleys, and giving them access to music-making equipment. A rice shaker for a toddler is cheap and easy to make; instruments for older children can be borrowed or hired through school and there are several free digital editing programs available online.

STRENGTHENING KINAESTHETIC LEARNING SKILLS

Supply your child with materials to make and build. Cardboard boxes and tubes, cotton reels, tin lids, bits of fabric – plus safe scissors and enough sticky tape and glue to hold it all together. Give them easy access to construction toys even when you might think they're too old to enjoy them. Let them know where at home is safe for them to make a bit of a mess building things from their imagination or from kits.

Prompt them to describe events and ideas through the language of touch and movement:

'What textures can you remember from your nursery school?'
'How many different ways did you move around school today?'
'What would you do to turn that box into a home for your pet dragon?'

Play a game of 'I feel': 'I feel something with my little finger that feels... bumpy/sticky/warm/breakable'.

Find opportunities to link learning with doing. Use gestures when you're explaining or giving instructions, and encourage your child to make up actions to back up the key ideas. Show them how to clap out syllables or number sequences and write new spellings in the air. Get them to point to each of their major organs when they're studying the human body; run on the spot for a moment and feel their heartbeat increasing; act out the effects of different food groups.

Celebrate the importance of kinaesthetic learning by:

- *enjoying sports and physical activities together*
- *joining a drama club*
- *letting your child help with jobs and practical projects*
- *watching professional craftspeople at work.*

So what sort of learner is your child? The activities in this book are about getting to know your child's learning 'character', their abilities and attitudes, and then supporting them appropriately. You can help them to use their natural talents, and to develop new ones.

LOST IN LEARNING

It's great when children find moments of pure engagement – when whatever they're doing is so interesting and involving them so deeply that they're almost lost in it.

In the sixth century BC, the Greek philosopher Heraclitus wrote: 'Man is most nearly himself when he achieves the seriousness of a child at play.'

When children are absorbed by an activity they achieve a wonderful state of mind: creative, focused, confident and free. It may happen during an imaginative game with others, or by themselves. A hobby is often the source of such moments, allowing a wonderful level of engagement in the activity. Many of us also experience this kind of state when we're reading; powerfully focused at the same time as being completely relaxed.

It's a state that psychologists label 'flow': thinking and learning that's fluid and natural but also direct and effective. There are many similarities with the 'zone' that sports people inhabit in their moments of brilliance. Body and mind are calm, movement is easy, focus is pure, and amazing results are achieved.

Insight

A study of American teenagers showed a clear link between 'flow' and mental wellbeing. Those who enjoyed these moments of engagement were the ones most likely to achieve well in school and to be happy and fulfilled in life as a whole.

By playing, exploring their interests, thinking creatively and doing practically, your child can find their own moments of 'flow'. As well as helping you to understand their passions and skills, these moments are vital for developing children's love of learning and their motivation to achieve their best. 'Serious play' is a great way to describe whole-brain thinking: organized and creative, conscious and relaxed, effective and fun.

Take all the chances you get to investigate your child's natural intelligences, learning styles and other characteristics as a thinker. You could set them a challenge – planning a party, helping you to organize a family day out, being project manager when you decorate their bedroom – then watch closely to see how they respond, focusing on the following ten questions:

1 *How easy was it to motivate them to take part?*
2 *Were they able to concentrate throughout each part of the task?*
3 *Did they understand what they were being asked to do?*
4 *Could they see the 'big picture' as well as the small details?*
5 *How easy and enjoyable did they find the creative process?*
6 *What part did memory play in their approach – perhaps suggesting ideas based on past events, or helping them to organize new information?*
7 *Was there evidence of their preferred learning style: visual, auditory or kinaesthetic?*
8 *Were they able to combine learning styles, or switch from one to another?*

9 *How well did they communicate with other people involved in the task?*

10 *Could they reflect honestly on their own performance, analysing their actions, feelings and thinking skills?*

Activities like this let you explore your child's thinking at the same time as strengthening and extending their abilities. You'll notice natural talents that can be nurtured and used elsewhere, as well as areas that need to be developed to benefit their whole approach to learning.

Insight

Talk to your child about their interests and make three different lists: what they used to enjoy doing, what they love now, and what they would like to try in the future. Spotting the themes and patterns that emerge helps you to understand what makes them tick.

Many other factors affect how ready your child is to learn, and what form that learning will take.

Left-handed children

Traditionally, people who prefer to use their left hand have been viewed with suspicion. It's not so long since many school children were forced to use their right hand instead, to be 'normal'. Thankfully, in recent years our understanding, acceptance and appreciation of left-handedness has improved. We know that left-handers have particularly connected and flexible brains. Unlike right-handers, who process language in the left hemisphere and handle many creative and visual tasks with the right, left-handed people have much less specialized brains. There are more natural connections between their right and left sides, suggesting that left-handers will be less rule-bound and more inclined to free creativity. Certainly many famous creative pioneers have been left handed – Leonardo da Vinci, Michelangelo, Albert Einstein, Lewis Carroll,

Charlie Chaplin, Paul McCartney – proving at the very least that being left-handed doesn't limit your child's potential for success. If anything, it improves their likelihood of being an imaginative, inquisitive, ingenious thinker – although their tendency to challenge and change rules may sometimes bring them into conflict with authority.

Insight

Bart Simpson is left-handed – like his creator, the multi-talented cartoonist and writer Matt Groening. He's a great example of the 'spirit' of left-handedness: creative, rebellious, and very different from his organized, obedient and right-handed sister Lisa.

Left-handers will need help with handwriting, and specially designed pens, rulers, pencil sharpeners and scissors can make life much easier in school. They may also need support to recognize when rules do need to be followed, although their natural instincts to invent and rethink can certainly be used to activate their learning. Tests have shown that left-handers are better at remembering the details of events and experiences, so they should be extremely good at many of the visual, story-based thinking techniques explored in this book. At the same time, the strategies for ordering and structuring information may be particularly important for helping them retain control of their ideas – and sometimes, their behaviour.

Boys and girls: learning differences

There seems to be a greater range of ability amongst boys than girls. Boys are much more likely to be at the extreme ends of the scale, and many reasons for this have been suggested. For example, girls' roles have traditionally been more 'fixed', governed by particular expectations, while boys have had more avenues open to them – and so more scope to succeed or fail in extreme ways. On a physiological level, male hormones have also been blamed for boys' incompatibility with many traditional 'sit still and study' learning tasks, along with many of the techniques designed to measure ability. A range of developmental problems affect three to five times more boys than girls. And while girls are often observed to be 'eager to please', boys have always tended to take the most risks.

We know that girls develop language skills faster than boys. The language area of their brain is larger; but research also shows that mothers (still more likely to be the main caregiver) talk more to their girls than their boys. Girls also have more acute senses. As babies they can pick up much quieter sounds, and one-year-old girls have been shown to prefer soft classical music, while the boys respond more positively to loud rock. Professor Michael Rutter has demonstrated that boys are more sensitive to tension between their parents – perhaps another reason why boys' achievement is more 'volatile', more extreme.

So girls and boys have some important in-built differences, but they're also affected by the attitudes towards them and the opportunities they get. It's important for parents to understand what makes boys and girls special, and at the same time to avoid limiting them with particular gender expectations. Children copy so many of the behaviours and attitudes they see close-up. A household where everyone has opportunities and choices is likely to foster the healthy sense of freedom that all children need to succeed.

Does birth order affect achievement?

In a famous experiment, 400,000 men in the Dutch army underwent intelligence tests – and the results showed an unmistakable link between family position and thinking skills. The older a man was compared with his siblings, the better he performed in the tests. The experiment also revealed that, for children further down the pecking order, the larger their family, the worse their score.

Francis Galton had highlighted this link between family order and success back in the late 1800s. The eminent scientist had noticed that fellow members of the Royal Society were mostly firstborns. Many studies since have supported this link between family position and achievement. Statistically, firstborns come out clearly on top. Last born siblings have a good chance of being very successful, while middle children seem to face the greatest challenges.

So why does birth order make such a difference? There could well be hormonal factors in play. The blood of eldest children has been shown to contain higher levels of hormones, possibly resulting in physical differences between siblings. We do know that larger babies, and those seen as more attractive, tend to be treated as more 'mature' by their parents, challenged more and expected to do better. Firstborns' parents have more time to devote to them, and are more likely to be doing everything 'by the book'. First children are held more, talked to more, given more individual opportunities and focused support; in short, all the things that seem to make the most difference to children's success.

But there are also challenges to being first. As Charlie Brown said, 'There's no heavier burden than a great potential.' Firstborns tend to have the most expectation heaped on them, in terms of behaviour as well as success in school. They may be pushed more towards typically 'educational' pursuits, expected to be more responsible, and influenced by more worried parents to develop worries of their own. Studies of friendship and sociability have shown that first children are actually the least popular amongst their peers.

Middle children may feel the need to fight to be seen and heard. Evidence shows that they're most likely to rebel against authority and assert their right to go their own way. In the popularity stakes they still do well – but not as well as the last children in the family. They're the ones who receive most warmth from teachers and friends; the ones most likely to be the relaxed and happy children in the group. Their parents have had the time to temper their expectations, to learn from their mistakes and to develop a balanced approach to bringing up children according to their needs. Last born children have a range of role models to choose between as they develop their approach to life and make key decisions, and they benefit from having the security and structure of a well-established home.

Of course none of this is set in stone. Every family is different, and children can react to their upbringing in any number of ways. We all know firstborns who are the low achievers, relaxed middle children and youngest siblings who are frustrated and uptight. The important thing is to realize the potential impact of family order, and to make sure that all your children receive the support they need. Their experiences will necessarily be different, and there are clear advantages to each place in the family order. With awareness of their particular challenges, all your children can be brilliant in their own way.

The importance of friends and social life

Your child's social life is a crucial factor in balancing any effects of family position, character or temperament. Friendships show them other ways of being, letting them try out different viewpoints and teaching them to have empathy and understanding.

It's good for your child to mix with children who are different from them, just as it's important for them to find like-minded friends who share their interests. With both of these 'groups' there are challenges as well as pleasures. The sooner your child can operate confidently within a mixed collection of their peers – and cope with children older and younger than them – the sooner they'll develop the 'people' skills required to thrive in their community at school.

There are two main skills for parents, which need to be balanced.

ORGANIZING YOUR CHILD'S SOCIAL LIFE

Your child doesn't need to be with other children all the time, and you certainly need a break from other parents; but early mixing is essential for children to develop the social skills that will in turn boost their learning. Try to give them a range of play experiences: with close friends and new acquaintances; in groups of different sizes; indoors and out.

LETTING YOUR CHILD MAKE CHOICES OF THEIR OWN

As well as coping with the friends you provide, your child needs to pick the people they want to play with. This becomes more and more important as their interests develop and they want to join in activities with children who enjoy the same things. There may also be children they really *don't* want to play with, and you need to respect that: talking to your child, trying to get to the bottom of the problem, but ultimately showing respect for their opinion.

Support them to tolerate difficult children and give them strategies to avoid conflict. Your child needs to know how to exist peacefully alongside people they don't particularly like, as well as being able to form close friendships of their choice.

Boys and girls tend to be quite different in their friendships. While some boys have extremely close friendships, many are 'friendly' with a large group, gaining their confidence from being able to talk and play with a range of different characters. Girls often need specific, closer friendships. They fall out more, but also have deeper connections with their friends.

Insight

There's an evolutionary theory that men out hunting needed to get along with other men practically and easily; but for the women, left together in the community, social interactions were intimate, complex and of huge importance.

Whatever the causes, males and females clearly have different tendencies when it comes to friendships; but children are individually different, and parents need to do their very best to support them appropriately. Good communication is the key. Your child may be perfectly happy with several interchangeable friends, confident to deal with all sorts of people and glad sometimes to have their own space. Or they may be deeply lonely and worried that they don't have that one 'best friend' they need to feel secure. As always, parents – in communication with teachers – are best placed to discover the truth, working with their child to achieve the right balance for them.

Dealing with emotions

Knowing your child is vital to supporting them as they grow. But of course your child can also change from minute to minute, depending on their mood. Their emotions play a major part in their learning.

The simple truth is that they learn better when they're happy; we all do. Studies have shown that it's much easier to learn information that makes us feel good, while our brains have an inbuilt tendency to repress negative memories. If children are unhappy, distracted or troubled in some way, their learning suffers – and the more that happens, the more learning itself becomes a source of unhappiness. It can set in motion a very negative cycle. You need to be alert to your children's emotional state and ready to alter even the best-laid learning plans accordingly.

Insight
The brain's ultimate job is to help us survive. If we're unhappy, insecure, worried or scared, mental energy is automatically directed towards those issues – and away from other tasks, such as learning.

During childhood the pre-frontal cortex is still forming; the area of the brain that helps to control powerful feelings. Children are not born with good skills of 'emotional management'. They need to learn how to cope with the stresses and strains and disappointments of life, to calm themselves down and to see the bigger picture. Many of the activities and games in this book will actually help them develop these skills, giving children practical techniques for keeping their emotions in check.

Concentration and focus

Whatever their character and natural style of learning, some children have a problem with focusing on learning. They get distracted easily, lose energy and find different sorts of information confusing. By putting their skills and attitudes to the test you can gather evidence about their particular abilities and unique approach to learning. That evidence may point to issues that need further investigation and guidance. But all children will benefit from a safe environment, a positive approach to learning, and strategies to help them get the most out of their thinking skills.

The creative learning techniques explored in this book can help your child to control their attention and keep their behaviour in check. Distracted, overactive children may look like they need to be calmed down, their imaginative energy reined in; but the classic drug treatment for ADHD is actually a stimulant rather than a sedative. Children like this are likely to need more stimulation, not less, to stop them seeking out distractions to satisfy their needs. Give them the ability to stimulate their own mind, to use fun, energetic and sparky ideas to drive their learning and you reduce their need to search for distractions.

Insight

A stimulating lesson is usually the best way to control children's behaviour. If they're engaged, interested, excited and actively involved with all their brain power, they behave better and learn more. So if the lesson itself isn't stimulating enough, make sure your child can generate their own exciting and engaging ideas.

Happiness and learning

The more time children spend being happy and relaxed, the more opportunities they have to learn. How often does your child smile? How young were they when they first enjoyed being tickled? Studies have shown a link between children's laughter and their intelligence. Many of the learning strategies in this book are designed to be funny, to make children smile, boosting their enjoyment of learning and using happiness to strengthen memories. Incorporate them into a family life that's humorous and warm.

- ▶ *Listen patiently to their jokes and laugh like you're hearing them for the first time. Tell them jokes of your own: from your childhood, from lolly sticks, or from your own imagination.*
- ▶ *Take them to see comedy at the cinema and theatre, where the experience of shared laughter can be powerful and infectious.*
- ▶ *Talk about funny memories that involve you both.*
- ▶ *Inject a bit of silliness into family life from time to time: 'How about, just this once, we have our pudding before our main course?'; 'I've always wondered what this jacket would look like back to front...'*
- ▶ *Tickle them – if they enjoy it – and let them experience the thrill of uncontrollable laughter.*

Experiments on rats have shown that mental ability is boosted by regular physical affection, within a stimulating learning environment. Make sure you give your child plenty of hugs as part of their fun, warm family life.

Looking after your child's social and emotional wellbeing puts them in a great frame of mind for learning: happy, secure and supported – but also mentally warmed up and ready to use their brain brilliantly in school.

10 THINGS TO REMEMBER

1 By focusing on language and logic, traditional intelligence tests analyse only part of your child's mental ability.

2 Explore and enrich all your child's different intelligences: musical, kinaesthetic, spatial, interpersonal and intrapersonal; plus naturalist and spiritual intelligence.

3 Be aware of your child's preferred learning style – visual, auditory or kinaesthetic – but avoid limiting 'labels' and work with them to improve their skills in all three areas.

4 Boost visual learning by playing observation games, encouraging writing and drawing, and using pictures to understand and remember abstract ideas.

5 Strengthen your child's auditory learning with activities that stretch their listening skills, and by using imagination to add sounds to memories.

6 Make the most of their kinaesthetic learning, giving them a range of opportunities for touching, holding, making and doing, and helping them to use physical actions to activate their recall.

7 Give your child absorbing challenges that stimulate all their thinking skills and let them sample moments of 'flow'.

8 Consider all the factors that affect your child's learning success – including gender, right/left hand dominance and family position – and focus on the benefits as well as the challenges.

9   *Children vary in their attitudes to friendships, but they all need to feel secure with others if they're to learn at their best; so show them how to achieve the right relationships for them.*

10 *To learn well, children need to feel happy, enjoying jokes, games and shared activities, and receiving affection from others.*

3

Working with others

In this chapter you will learn:
- *that working with others offers many benefits for children, as well as challenging all their emotional and learning skills*
- *activities to support your child's natural approach to joint tasks, and to teach them new ways of thinking and learning with others*
- *strategies to prepare them for the unpredictability of teamwork*
- *techniques for exciting children about everything that's different and new.*

Going to school presents children with wonderful opportunities to learn and grow as part of a group. It also comes with many challenges. Chapter 2 explored ways of getting to know your unique child, understanding their distinct characteristics as a learner and starting to enrich and extend their skills. But what happens when they take their place within a community of learners? What will their particular approach mean in terms of their behaviour, confidence, happiness, and levels of achievement in school? What can you do to help your child succeed?

Insight
Family life gives children their first and most powerful experience of being part of a team. The way your family operates shapes your child's entire approach to working with others. Get it right at home, lead by example and they'll be programmed with some of the most important skills of all.

Success in school is built on a foundation of working with others, making allowances for other people, while also pursuing your own needs. It's about understanding others, and understanding yourself. With help from you, your child can pursue their own interests and achievements as part of a large and ever changing group. In fact, a well-supported child succeeds because of – not in spite of – their experiences at school.

Analysing your child's character

Your child's character as a learner becomes even more apparent amongst a group of 20 or 30 other pupils. The challenges of school bring out very clear differences between one child and the next – beyond just being strong in particular subjects or having certain interests. When it comes to learning there are some useful stereotypes: character descriptions that many teachers will recognize instantly. Your child may fit one of these types perfectly, or be a mix of several. Other characteristics are important – such as how artistically minded they are or how much interest they have in computers – and the list is certainly not finite; but it's a useful guide to the typical learners found in any primary school class.

Analysing your child in this way helps you understand how their friends and teachers may see them. It gives you a chance to make the most of the benefits and negotiate the potential difficulties arising from their particular approach to learning.

When working with others, which of the following descriptions most closely matches your child?

THE LEADER

These children are charismatic and popular, commanding attention and showing real presence amongst others. Often physically mature, they love taking charge of group activities – sometimes to the point of bossiness. But they tend to be able to receive instructions well too, understanding how useful it is for different people to be given different jobs and for everyone to know what they're doing. A child like this enjoys taking on new roles and responsibilities. They may end a project with little written evidence of their own work, because they've spent so much time delegating tasks and enjoying being the boss.

THE PUZZLE SOLVER

This is the child who adores the challenge of school. Logical and strategic, they love clear instructions – and may actually be confused if things don't quite fit the rules. They lean towards numeracy rather than literacy, but enjoy tackling letter codes and word puzzles. Then tend to be fairly slow at completing tasks and can take too much time ironing out details along the way. They may also find it hard to see the benefits of working with others. This kind of child needs to be stretched by school; motivated to solve 'puzzles' in every subject and taught to recognize the power of creative teams.

THE INVESTIGATOR

These children come to school with natural inquisitiveness and a real eagerness to learn. They love gathering facts and amassing details, and may have particular areas of interest – like space, transport or the natural world – that result in collections of objects and resources. They have endless questions about the topics they're studying and the world in general, but sometimes they need help to ask them in the most appropriate ways. They can struggle to choose 'edited highlights' of their knowledge to share, and working with others doesn't always come easily.

THE VISIONARY

Visionaries see the big picture. They take school seriously and have a very mature understanding of rules and choices, along with a range of strong opinions – whether or not they choose to express them publicly. When they do present their thoughts, they can seem over-confident, even blunt, and they need to recognize the impact their views can have on others. Children like this also tend not to worry about the details, making needless mistakes as they concentrate on the main ideas and the overall success of their work.

THE BUILDER

When these children start school, they quickly see the opportunities to make and build. They love trying out new tools and materials and they relish the chance to work with other like-minded people, as well as taking on projects of their own. They can find it hard to get down to writing tasks and to stay motivated in lessons involving more abstract thinking skills, such as maths or RE. Builders may need help in setting realistic objectives for their practical work – since they'd happily spend all their time attempting the most ambitious construction plans.

THE STORY TELLER

This is the child who loves listening to and telling all kinds of stories, particularly fantasies, fables and fairytales. They enjoy drama and puppetry, but may prefer playing the narrator to acting any one role. Keen to play in groups, they have imaginative ideas for games, and sometimes feel frustrated when others don't share the same vision. They prefer the practical application of maths – areas like money and data handling – to solving abstract questions. This child is likely to have an excellent memory for events and experiences and a sensitive understanding of other people's feelings.

THE REBEL

Aside from their behaviour (which may also tend towards the rebellious) this kind of child is rebellious and unconventional in their thoughts and ideas. There are many positive elements to their approach, and the rebel can be a very interesting and appealing child, both to friends and teachers. They bring great enthusiasm to their work and find surprising and insightful ways to tackle projects. They can also fail to meet the criteria they've been set. Their work tends to be untidy, and they need help balancing daydreaming and originality with the ability to produce appropriate and useful results.

THE ENTERTAINER

This child loves school because it gives them an audience. They relish every chance they get to play, act and sing and they bring a real confidence to every kind of performance. Their work tends to be unconventional, but they can take constructive criticism well and find ways to improve. The entertainer may sometimes overstep the mark and need reminding about appropriate behaviour – and that certain tasks need to be taken more seriously than others. They may also be a little over-dramatic in their relationships in school and need help keeping things in perspective.

THE TALKER

This child settles in quickly to new schools and new classes – because they've talked it all through at home. They're sociable and popular, although they can get into trouble for talking when they should be silent. Their internal dialogues and self-talk are excellent, allowing them to handle a wide range of subjects and to cope with feelings and friendships. Sometimes their writing doesn't reflect their understanding and ability, and they need help checking the details of their work and pushing themselves to achieve top quality, tangible results.

THE ENTREPRENEUR

If your child loves reward systems and incentive schemes, and can turn anything into a competition, then they have skills that will help them achieve in many areas at school. Children like this motivate themselves well and love involving others in their plans. Their competitive spirit can be divisive, though; very attractive to like-minded friends, but off-putting to others. Their favourite lessons tend to be maths and PE, but they love all opportunities to tackle a project that will have quantifiable results. Entrepreneurs sometimes work too quickly and miss opportunities to enjoy experimenting or learning for learning's sake. They can also get a name for themselves for bending the rules – in their determination to maximize their chances of success.

This list of ten 'types' is by no means exhaustive, but it features the key traits that children demonstrate in school. No child matches one description perfectly, and although their predominant character will be clear, they're likely to share characteristics with other types on the list. What's particularly important to realize is that no type is necessarily any better or worse than any other. They all have benefits as well as challenges, and successful children find ways of tapping into the advantages of all of them: being a leader when necessary, using their talking skills when appropriate, becoming a rebel in their thinking when that's the most effective approach to take. It's this sort of flexibility, self-awareness and confidence in learning that marks out the truly brilliant children in school.

Insight

As with learning styles – visual, auditory, kinaesthetic – these character types must never be used to limit a child's learning. Your child may well be a clear investigator, but that doesn't mean they can't also develop subtle communication skills to help them present their knowledge. An entertainer can be helped to learn the skills of silent, individual working; a visionary encouraged to make practical, detailed enquiries.

Children can be helped to find interest and excitement in areas they might otherwise have avoided, but they can also be shown how to get more from their favourite subjects. As Marcel Proust wrote,

'The voyage of discovery is not in seeking new landscapes but in having new eyes.'

The challenges of working in groups present many opportunities to experiment and grow. Here are some ideas for helping your child make the most of their natural approach to school, while also learning the benefits of other ways of thinking and behaving.

These are important concepts. So much of your child's success depends on their ability to work with others. All these techniques will develop their repertoire of thinking skills as well as equipping them for group learning in school.

The leader

Make sure they continue...

... feeling confident in controlling a project. Give them activities to 'manage' at home. These children love to be in charge of tasks like setting the table, getting their siblings ready to go to the park or explaining a board game to relatives. Don't be afraid to give them jobs that are challenging. Talk to them afterwards about what worked and what didn't. Pay attention to their communication skills, and to how well they motivated and supported the other people involved in the activity. Keep praising their confidence and skill in making things happen and strengthen their natural abilities to take a leading role in group tasks.

Help them learn to...

... take a back-seat role when required. Show them that, sometimes, they need to focus on just one part of the project.

(Contd)

Encourage your child to negotiate the details of their role, but also to accept the job they've been given, for example:

▶ *'Someone needs to work out how many sandwiches we're going to need for the picnic. How are you going to do that?'*
▶ *'I've got a notepad here, and I want you to be in charge of that bit of our holiday packing. So what do you think you need to do?'*

Your child can still be confident and make sure the activity succeeds, without always being the one in overall charge. Give them different roles every time you go shopping, build sandcastles or decorate the Christmas tree. Ask them to show you evidence that their 'bit' of the project has been achieved, encouraging them to concentrate on details – and when appropriate, to produce written results. The supportive way you talk – understanding any difficulties but also expecting them to do their best – will help them achieve a similar balance in their group work in school.

The puzzle solver

Make sure they continue...

...using their ingenuity and inquisitiveness to motivate their success. Take every opportunity to set them puzzles and challenges, especially those that activate their natural talents for science, maths and logic. These are the key skills they'll bring to group tasks. For example:

▶ *'Where did the rattle go? It was in this hand, so now where is it?'*
▶ *'Why did your lolly start dripping?'*
▶ *'Why are flower petals brightly coloured?'*
▶ *'How many legs would two of those donkeys have?'*

- ▶ *'How many prime numbers can you find between 0 and 30? How do you know you've got them all?'*
- ▶ *'What letter comes next: D, E, F...?'*
- ▶ *'I've just written these letters down in my diary. Can you guess what the next one will be? M, T, W, T...' (F for Friday)*

Being able to share their answers and explain their thinking will be essential to your child during all their group work in school.

You can use puzzles to set up an intriguing dialogue between the two of you. When they're old enough, puzzle solvers adore secret codes, so write codes on slips of paper and hide them in their lunchbox, their coat pocket or their socks, for example:

- ▶ *Codes can simply be jumbled up letters: YPAHP AIYTBHRD (Happy Birthday)*
- ▶ *Another code can use numbers to represent letters: 1 for A, 2 for B and so on: (8, 5, 12, 12, 15 = Hello)*
- ▶ *For older children, give every letter of the alphabet a random number, or move all the letters a certain number of places forwards or backwards in the alphabet.*

Help them learn to...

...enjoy tasks where there's no particular 'answer' to find or puzzle to solve: tasks that encourage conversation, collaboration, and shared enjoyment in the thinking process itself.

Questions beginning, 'How many different...' or, 'What's the best...' are particularly good for leading children away from the 'one answer' approach. They encourage them to consider the details, to compare and contrast and to discuss their ideas with others. Throw in a few questions about specifically creative topics such as music and art:

- ▶ *'How many different ways could you use a paper clip?'*
- ▶ *'What's the best way to stay friends with someone?'*

(Contd)

- ▶ *'Which other singers could perform that song really well?'*
- ▶ *'Which paintings from the gallery will you remember most clearly?'*

Use this kind of questioning to strengthen your child's communication skills. Add some of your own opinions into the mix and give them time to reassess their ideas.

Help your child to pursue creative solution to problems, trying different thought processes until they find the answer. Share puzzles with them that require a mixture of logical and 'lateral' thought:

- ▶ *'What looks like a cat, smells like a cat, sounds like a cat, but has eight legs?' (Two cats)*
- ▶ *'How can you remove a coin from an empty glass bottle without damaging the bottle or pulling out the cork?' (Push the cork into the bottle, then let the coin fall out)*
- ▶ *'Mrs Jones has three children, and half of them are girls. How come?' (They're all girls!)*

Give your child a flexible approach to problem-solving that helps them tackle many different challenges in school.

The investigator

Make sure they continue...

...exploring the areas that excite them, and finding new topics of fascination.

Research into the childhoods of eminent scientists has shown that the vast majority of them started young, building up large collections of objects and facts. Support your own child by taking them to visit the local wildlife pond or free town museum. Libraries as well as bookshops are wonderful sources of information, and of course the internet – used carefully and safely – will help them with their research. Be as patient as you can with their growing collections, encouraging them to organize and store things as carefully as possible. Look for opportunities for them to meet with like-minded learners, either online or in clubs or societies. Subscriptions to appropriate magazines or newsletters make fantastic presents for the investigator in your family.

Help them learn to...

...develop general knowledge and common sense. Help them find ways of putting the information they learn into context and connecting it with their own life, for example:

▶ *'And just think, that palaeontologist was once a school child like you. Maybe you could find out what sort of family life he had?'*
▶ *'You know so much about the Apollo astronauts. I wonder how many people are training to go into space right now. What would it take for you to join them?'*

Conversations like this help your child to think about the real significance of the details they're amassing, and to connect different topics of research. Encourage them to link new topics in school with the information they already know. A Science lesson about habitats might enrich their understanding of dinosaurs, and tap into their general expertise about animals and plants. Art work on movement could draw on their wealth of knowledge about F1 racing, as well as giving new insights into their favourite sport.

(Contd)

Make sure you celebrate their less 'specialist' understanding, for example, of games, day-to-day tasks or other people's feelings. Give them opportunities to talk about their passions to people of different ages, and to reflect on how well they did. Which were the most interesting bits? Was there too little or too much detail? How could they make the same information even more exciting and useful next time?

The visionary

Make sure they continue...

...believing in their big ideas, and forming and communicating new theories about the world.

Celebrate their understanding at different stages in their development:

▶ *'Yes, maybe every grumpy person should be given a pet to stroke!'*
▶ *'You're right: we're all much more tired by Friday night. I love your idea to relax some of the mealtime rules.'*
▶ *'What an interesting plan to stop people dropping so much litter. What sorts of advertising would be best for getting your message across?'*
▶ *Talk to them about ideas you've had and why you felt so strongly about them.*
▶ *Tell them about great visionaries and architects of change: Gandhi, Nightingale, Obama.*
▶ *Help your visionary child to start a blog about children's rights or join an internet forum about the environment.*
▶ *Encourage them to read responses carefully and to consider other people's points of view.*

▶ *Remind them of the times when they and others had to adjust their views and reassess their vision.*

'Prediction' games are good for this. You both have a go at predicting how a football game or maths lesson or walk in the countryside will go, then you observe events closely before discussing whose vision was closer to the truth. How useful did the predictions turn out to be? Did they help with the activity – and how could they be made even more accurate and useful in the future? Your child needs the self-belief to put forward their big ideas to others, as well as the flexibility and confidence to adjust their thinking in the light of experience.

Help them learn to...

...understand the impact of their words and to use their visionary skills in the most appropriate ways.

Use role play. Tell your child that you're the choreographer and they're the dancer. They have to show how their character feels – using just facial expressions and body language – when they receive different sorts of news.

First, you (the choreographer in this scenario) tell the dancer that tomorrow's performance has to be completely different. Everything about today's show was off the mark: wrong movements, wrong emotions, wrong interpretation altogether. So what would the dancer look like when they heard that? Depressed, confused, angry, crushed?

Next, you describe a moment before the rehearsal process even started. The choreographer is describing a vision for the dance, but talking about how hard it will be to achieve. Again, your child needs to respond appropriately: unsure, nervous, co-operative but not hopeful.

(Contd)

And what about during the performance? How would the dancer react to a frown, thumbs up, pointing, head shaking – or no direction from the choreographer at all?

Try different approaches to this imaginary relationship and let your child play both roles. There are plenty of other 'visionary' scenarios you could explore: coach and player, boss and worker, architect and builder. Show your child the effects that different ways of speaking can have. Help them to understand that great visionaries are confident and clear enough to inspire others, but also gentle and reflective, supporting others and adjusting their big ideas when necessary.

The builder

Make sure they continue...

...being excited and motivated by physical building projects. Get them using 'free' materials, like cardboard boxes and off-cuts of wood, as well as manufactured construction kits. Encourage them to explore different subjects through the objects they build:

▶ *'Can you make the castle where the princess lives?'*
▶ *'Let's try to build a model of the solar system.'*
▶ *'How about constructing your own Tudor house?'*

Invite other children round to help. Get involved yourself from time to time and show off some of your own craft skills.

By reading library books, exploring internet sites, speaking to some of your friends, and maybe even visiting workshops, studios or building sites, your child can develop a rich understanding of many different construction roles: architect, chef, instrument maker, potter, tailor, engineer... Give them ideas for their own projects as well as inspiration for where their skills might take them.

Help them learn to...

...think through their plans before they start to build, and to discuss their work before, during, and after the physical construction process.

Natural builders often dive straight into *doing*. They benefit from developing their abstract thinking skills, which are usually strong but underused. Talk to your child about the reasons behind a project as well as their overall vision for the finished work. What are the things that will make it successful? What alternative approaches might they take? How will other people react to it, use it, and benefit from it in the end?

Use construction tasks to extend your child's writing, speaking and interpersonal skills. Show them how a simple design brief will help them organize their thinking, explore alternatives and present their ideas. It can be fun to make yourself the 'client' and set a particular challenge: something practical, solving real problems or something creative or artistic:

▶ *'You could do with something to sort out all your comics.'*
▶ *'We need some exciting new Christmas decorations for the hallway.'*
▶ *'Build me a natural sculpture with those twigs, stones and shells.'*

Before the building work starts, tell them you'll need to see notes and plans and a few different options to choose between. Encourage them to talk to you as well as to show you their writing. Gently challenge some of the ideas they've come up with. Keep reminding them of your needs, both practical and emotional:

▶ *'Is this bit going to be big enough?'*
▶ *'How will that material make me feel when I touch it?'*

(Contd)

- ▶ *'What words will people use to describe your creation?'*

Once the work has been finished, constructor and client need to discuss how well it's been achieved. Make sure you praise them for their hard work, but also help your child to assess their success. Encourage them to describe what they were hoping to do and to compare their vision with what they actually came up with. How do they feel about it now? What could they do next time to make it even better?

Use the project to stimulate writing. Young children often enjoy writing on sticky notes that they can fasten to their work, labelling different parts or explaining what they do. Older children can record the story of their project in diary or newspaper form.

Models provide great stimulation for creative writing:

- ▶ *'Write me the story of the king who lives in your castle.'*
- ▶ *'What sort of poem would go with your sculpture?'*

To work well with others, an approach that blends practical skills with confident communication is hugely beneficial to your child.

The story teller

Make sure they continue...

...reading and telling a wide range of stories, helping to boost their imagination, understanding and memory.

Stories represent a powerful combination of creativity and structure, essential for powerful thinking and learning. Give your child access to stories from different ages and cultures and show them the recurring themes and key features that make stories universally popular. When sharing one story, ask them about other stories they've read or heard that are similar. See if they can use their 'story sense' to guess what happens next, or to say why a surprise ending is so unexpected.

Find time to read and listen to your child's stories. Celebrate their effort and imagination and be specific in praising the aspects you really like. Offer constructive criticism, discuss their own assessment of the story's plot, characters, language use and so on – but always make it clear that you're helping them because they're already so talented with stories.

Help them learn to...

...respond positively to other people's ideas. Confident story tellers are sometimes reluctant to let others into their creative process, certain that they have the perfect plan for a game or activity. They can miss out on opportunities to learn from others.

Adding random elements to story-telling can help. You could put several interesting objects in a bag and ask your child to reach in and pick one. Whatever comes out has to be mentioned at the start of the story; the next thing must belong to the first character to appear; then each new item has to be included in sequence as the story progresses.

Dice are also useful for improving your child's flexibility and their confidence to change plans. At key stages in the story – for example, describing the character or choosing

(Contd)

an ending – write down six options. Rolling the die then makes the decision, and the rule is that you have to follow it, however hard it may seem.

The die could rule between different character names, homes or modes of transport; details of potions, fights, dreams; or the big things that motivate the characters or cause important turning points in the plot.

Encourage your child to use their creative story-telling skills in seemingly logical subjects like Numeracy and Science. Young children have always been helped to count and calculate by rhymes and songs, so why not continue this when they start grappling with abstract concepts like division, percentages or averages? Ask your child to tell you a story about the numbers in a fraction and you'll both see how much they really understand. Thinking up a memorable story about triangles, 3D shapes or co-ordinates really will strengthen your child's knowledge and skills.

Challenge your child to tell you the 'story' of pollination, from the perspective of the flower, an insect or even the wind. See if they can talk or write about each stage in an experiment – perhaps as the diary of a scientist, in comic strip form, or as a film screenplay. The more creativity they can inject into every subject, the better. It boosts their understanding and memory as well as helping them to work in an imaginative and organized way with others.

Insight

Encourage your child to extend their range of story types: short stories, different genres, stories told using film, MP3, comic strips, puppets... When they write their own stories, push them to try new forms – sometimes producing several different treatments of the same story. This will be a very valuable skill in collaborative work.

Make sure they continue...

...attacking problems from different angles and having the
bravery to produce unexpected results. Whenever they do
have moments of brilliant insight, make sure you celebrate
them and put them to good use. Be very clear about what
they've achieved, for example:

▶ *'Your idea about the route to take saved us so much time.'*
▶ *'That's a great arrangement for sharing the toys: it'll
really help you all get along.'*

Talk to them about the process that led up to their clever ideas:

▶ *'You didn't go for the easy answer; you used your
imagination to see things from back to front and
came up with a brilliant plan.'*

Give them puzzles to solve that will suit their creative brain:

▶ *'A girl bought a pair of socks, and found that each sock
had a hole it in. But she didn't take them back to the
shop. Why not?'*
▶ *'Jim and Joe were born to the same parents on the same
day, but they're not twins. How come?'*

There are many sensible responses to both of these questions,
as well as a perfect solution to each one. Encourage your
child to ask questions so that you can take part in the
solving process with them:

▶ *'No, she wasn't afraid of the shopkeeper.'*
▶ *'Yes, they definitely have the same mother and father –
and they're not adopted.'*

(Contd)

Encourage your rebel thinker to trust their instincts, to follow up questions and to listen carefully for clues that might just connect them to the answers. (Which are: 'Because all socks have holes in, otherwise you wouldn't get them on your foot'; and 'Jim and Joe weren't twins because they were triplets – you just weren't told about their brother John.')

Help them learn to...

...use logical thought when necessary, organizing all their work, checking the details, and presenting it as neatly and attractively as they can.

Show them pictures from the notebooks of Leonardo da Vinci. He had remarkable ideas, demonstrating new ways of seeing things and creating wild, world changing inventions. His books are a fascinating mixture of free creativity and detailed logic. His imaginative drawings are labelled carefully, the colours of his paintings considered and noted with absolute precision. On the other hand, his technical diagrams are decorated with energetic notes and doodles and drawn with real imaginative flair. Talk to your child about the importance of combining both these approaches in one.

Encourage them to keep a notebook or their own. They can jot down random thoughts and start ordering them into lists, choosing some to work on and others to discard. Like Leonardo they can use their creative skills to record their thoughts quickly and imaginatively, but they can also use the book as an 'instruction manual' for putting their thinking to practical use. Show them how to grade their ideas, ticking off any particularly good ones that can be put into action.

'Simon says' is an excellent game for encouraging rule-following in a relaxed and fun way. Once your child has had a go at following your instructions (doing an action only when they hear the words 'Simon says...'), they can have a go at telling you what to do. Let them be as creative, funny and challenging as they want, exercising that side of their character at the same time as dealing with logic, rules and the adjudications that have to be made.

Insight

Help them to use their notebook to develop their handwriting and presentation. Follow Leonardo's lead and sprinkle in some secret codes and backwards writing. Children with the rebel character type will really benefit from seeing the value in written work, and realizing that they can still use and show off their interesting personality and quirky thoughts.

The entertainer

Make sure they continue...

...exciting themselves and others with their performance skills.

Encourage your child to develop their acting, singing and dancing. When they're young, read stories with them in funny voices and get them to play along. Teach them songs, give them pots and pans to use as musical instruments, provide different sorts of music for them to dance to.

When they're older, find out about drama clubs, dance sessions, choirs, bands: opportunities they'll love and learn from. Take them to plays, ballets, operas, pantomimes – either professional productions or more affordable amateur shows.

Encourage them to inject drama into their learning. Show them how reading information aloud or acting it out makes

(Contd)

it instantly more memorable. Challenge them to use their imagination and put themselves in historical roles. Can they talk to you as Henry VIII, using the facts they've learnt at school to get into character? Can they mime a role in the Battle of Hastings, a medieval joust or a ritual from Ancient Egypt?

Develop their dramatic skills alongside their creativity. Give them and their friends a set of random items to use as props in three different scenes. Challenge them to think up a variety of ways to move across the room, dance with an umbrella or put on a pair of imaginary Wellington boots.

Help them learn to...

...take their turn, fit in with others, and feel as confident with written work as with performance.

Try the following turn-taking drama activity. A group of children sit in a circle, and they're given a simple object, for example a wooden brick, a hairbrush or a pen. The first person takes hold of the object and uses it as a prop, presenting an action to the rest of the group before passing it on in silence to the next person. They have to think of a new use for the object, act it out and then pass it on – until everyone has had a turn.

After that, the person left with the object tries to describe from memory what everyone did, for example, 'Jamie, I think you used the brick to take a phone call; then Kate turned it into an ice cream to lick...'

If they forget or wrongly describe someone's action, that person takes over and tries to get around everyone correctly.

It's a great activity for reminding strong performers that everyone in a group can use their dramatic talents. It helps them to watch and listen as well as to entertain, to change their plans to fit in with other people's choices, and to connect their drama abilities to their creativity and memory skills.

Although written work may not be your child's favourite form of expression, you can show them how drama can inspire brilliant ideas. Before they start writing a story, role play some possible scenes. Ask 'How might the main character walk?'; 'What would an evil queen's voice sound like?' Your child may well enjoy visualizing the story as a play or film before trying to put it into words. Show them playscripts to help them understand the importance of carefully constructed written language, and encourage them to see writing and performing as two sides of the same creative process.

The talker

Make sure they continue...

...using their communication skills to explore information, share ideas with others and boost their learning.

The more conversations you have with your child about their learning, the more they'll value talk and use it positively themselves. Sometimes be explicit: 'Let's talk about your history topic, the Victorians.' Sometimes let the conversation shift naturally in the direction of learning: 'And on the way home we'll have a go on the slot machines on the pier – which you're learning about in History, aren't you?' Don't force conversations, but also don't miss opportunities to chat to your child about their interests in and out of school.

(Contd)

Challenge your child to speak for a minute about a topic from any area of school: multiplication, festivals, hockey, biscuit making. Review their performance (perhaps even recording and playing it back). Agree on marks out of ten for interest, fluency, content and so on, and then have a go yourself, on a subject of their choice! Encourage your child to connect talk with learning, to reflect on the quality of communication, and to consider the benefits of being focused, organized, interesting and clear.

Help them learn to...

...work in silence when required, confidently producing written work that powerfully communicates their thoughts.

Letter writing is a good way to encourage talkers to become writers. As soon as they start to write, give your child sticky notes, postcards and labels to use for sending messages – to you, brothers and sisters and other family and friends. Reply by sticking your own notes to their bedroom door or tucking them in their school bag. You'll begin a fun dialogue and excite them about putting their thoughts into writing.

Older children can send full-blown postcards, letters and emails. As well as thanking them for their messages, don't be afraid to mention any bits that you found unclear or confusing. Help them to see that spelling, grammar and punctuation matter, along with overall presentation and the 'voice' of the writing.

Give them opportunities to write to others outside the family. Perhaps they could write a thank you letter to a restaurant, or send some suggestions to the local zoo? Work with your child to get the tone right; not too formal, not overly familiar. Sometimes let them watch you composing letters or emails. Show them how careful you are to convey the right information in the most appropriate writing style.

A natural talker finds speaking fun, so make sure they know that writing can be fun too. They might like to start a diary, draft a plan for a day out or make their own party invitations. Find opportunities for them to write lists, reports, reviews – and any other ways they can think of to communicate and collaborate effectively with others.

Insight

When you're watching TV or listening to the radio with your child, discuss the different sorts of talk you see and hear. Which famous people are really good communicators, and who's less talented at using their voice?

Simply by providing your child with a range of people to talk to, you will boost their speaking and listening skills and their confidence to alter their speech to suit different situations. This becomes vital when they start using their talent for talking in school.

The entrepreneur

Make sure they continue...

...pushing themselves to succeed and valuing their achievements.

The young entrepreneur will naturally seek out ways to challenge their abilities and win rewards; but keep your eyes open for ideas of your own. Check community newsletters, posters in the library and local and national publications for competitions your child might want to enter. Encourage them to take on roles in fundraising events, in and out of school. Challenge them to make and save the

(Contd)

money they need to buy that must-have video game or new bike. Celebrate their efforts as much as their successes. Their will to win is going to drive their success in school.

Your child's entrepreneurial projects can help them develop a range of skills. Discuss the ways in which they plan, research and finance their schemes. Whether they're making lemonade to sell on hot days, organizing a yard sale or persuading friends to sponsor them for charity, there are plenty of powerful learning opportunities. Ask them to explain the costs and profits (they'll be good at that!), their methods of communication and any art and design details involved.

Encourage your child to set up their own reward schemes. What sort of treats would they deserve if they kept their room tidy; improved their score in the weekly spelling test; or spent 20 minutes working on their mental maths? Being able to self-motivate helps children to build a strong, persistent and focused approach to work – all traits that will be very appealing to the people they work alongside.

Help them learn to...

...find pleasure in learning itself.

Sometimes learning is its own reward: the interesting research, the knowledge and skills collected, the enjoyment of working with others. Talk to your child about the things they've enjoyed about the learning process, rather than just highlighting their successes and failures. Discuss the topics they'd like to explore and the skills they'd choose to develop.

Make sure your child takes part in collaborative activities where there are no specific rewards, just the experience of working in a group and the pleasure of a job well done. Dance troupes, choirs and 'secret clubs' with friends all help children to balance their competitive instincts with the intangible benefits of being part of a team.

Show your child that they can set themselves competitively high standards for their behaviour. They'll probably enjoy writing up lists of rules to work to, about their approach to school or friendships or household tasks. Discuss their 'golden rules' for success. Get to know more about their priorities by talking through the things they've included on their list, and those they've left out. Sticking their finished lists in clear view – on the fridge, family message board or living room door – shows you think there's great value in scoring success by these criteria, as well as using all the more obvious markers of profit and victory.

Most schools have very clear rules regarding children's attitudes and behaviour. The sooner your child can match their energy and ambition to these standards, the easier they'll find it to succeed within their school community.

NEW EXPERIENCES

For all children, learning to work with others means stepping into the unknown. Other people are unpredictable, even when your child knows all the other members of their new class or school. The more you can build up their confidence about coping with the 'new', whether it's food, music, places or people, the better prepared they'll be to cope with the opportunities and challenges of school. By letting them try new things within the safety of their family, you show children that they can conquer their fears and give almost anything a go.

Insight

I always tell children in my class the motto of the mongooses in Rudyard Kipling's *The Jungle Book*: 'Run and find out!' I want them to relish new discoveries, bring energy to exploring and enjoy sampling the new – whatever happens.

People's attitudes to food are often very similar to their attitudes to trying anything that's new and unpredictable. Use family meal times to encourage your child's positive outlook and their strength of character in any unpredictable situation. It will rub off on their whole approach to learning. After all, a lack of knowledge about something can be either very scary, or very exciting. Confident children will learn to choose exciting. Here are some tips for introducing a new food.

▶ *They may love a new food or absolutely hate it, but it won't kill them, and they should never be worried or embarrassed about their reaction.*

▶ *Encourage your child to describe their opinion about each new food they taste. Be specific: What's the best adjective for it? What would improve the flavour?*

▶ *Celebrate the fact that they were brave enough to give it a try. This fearless, uninhibited attitude is so important for learning in groups.*

▶ *Push them to be positive. Wouldn't it be good if, one day, they did like this food and had more ways of enjoying a meal?*

▶ *Explain that trying a tiny bit of a food again and again helps you get to like it in the end.*

▶ *Tell your child about the 'new' foods that you hated when you were little, but kept trying – and finally enjoyed.*

Use dice to prepare your child for the unpredictability of learning with others, and to show them the fun they can have when other people get involved. Before an activity – a trip to the zoo, a piano lesson, a visit to the library to find out about aeroplanes – play a quick game. Think up a few questions, along with different decisions that the die could make:

'Where shall we start at the zoo? Throwing one will send us to the penguin pool, two to the lions, three to the chimps...'
'Which order are you going to practise scales today? Six is C major, five is D minor...'
'What sort of planes shall we learn about first? An odd number means we'll do jet planes, an even number will be planes with propellers.'

Games like these give children the confidence to cope when some of the decisions are taken out of their hands. They're a fun way to develop the relaxed and flexible approach that plays such a big part in learning.

As adults we can learn a lot from children's fresh, unprejudiced views. We can celebrate the open-minded way they approach new information and experiences, and mirror it in our own behaviour to show them it's an attitude to be valued and retained.

Insight

I like this quote from the nineteenth century biologist and educator Thomas Huxley: 'Sit down before fact as a little child, be prepared to give up every conceived notion, follow humbly... or you will learn nothing.'

Take your child to new places and talk to them about their feelings: the differences from home that they're worried about, the things they might miss but also the ways in which this place could be fantastic. Celebrate the bravery they show when they leave their comfort zone.

Your child will pick up so much from your approach to travel; in particular how you talk to the new people you meet. Make sure your own conversations with strangers are respectful but confident. Value their contributions and perspectives. Discuss the rules, languages and customs of a new place and how you might all fit in with them. Encourage your child to make friends on holiday, and share details about themselves as well as learning about other people's lives.

10 THINGS TO REMEMBER

1 *Give children opportunities to lead groups, and to take on different roles within learning teams.*

2 *Encourage their puzzle-solving skills as well as their interest in more open-ended questions.*

3 *Support their investigations into the subjects they love, and show them ways to put their understanding to practical use.*

4 *Celebrate your child's big ideas and help them to take other people's views into account.*

5 *Give them plenty of opportunities to make and build, using their practical skills to stimulate all areas of their thinking.*

6 *Widen the range of stories they hear and tell, challenging them to go beyond familiar patterns and to use stories to explore new information.*

7 *Celebrate unconventional thinking, but make sure it's balanced by logic and order when necessary.*

8 *Nurture your child's performance skills and their confidence to entertain, while also helping them to collaborate with others and to inject drama and flair into their written work.*

9 *Encourage them to be confident communicating with both the spoken and the written word.*

10 *Celebrate and challenge children's competitive spirit, but also teach them to find pleasure in learning itself.*

4

Putting your child in control

In this chapter you will learn:
- *how to equip children with a wide range of communication skills*
- *why talking to children affects the way they think and learn*
- *exercises to boost children's confidence and help them deal with worries and fears*
- *the vital link between self-control and success in school*
- *the impact of TV, computers and video games on children's learning.*

The confidence to be brilliant comes from a deep feeling of being in control. This doesn't mean becoming a control freak or needing to have things your own way all the time. In fact you can still feel confident, while acknowledging that there are plenty of things you're not sure about and want to improve. You're not desperate to push yourself forward, be brash or bossy. You just know that you can cope with new challenges, use your skills wisely and build on what you've already achieved. It's the confidence to be flexible and resilient, to make good choices about what you do and how you do it, and to take responsibility for driving forward your own success.

This chapter is about putting your child in control of their learning: giving them effective communication tools, active enquiry skills, and enough understanding about their brain to start using it powerfully in school. By developing their speaking and listening, their appreciation of the senses, and their ability to think both logically and creatively, your child can become a relaxed, ambitious, confident learner.

Taking control of communication skills

Communication skills are vitally important to your child's success and happiness in school. Good communicators:

▶ *have more friends*
▶ *feel more at ease in a range of social situations*
▶ *have a healthy awareness of their own feelings and 'inner talk'*
▶ *work well with others to the benefit of all*
▶ *discuss their learning with teachers and access the most appropriate support*
▶ *strengthen their memory skills by vocalizing their knowledge*
▶ *become active participants in the flow of information and ideas.*

From the day they're born, the way you talk to your child plays a huge role in shaping their communication skills. Children spoken to with care and respect will develop the same skills for dealing with others. When parents calmly outline their perspectives, discuss ideas and negotiate patiently, their children learn the importance of this approach and start using it. The more your child hears language being used in positive ways, the better they'll be at building up a repertoire of beneficial language skills.

WALKING AND TALKING

Taking a walk in the countryside is an excellent way to promote good communication with your child. Away from the distractions of home you can relax in the fresh air, gain some perspective on

everyday life, and let all the interesting sights, sounds and smel~
inspire your conversation.

The rhythm of your walking can help to regulate your words.
So often our communications in families are rushed and chaotic:
snatched moments on the move or stressed instructions and
complaints. Enjoy the chance to settle into a much more
comfortable rhythm of thought and speech.

Use the natural world as a source of interesting questions. Your
child may well have questions about the names of trees and birds,
the laws of nature, along with the inevitable 'How much further
is it?' Vary your answering style, sometimes supplying a factual
response ('That one's a silver birch'), sometimes nudging them into
answering their own question ('It looks very similar to that bird
Grandpa told you about – remember?') and sometimes replying
with a question of your own ('How far do *you* think it is, bearing
in mind we're more than half way there?')

Encourage your child to talk to you about their surroundings.
You might gently challenge them to describe every different colour
they can see, or to choose their favourite textures and tell you
why they're so appealing. You can still talk about everyday things;
just take the chance to sprinkle in a few bits of 'communication
training' along the way. The ability to take inspiration from their
senses and to talk freely and confidently will be hugely helpful to
your child in school.

Walks outdoors also involve times of silence: opportunities to
communicate with yourself, to ponder and collect your thoughts and
to consider the next thing to say. Our hectic lifestyles often infringe
on these moments but they're a vital part of communication.
Without them, children find it hard to hear the voice in their own
head. We can all benefit from time to think before we open our
mouth.

As you walk together, enjoy the opportunity to share ideas,
memories and jokes. However old your child is – from a baby in

wards – a nature walk is a great chance to learn
...er. Enjoy answering questions as well as asking
...nonstrate how much you value time spent talking

wi...

These principles of good communication can be nurtured in
many other ways. Especially with young children, many of your
conversations will be motivated by the question 'Why?' I remember
one 15-minute walk to the shops with my four-year-old son
during which I was asked 'Why...?' 39 times! It's a very powerful
question; the starting point for huge discoveries in science,
mathematics and philosophy.

SOCRATIC QUESTIONING

Socrates, the great Athenian philosopher, developed a style of
learning through asking carefully chosen questions; questions that
probe much more deeply than simply asking for factual answers.
This 'Socratic' questioning is a very powerful technique to try
with children, strengthening their confidence to be persistent and
creative as they pursue the answers themselves. It also prepares
them for the dynamic question and answer relationships they'll
need to develop in school.

Socrates used six main types of question.

1 *Questions that clarify the enquiry and encourage deeper
   thinking:*
     ▷ *'Can you tell me exactly what you mean?'*
     ▷ *'What's made you so interested in that?'*
2 *Questions that challenge assumptions:*
     ▷ *'How will we know for sure?'*
     ▷ *'What other reasons could there be?'*
3 *Questions that test the evidence:*
     ▷ *'Can you prove that's true?'*
     ▷ *'Are there any clues that say something else?'*

4 *Questions from different viewpoints:*
   ▷ *'Is there another way of looking at it?'*
   ▷ *'What if you tried a different experiment?'*
5 *Questions that test logic:*
   ▷ *'So what do you think would happen then?'*
   ▷ *'How does it fit in with what we learnt yesterday?'*
6 *Questions about questions:*
   ▷ *'Is that the best question to ask about this?'*
   ▷ *'Why do you think I asked you that?'*

Rather than ending a line of enquiry, questions can be powerful starting points for learning. Children need to get used to asking and answering a variety of questions, developing the confidence and flexibility of thought to use them to structure their thinking and move it on. And if nothing else, varying your question and answer style removes the responsibility for you to do all the work!

Insight

I know from experience how exhausting this and other forms of question can be, however much you appreciate their significance in children's development. It made a big difference to me when I realized that I didn't have to provide an immediate answer to every single question I was asked.

Here's an example of Socratic questioning in action, based on a real conversation with my eight-year-old son.

Noah: *'Why can't we see around corners?'*

Dad: *'That's interesting – what do you mean?'* (Clarifying the question)

Noah: *'Well, I know the park is just over there, but I can't see it. Seeing doesn't go around corners.'*

Dad: *'How do you know that?'* (Testing the evidence)

Noah: *'Because I'm looking that way now but I can only see as far at the house on the corner. I can't look around it.'*

Dad: *'What would happen if you could?'* (Testing logic)

Noah: *'The world would be crazy! You'd see everything, all the time.'*

Dad: *'So what question do you really need to ask?'* (Questioning questioning)

Noah: *'I suppose... why can't eyes bend around corners?'*

Dad: *'Are you sure it's your eye that bends around?'* (Challenging assumptions)

Noah: *'No, your eye stays where it is. I mean the light.'*

Dad: *'So think about where the light comes from, and how it travels to your eye.'* (Seeking new viewpoints)

Noah: *'It comes from the Sun really, then it hits something and bounces straight to me.'*

Dad: *'Yes! It travels straight to you, in straight lines. So it can't go round a corner, unless...'*

Noah: *'Unless it bounces off something else. So could you look round corners with mirrors...?'*

Questions are such an important tool for learning. Play games with children that develop their ability to choose effective questions themselves, to hear and remember the answers, and then to use the information they get to drive forward their learning. Children with these skills are able to see problems from different sides, weigh up the pros and cons, and refine their own ideas and opinions.

TWENTY QUESTIONS

This is the classic 'Who am I?' game. Either one player thinks of a person known to the others, then challenges them to work out the name by asking no more than 20 'Yes' or 'No' questions. Or, more elaborately, each player is given a famous person to 'be' – with the name written on a badge or headband that they can't see. In this version it's up to them to ask the questions until they've worked out who they are.

It's a great game for teaching children the importance of carefully chosen questions. To begin with, they may struggle to think of questions that require only 'Yes' or 'No' answers ('What colour is your hair?') or go straight for very limited questions ('Are you the Queen?'). But with some gentle direction, and by listening to others, they can learn to plan ahead and take a more methodical route to the answer. They'll soon see that the best questions give them useful evidence, whether the answer is 'Yes' or 'No', and learn to use each response to help them formulate their next question.

To do well in 'Twenty questions' you need to ask questions that are both accurate and creative, remember each answer, use logic to narrow down the list of possibilities, and have the confidence and persistence to keep thinking clearly even under the pressure of the last few questions. Whether asking or answering, this game teaches so many vital skills for successful communicating, thinking and learning.

Encourage your children to incorporate careful questioning into their everyday conversations, with adult friends and relatives as well as children of their own age. Give praise when you hear them asking their grandparents how they're feeling or questioning a neighbour about their pets. If they find this hard, prime them with ideas for good questions to ask. Let them know that adults often have to prepare a few questions beforehand to ease social situations.

TALKING TO CHILDREN

Ensure that you speak as clearly as you can, slowly enough to be understood, and use gestures and actions to help you get your meaning across. Even older children will appreciate it when you use short sentences for important messages and repeat the key points.

Try to see the world through your child's eyes, physically as well as metaphorically. Sometimes get down to their level to make your communication more equal. See the situation – the mess you want them to tidy, the game that needs to be refereed – from the same physical vantage point as them. There will be times when you need to stand above them to maintain your adult authority, but there's also great benefit in being able to communicate with your child on their own level.

Imagine how your words sound to your child. If you're brave, record yourself speaking to children in different situations, especially when you're helping with their learning. It can be an unsettling but very useful experience to listen back to what you actually said and how you said it. What messages were you *really* giving to your child? For example:

'I'm interested in everything you've got to say.'
'I'm just trying to help you improve.'
'You're getting it wrong and making me frustrated.'
'I wish you'd stop asking so many questions.'

> **Insight**
> Modelling good talking is the best way to develop your child's speaking skills. They'll copy the way you talk to them and use similar strategies to communicate well with friends and teachers.

LISTENING TO CHILDREN

If you're listening to your child speak, make sure they *know* you're listening. Sometimes you'll have to continue driving or making the dinner, but you can always respond with glances and comments that prove you're attentive and interested, valuing what they have to say. If their words turn out to be particularly important, either stop what you're doing to sit face to face and give them your full attention, or agree to wait and talk properly as soon as you can.

When you feel the need to correct something your child has said – the pronunciation of a word, for example, or a bit of grammar – think carefully about the best way to do it. Stop your child in their tracks too many times and they'll become incredibly frustrated and nervous; but ignore every mistake and they're liable to develop some very hard-to-break habits. Casual correcting is the best way to strike the right balance. Choose your battles; focus on one language rule at a time. We spent several weeks gently turning our daughter's 'I done' into 'I *did*'. Let your child know you value what they have to say, but that how they say it is also very important.

Show your child that you've listened and responded to their words. If you agree to do something for them, make absolutely sure you do it. If you like their idea, put it into practice:

'Look, I remembered what you said about turning the DVD off standby.'
'I thought we'd try that tip you heard about putting mint on our strawberries.'

Let your child know that their words have power.

As with talking, your child's effective listening skills are best learnt from you. Take the time and care to lead by example and you'll help them learn to listen politely and effectively, in school and out.

BODY LANGUAGE

How well can your child understand non-verbal clues? It's a vital part of their communication, helping them to work with a range of other people and to build strong relationships. You help them develop it by using exaggerated facial gestures, actions and contrasting tones of voice when they're babies, but then you keep doing it, in more subtle ways, throughout their childhood.

Sometimes pause before you speak, using facial expressions to show what you're feeling. A big grin, raised eyebrow or questioning scratch of the head will fire your child's thought processes and get them ready for whatever you need to say. It trains them to read these signals and to use expression and body language to strengthen their own communication.

Try an experiment with your child. First, discuss which they think is most important: *what* someone says or *how* they say it. Push them to be specific. If one is more important than the other, how *much* more?

Then give them some 'neutral' lines to read out. For example:

'I'm going to the shops.'
'Tomorrow it's Thursday.'

Ask them to read the lines aloud with no particular expression in their voice, and then you do the same.

Next, both try reading the lines with some very extreme expressions. Imagine you're incredibly excited. How will you say the lines now? What about if you're furiously angry, terrified or overjoyed? Have fun experimenting with the way the lines sound now and the effects they have on you as listeners.

After that, use lines that should convey a particular emotional message – but say them in a way that expresses something very different.

So you might shout, 'I love you!' as angrily as you can; mutter 'I'm so excited, I've just won a million pounds' in the most bored voice you can manage; or merrily say, 'I'm in terrible pain, I'm so unhappy', giggling and with a glint in your eye.

Try different forms of body language too, testing out what happens when someone's words don't match their facial expressions or body postures.

After trying these activities, ask your child again which is more important: *what* they say or *how* they say it. It's likely that their views will have changed dramatically, now that they've seen what an impact tone and posture can have on meaning. And it's not just a slight effect. The words we hear become almost meaningless compared with the evidence we take from how someone speaks to us.

Realizing this can make a huge difference to how your child communicates with others.

Trying this activity together gives you something specific to refer to when real-life situations need unpicking, for example:

'Why do you think she got so upset when you said that?'
'How are you going to discuss that with your teacher?'
'How should we break the news to Mum?'

COMMUNICATION GAMES

Many family games are great for strengthening communication. Playing 'Charades' with different generations can test everyone's skills to the limit. It's especially good for teaching children to communicate in different ways to different people. After all, you need to think very carefully about which references and clues Grandma or six-year-old Charlie will understand. You also need to ask questions very carefully, think logically and creatively, and exercise so many of your thinking skills under pressure.

You can even inject a bit of mime into everyday life. At school, with 32 children eager to ask questions and find out what's happening next, I often rest my voice and mime the answer, or ask them to put their requests to me in the form of a mime.

Taking control of confidence-building

Strategies to strengthen communication with others are also
important for developing children's self-talk, their confidence and
their sense of self-worth.

If your child can see from different points of view, put issues into
perspective, and work through problems independently with a
balance of logic and creativity, then they'll be well equipped to
deal with many of life's problems. They'll build up useful levels
of resilience and mental 'toughness', along with the strategies
necessary for balancing their emotions and reframing their
thoughts. They'll learn how to take an active role in promoting
their own mental wellbeing and do wonders for their overall
self-esteem.

Use Socratic questioning to challenge children's limiting beliefs:

- ▶ *'What exactly are you saying about your handwriting?'*
  (Clarify the concern)
- ▶ *'Do you think that's what all your teachers would say?'*
  (Challenge assumptions)
- ▶ *'What did your last art assessment actually tell you?'*
  (Test the evidence)
- ▶ *'What would Leonardo da Vinci say about your science?*
  (Take different viewpoints)
- ▶ *'What's the worst thing that could happen on sports day?'*
  (Use logic)
- ▶ *'What would be a better question to ask about your new
  school?'(Question questioning itself)*

There are plenty of other practical measures you can take to ⟨…⟩ children's confidence and self-esteem, encouraging them to t⟨…⟩ new things, to set higher targets, and to enjoy all their learning experiences.

Take every opportunity to display the best examples of your child's work. It can be counter-productive to praise everything, suggesting that the quality of the work isn't actually that important. Instead, choose their most impressive pieces:

▶ *Put pictures into good-quality frames and hang them up in prominent places around the house.*
▶ *Find effective ways of storing and displaying all their certificates, medals and rosettes.*
▶ *Take photographs of art, models, sports events, even bits of written work, and use them as screensaver images on your laptop or mobile phone.*
▶ *Turn your child's best work into a calendar, mouse mat or your family Christmas card.*

Make sure that everyone with a stake in your child's wellbeing knows when they've enjoyed a success worth celebrating.

THE 'WHAT IF?' GAME

This is a quick and fun activity to boost your child's resilience and acceptance of change, as well as strengthening their key skills of communication and creativity.

Start with a simple proposition, for example: 'What if… it rained this afternoon?' The response from your child is likely to be fairly straightforward: 'Then we'd have to wear our raincoats on the way home from school.' But now it's their turn to add a bit more imagination to the game: 'What if our raincoats all had big holes in them?' The creative process could continue:

'Then we'd get really wet. And what if… we got so wet that we caught a terrible cold and had to be rushed to hospital?'

'We'd have an exciting ride in the ambulance. But what if the ambulance driver couldn't find the hospital in the rain?'
'Then he might have to stop and ask for directions. And the person he asked would offer to come along too, to show him the way. What if he was really a robber and tried to steal the ambulance...?'

In no time at all you're working together to write a weird and wonderful story, your questions opening up interesting possibilities. In a very natural way your child is encouraged to consider both positive and negative ideas, to think logically and creatively, and to keep imagining *beyond* each event. It's a really useful habit to get into, helping them to put problems into perspective. Things that might at first seem like crises can actually turn out to be opportunities. When everything's going well, you need to be ready to cope with challenges. And in the midst of disaster, you can use your flexible thinking skills to find solutions – and to *feel* better about whatever happens next.

Insight

Laurence Shorter's book *The Optimist* reveals that a key characteristic of optimistic people is actually their realism: the ability to recognize failures as well as successes, and to keep both in perspective. Your child's optimistic outlook will be boosted by their ability to think creatively, to visualize situations from different angles, and to focus on details.

The term 'cognitive flexibility' is increasingly being used to describe the most effective way of challenging anxiety and low self-esteem. If your child can find different ways of viewing events, and take some control over how they process their experiences, it will be good for their mental health in general as well as having a profound effect on their confidence to think and learn in school.

Games like these help your child to stretch their imagination as they explore and learn. The Mad Hatter from *Alice's Adventures in Wonderland* is a good role model for this sort of thinking: 'When I was your age, I always did it for half an hour a day.

Why, sometimes I've believed as many as six impossible things before breakfast.'

Research shows that children with high levels of self-esteem are less likely to suffer badly when things go wrong. If they have deep-seated confidence, a wide range of interests and a repertoire of strategies to try – plus, of course, a supportive family – then they'll feel able to keep going and to try again.

> ### Insight
> The Nobel Prize-winning scientist Peter Medawer once wrote that the secret of his success was 'treasuring his failures'.

Often, talent in a certain area comes from a particular sensitivity to it – so a child risks suffering a major dent in their confidence if things go wrong. The more they can back up their natural talents with a strong set of thinking and learning skills, the more robust their abilities and their self-esteem will be.

Henry Ford wrote: 'Whether you think you can, or think you can't, you're probably right.' Boost your child's self-belief and you're sowing the seeds of their long-term success.

THE POWER OF PRAISE

Experiments with rats have shown that intermittent praise works best. The animals rewarded constantly were less motivated than those given treats only when they'd performed a task particularly well.

Praise your child for their efforts as well as their achievements. In an experiment at Columbia University, children were given a test and then praised either for their cleverness or for the effort they'd put in. They were then allowed to choose the level of their next test: about the same, or harder than the first. The children praised for being clever tended to opt for the same sort of challenge, but those praised for their effort were motivated to attempt a harder task.

Specific praise is good, but make sure it doesn't encourage your child simply to repeat the same achievement over and over again.

Ultimately, you want your child to be able to motivate themselves. They need to know that they can achieve great results, enjoy working hard for them and have a positive outlook on their chances of success.

The best learning strategies are also rewards in themselves. They give children access to favourite areas of knowledge and allow them to master desirable skills. The activities explained in this book will help your child know when they've done their best and how to reward themselves appropriately.

Studies have shown that mothers and fathers tend to motivate their children differently. While mothers give reasons to work hard and plenty of verbal advice about strategies to try, fathers are more likely to take a 'hands-on' approach, leading by example and offering instructions that are much more logical and precise. It's interesting that these two approaches reflect 'right brain' and 'left brain' thinking. Clearly children benefit from a good balance of both.

WORRIES AND FEARS

Children are naturally inventive and obedient, exploring their world but also looking for boundaries, structures, patterns. With support, this powerful combination can help them to learn; but it can also help them to learn worries and fears in a way that can be very hard to change. It's not surprising that phobias, the most deep-rooted fears, are created almost exclusively in childhood.

The good news is that the answer may well lie inside the problem. In a safe and comfortable setting, your child's imaginative brain can be used to explore the things that trouble them. The recall strategies explored throughout this book can help to pinpoint the cause of a fear – the experience that laid down the 'danger warning'. And the visualization techniques can be extremely helpful in putting the events into perspective, gaining new understanding of them, and even changing them to make them less troublesome.

To take control of troubling thoughts and memories:

▶ *talk about them, encouraging your child to describe them in detail*

▶ *shift the mental 'camera angle' to show the incident from different points of view – then choose the angle that feels most positive*

▶ *re-size any negative details, removing their power and decreasing their importance – and increasing the size of all the positive ones*

▶ *replay the memory and alter the pace of different moments, speeding up the bad bits and slowing down the details that are more pleasurable to watch.*

This approach works for events that haven't even happened yet. If your child is scared about a test or class party or starting school in general, it may be that those thoughts can be analysed and reframed.

Worried about getting on with the older children? Why not ask your child to picture the playground with them and their friends as the biggest and most confident kids there – or the smallest, if that helps them feel inconspicuous and safe.

Nervous about the residential holiday? Perhaps you could ask them to imagine a couple of activities they might enjoy – as if they were watching them on a DVD years later with their own children. Focus on their smiling face and make that the clearest detail. Turn up the volume on the laughter. Make this the version of events that they return to again and again. They will enjoy feeling their confidence grow.

A fear doesn't have to be eliminated completely, but visualization can remove some of its negative impact and help your child direct their mental energy towards their learning. And helping children take some control over their thoughts and memories may also boost their self-control, which in turn has a major effect on their learning success.

SELF-CONTROL

It seems that the children who can see beyond the immediate moment and focus on long-term benefits are those who motivate themselves more, make better choices and enjoy greater success in the long run.

The classic experiment is the 'marshmallow test', designed by psychology professor Walter Mischel in 1968 and repeated numerous times since. A child is given a plate with a marshmallow on it and told that they can choose to eat the sweet now, or wait for 15 minutes and have two. The children who wait, delaying their gratification to get twice the rewards, are much more likely to do better in school. Nurturing children's self-control is clearly an important way of boosting their brilliance.

Visualization can definitely help. If all you can see is a tasty marshmallow, the computer game that's preferable to doing your revision, or the time your mistake gave away a goal, then it's hard to resist the temptation to eat or play or sit out the match. But if you have a clear picture of something bigger and better, you're much more likely to put up with short-term pain for long-term gain. And with a bit of imagination, that picture can be made irresistible: two giant marshmallows; the theme park trip to celebrate passing an exam; the cheers of the crowd when a soccer team has done its very best.

The more that children challenge themselves, use their thinking skills to make positive choices and reap the rewards, the more this approach becomes habit.

To do well in school, children need to carry with them the deep-seated sense of confidence and safety they get from their family. They need parents who support and guide, but who also give them the space to pursue their own learning – and to talk about it with people that they love.

Researchers watched five-year-old visitors to the Jewish Museum in New York as they received a short lesson and then searched for artefacts in a sandbox. Six years later the children could still remember much of what they'd seen and done – up to 87 per cent – but only when they were engaged in conversation about it and gently 'cued' to trigger their recall.

Other studies have demonstrated the importance of this relaxed, conversational approach, where adults provide opportunities to learn and chat rather than 'teaching' in an explicit way. It makes learning easier and more enjoyable, and it means that children want to do it more.

You give your child so much of their attitude to thinking and learning. It's tempting to focus on their behaviour at school, but make sure you also tell them to do their very best learning. Send them off in the morning looking smart for others to see, but also with a positive picture of themselves and their abilities. Make sure they're provided with the right physical equipment for school, and also equipped with the thinking skills that will help them take a confident, energetic and ambitious approach to every challenge they meet.

Taking control of concentration levels

As well as feeling good about their learning, children need strong skills of concentration to let them use all their thinking strategies to the full. The children who do best in school can learn well during relaxed, collaborative activities, but they're also able to switch on focused concentration and to work silently and independently when required.

> *There's one fault that I find with the twentieth century*
> *And I'll put it in a couple of words: too adventurey.*
> *What I'd like is some nice dull monotony*
> *If anyone's gotony.*
>
> Ogden Nash

Some research suggests that modern life is ruining children's ability to concentrate. Hectic family schedules, fast-paced computer games, TV programmes that whizz from one subject to another every few seconds: it all gets children used to thinking in bursts and to expect a constant level of stimulation and high-energy entertainment. You may see your child watching TV at the same time as playing a computer game, or listening to an MP3 player while surfing the internet, and wonder how they'll ever manage to read quietly, to concentrate on a straightforward lesson in school or to focus on a pen-and-paper test.

But other research has shown that these factors also challenge children to have quick-thinking, flexible brains. Their lifestyles and the technologies they use train them to work on several tasks at once and to connect different activities in useful ways. They respond well to stimulation, and they're ready to be excited about new ideas and to work quickly and efficiently.

As ever, balance is the key, and parental support is essential. More than ever, children need help developing the ability to concentrate on just one thing and to motivate themselves, rather than relying on constant stimulation to interest and entertain them; but the skills required to cope with the fast pace of modern life can also give a huge boost to their learning.

The imagery, sounds and exciting action of video games can be used to stimulate creativity and strengthen memory, and many games promote persistence, problem-solving, and the ability to think under pressure. Children's internet skills train them to process information quickly and make choices about what's useful to know, accessing material from many different sources to widen their knowledge and excite new interests. By multitasking they can actually hone their concentration skills and achieve more with their brains.

With the support of their parents, children can tap into all the benefits of the modern world, while also learning to do without them.

Choose video games wisely. Look for products with opportunities for problem-solving. Help your child to regulate the amount of time they spend playing, but also suggest ways of being successful when they do. Socratic questioning techniques can give them insights into how to break through the next level, and all the other thinking skills developed in this book will increase their chances of solving all the puzzles on the way to completing the mission. Talk to them about how they're using their logic, creativity, memory.

> ### Insight
> Even the most committed video game player will probably enjoy receiving a notepad to write down their thoughts and strategies, widening the range of thinking skills they're inclined to use.

Playing with them sometimes and talking about all the skills involved will help your child keep their electronic activities in perspective, spot parallels with other forms of learning, and be able to readjust to the real world when they turn off.

Find ways to use children's multimedia experiences in their school work. If your child is motivated by the progressively more difficult levels in computer games, perhaps you could structure some of their learning tasks in a similar way, for example: 'Every spelling you remember today counts for one enemy robot. Get at least nine out of ten and you'll be onto the next mission: to beat the alien warlord with your times table speed...'

Help children to access their vivid imagination by reminding them of TV programmes, films, internet sites and computer games. They might try planning a story as if they were going to film it; make their page of notes for a history project look like a brilliant website; or invent a game idea for making percentages exciting. As your child starts using powerful techniques to remember and learn, use the images and structures they're most familiar with to improve their success. Adventures on screen can form the basis for memorable learning adventures in your child's imagination.

Insight

Research in the UK by the charity Childline discovered that children's TV watching has reduced in recent years, but that much more of their time is now being spent looking at computer screens. The average total 'screen time' for 5–16-year-olds was found to be 5 hours 20 minutes a day.

Observe your own child's screen time. Monitor them over a day, a week and a month. Make a simple record of how long they spend at TV and computer screens, the activities they're doing – and any effects you notice on their mood, health or learning ability. Use your research to decide how balanced their multimedia experience seems to be. Ask yourself:

▶ *How does their use of the internet compare with their time spent reading?*
▶ *Are their 'virtual' sports balanced with real, physical, collaborative games and exercise?*
▶ *Are there particular screen activities that frustrate or tire them?*
▶ *Which websites, games or TV programmes seem to improve their concentration or give them interesting ideas?*
▶ *Do any patterns emerge in relation to when, in the day or week, your child sits in front of a screen?*

In my experience in school, children who've enjoyed a wide range of stimulating activities are particularly good at using them to structure and enliven their learning. But they also need the ability to work with others, to concentrate in silence when necess[ary] sometimes, to think carefully about just one thing at a time

Simple games like 'rhyme tennis' promote these essential skills.

RHYME TENNIS

For this game you need two players or two teams. The first player picks a word, then the two sides in the game take it in turns to find a rhyming word that hasn't been said already. The words become the 'balls' that are batted back and forth until someone makes a mistake.

Start slowly. Like real tennis, the players need to warm up. Have a few rounds where you're fairly relaxed about how long each side has to think of their rhyming words. But then step things up a bit. Establish a rhythm, either by using a metronome, some rhythmical music, or by getting the players to clap or stamp their feet. Set the rhythm clearly each round and make it slightly faster for the next one, ramping up the tension and challenging the players to maintain total concentration:

> *'Box' (clap clap) 'Fox' (clap clap) 'Locks' (clap clap) 'Clocks' (clap clap) 'Er...' 'Out!'*

You can score like a real tennis match (love, 15, 30, 40, deuce, advantage, game) or just give keep a running total of the points accumulated by each team.

A stopwatch is a useful tool for improving children's concentration. It can be particularly appealing to them because of its links with sport and physical training at the highest level.

Engage your child by make their own 'training' challenges very explicit:

'You're going to work on your science homework for exactly 15 minutes.'

'We're going to practise your sentence writing for three minutes longer than yesterday.'

> ## Insight
>
> Like a sports coach, use timings to focus and motivate. Get children used to what the passing of time actually feels like, and train them not to waste energy worrying about it. The watch will tell them when the time's up. All their mental energy can go into giving their very best performance.

Start with shorter times for younger children and increase the length of each 'concentration challenge' as their abilities improve. Discuss what you expect them to do within the time, involve them in setting their own manageable targets, and talk about how they're going to succeed.

It's great when children learn to take responsibility for sorting out their own needs: where they want to work, how they're going to minimize distractions, what sorts of thinking they'll be doing to achieve the desired results.

As long as your child can concentrate well in this quiet and focused way, there's no reason why they can't also reap the benefits of hectic multitasking and electronic stimulation. They can learn to enjoy both in a balanced and interconnected way. Having a brilliant book to read after switching off a frustrating computer game might provide the perfect release. Finishing half an hour's quiet maths homework could be rewarded with some time in a busy chatroom catching up with friends.

Your child's ability to concentrate is certainly influenced by their genetic make-up, their character and all the influences that have shaped the way their brain works. And the physical characteristics of their brain are also important, since concentration is controlled by specific areas. Research has shown that these areas differ from child to child in size and complexity. We also know that boys in general have poorer concentration skills than girls; and that boys are much more likely to show signs of conditions such as ADHD (attention deficit hyperactivity disorder) in which they need greater level of stimulation. Observing and understanding your unique child's ability to concentrate is essential to finding the ways to support and improve their success.

As you try out some of the activities suggested in this book, make sure you promote concentration by keeping interruptions to a minimum. Give your child a good chance to get their teeth into a task and try to keep your supportive touch as light as possible. It's easy to get impatient about children's development – but try to hide it, or it will rub off on them and ruin all the good work being done to build their concentration and confidence.

At the same time, teach your child to take short breaks when their concentration is flagging. In school, 'brain breaks' may involve brief exercises to stimulate the body and the brain, boosting alertness and left brain/right brain connections, for example:

▶ *Rub circles on your stomach with one hand while patting your head with the other.*
▶ *Draw the letter A in the air with your left finger, followed by B with your right foot on the floor; then C with your right finger and D with your left foot, and so on.*
▶ *Touch your shoulders so that your arms cross in front of you, right on top of left; then switch to left on top, and back again; several times, faster and faster...*

Play board games with your children. They're a brilliant way of achieving the balance between active stimulation and focused thought. They encourage turn taking, co-operation, patience, friendly competition, and the best games strengthen a wide range of logical and creative thinking skills. They provide a great chance to share natural conversations with your child and to monitor and discuss their developing abilities. At their best, family games represent so many important features of enjoyable, collaborative learning, training your child to achieve the right balance between exciting stimulation and relaxed, controlled concentration.

10 THINGS TO REMEMBER

1 *Give children the confidence to communicate in different ways and in a wide variety of situations.*

2 *Use 'Socratic questioning' to activate their full repertoire of thinking skills.*

3 *Talk and listen to children in a way that supports and extends their learning.*

4 *Correcting mistakes casually helps children to improve without denting their confidence.*

5 *Play games to sharpen their awareness of non-verbal communication.*

6 *Boost your child's 'cognitive flexibility', using imagination to gain some control over thoughts and feelings.*

7 *Re-frame memories that limit their happiness and chances of success in school.*

8 *Strengthening you child's self-control can have a huge effect on their educational achievement.*

9 *Use modern media to stimulate and challenge children's thinking and learning.*

10 *Play games that strengthen attentiveness and concentration.*

5

Key thinking and learning skills

In this chapter you will learn:
- *how to stimulate 'whole-brain' learning*
- *exercises for boosting visualization*
- *why the senses play a vital role in thinking and learning*
- *how to use the powerful 'memory journey' technique*
- *ideas for stretching your child's problem-solving and philosophical thinking skills.*

Information has never been easier to obtain. Most children are now completely used to gathering facts and figures online. Through laptops and mobile phones, the worldwide web is within our reach every second of the day, providing facts, opinions, and information of widely varying detail, quality and usefulness.

Children have to be incredibly organized and creative in their learning if they're to make the most of all the material at their fingertips. They need:

▶ *flexible brains to cope with information in many different forms*
▶ *a strong foundation of retained knowledge to help put new details into context*
▶ *the thinking skills necessary for judging, processing and applying information with accuracy and care.*

Poet and playwright Eden Phillpotts wrote: 'The universe is full of magical things, patiently waiting for our wits to grow sharper.'

How do we learn?

While the internet revolutionizes human knowledge second by second, the most powerful techniques for handling it have actually been around for thousands of years. The fundamental ways in which we learn haven't changed. Now more than ever we need to help children take control of their success by focusing on the ways in which their brains learn best.

1 *We learn by association, seeing the links between things.*
2 *We learn by imitation, copying to help us understand and remember.*
3 *We learn by exploring, amassing new experiences, knowledge and skills.*
4 *We learn by rote: doing specific things with our brains to sort and store information.*

The best learning strategies combine all these elements. They also use the whole of the brain. Your child has access to logical, left-brained principles of thought, as well as to the more creative right-brained processes; so it makes good sense to get them using both. They need a flexible and connected approach that helps them remember, learn, and apply what they know in clever and creative ways.

We know that the ancient Greeks taught their students *how* to learn as well as *what* they needed to know, discussing with them the benefits of particular techniques. From many different cultures and points in human history we can take learning methods that tap into the fundamental ways in which our brains work. We can also teach our children sound learning behaviours that will play a huge role in boosting their success in school – including the ability to reflect on their thinking and improve it.

Above all, your child needs to take an active approach to learning. They need the thinking skills to decide what they want to know, why it's important to them, and how they're going to store and use it in the most effective ways.

Learning is boosted by images (right brain) and structures (left brain). The more 'alive' information is to our senses, and the more personal connections we have with it through feelings and emotions, the more likely we are to remember it. It's not hard to teach children techniques for turning information into vivid pictures, then to weave them into memorable stories and scenes.

Here's an exercise to give both you and your child a taste of powerful, creative learning.

Start with a list of ten random words. For example: hat, church, dog, sandwich, CD, chair, carrot, box, book, telephone.

Next, choose a familiar route – a walk, a car journey, the rooms in your house – and give each item from the list a place within the route. Talk it through with your child and get their suggestions.

You might use the route to school and imagine a hat on the street light outside your house; a church appearing in the middle of the road; a dog sitting on a swing in the playground; a sandwich poking out of the postbox on the high street.

If you were using the rooms in your house there might be a new CD floating in the bath, an antique chair on the landing, a carrot tucked up in your bed.

Be as imaginative as you can, to make the pictures unusual and exaggerated and memorable as you 'fix' them into place in your chosen route.

This method of using places to structure and store information was a favourite of the ancient Greeks. Employing it in this activity helps to activate your child's visualization and creative imagination.

New memories are held in place by old ones, and they can be given extra sensory 'triggers'.

Start with colours and give a different one to each image. Go back through the journey, remind yourselves of the items and their imaginary locations, and choose a vivid colour for each one. Once again get suggestions from your child, then spend a few moments visualizing the red hat, green church, blue dog...

Next, work together to give each image a feeling or emotion. The red hat might be scared, sitting high up on the lamp post. The green church could be tired of sitting in the road. Perhaps the blue dog is hungry, embarrassed or proud.

How many other elements can you add to this surreal landscape? Try placing a famous person in each area, linking them to the information already there. What about a sport, a number, an adjective, a song?

As you return to each scene you train your child's mind to learn by rehearsal; but you also activate new areas of their thinking and encourage memorable cross-brain connections. You help them understand what this rich form of thinking feels like, sharpen their active memory skills, and improve their creativity and imagination.

After an activity like this, how much easier will they find it to write imaginative stories in their next Literacy lesson!

Insight

Anyone who's read Roger Hargreaves' brilliant 'Mr Men' books or the works of Lewis Carroll has seen what happens when the brain is liberated to make funny, colourful and memorable leaps. Confident creativity like this is the basis of all the most powerful learning skills.

But has this exercise worked? Help your child to explore the imagery they created and experience the strength of this kind of learning.

First, see if they can tell you the ten words on the list. Simply prompt them to retrace their steps along the journey you chose together and find a memorable picture in each place. And if they can do it forwards, what happens when they try recalling the entire list backwards?

Next, ask them about the colour that was given to each of the ten items.

Finally, can they remember the ten emotions you chose? Remind them to use all the clues available: the position of each word in the route, the image used to represent it, and the colour it became.

When they're ready you can also test the flexibility and 'pinpoint accuracy' of your child's learning.

If you give them a colour, can they tell you the appropriate word on the list? When you describe an emotion, can they say where exactly it appeared in the route – and give you the famous person, number, sport, or any of the other pieces of information you included? Encourage your child to keep exploring the ten spaces on a route until they've picked out all the information they put in. Celebrate the sheer amount of interconnected detail they're able to recall.

An activity like this provides a glimpse of learning at its most powerful. It proves that information can be made memorable, organized and visualized so that it suits the mechanisms of the brain. Give your memory what it needs and it can perform remarkable feats of recall, storing information in a way that stimulates flexible thinking.

By the same token, if material isn't inherently memorable, and nothing is done to change that, the brain is remarkably good at forgetting it.

So how do you get your child to think like this? How can they routinely explore and learn in such a richly creative and organized way?

Stimulating learning: warm-up activities

Good teachers know the importance of warming up children's minds before they begin. Just as an athlete would never go straight into vigorous exercise, so your child needs to limber up their mental muscles before starting work. Effective warm-up exercises will boost their alertness and concentration, as well as playing a vital role in energizing their learning skills. By stimulating different areas of the brain – and, crucially, by connecting and combining these thinking zones in particular ways – good warm-up activities put children in the best frame of mind for active, creative, whole-brain learning.

THE 'SAME DIFFERENCE' GAME

This can be a five-minute activity at the start of a classroom lesson or a quick challenge on a car journey or around the dinner table. It promotes creative thinking, right/left brain connections, and boosts your child's ability to visualize, organize and communicate their ideas.

Start by choosing two words. In the first round, pick words that are the same 'type', for example: two nouns, two people, two items from the kitchen. All the players then have to think of three things that are the *same* about these two words. Give everyone a few moments to generate ideas; then each player explains their three similarities, starting with the best.

For example, if you chose the words *tree* and *street light* (good choices to begin the game, both are similar in shape) your ideas might be:

*'They change colour: the tree in autumn, the street light when you
    switch it on.'*
'They're both tall.'
'Dogs could use them both as a toilet.'

Encourage players to explain exactly what they mean. Listen carefully to everyone's ideas without comment or criticism – yet.

The second player might continue with:

'People fix signs to them both.'
'You see them both on the roadside.'
'Both words have double "e" in them.'

If a player struggles to think of three ideas they can just use something that another person has said.

This first stage of the game encourages the brain to find connections and to explore learnt information in new ways.

Medical writer Rita Carter coined the term 'recognition unit' (RU) to help explain the way knowledge may be stored in the memory, dotted around in different file areas depending on particular associations and themes. The word 'house', for example, might be stored as an RU along with other buildings, but it could feature on the list of things you know about school (where children are often grouped in 'houses') and in your store of knowledge about bingo ('House!'). The shape of the house is stored as an image, while the feel of its bricks and its familiar smell sit in the memory within yet more collections of RUs.

The brain can be seen as a phenomenally powerful search engine, sorting knowledge by any number of criteria. Ask it to give you the words you know with double 'e' in them, cross-referenced with a list of living things, and you might quickly come up with 'tree' (and 'sheep', 'bee', 'weeping willow'…). Think about what you might see on a road side, or where you could stick a 'lost cat' poster, and 'tree' might appear again as your brain activates different RU locations. Each idea also comes with extra information attached: the colour, texture and smell of a tree; the sound of a sheep; your feelings about bees; paintings you've seen of weeping willows. Every RU spreads out its webs of connection in countless ways, linking with other pieces of knowledge as well as with personal memories and experiences, all stored in rich packages of detail.

So the 'Same difference' game begins to activate one of the brain's most powerful abilities: the capacity to file and sort information in complex and creative ways. Thinking of similarities sets in motion some wide and challenging searches of the memory. It warms up your child's powers of imagination, decision-making and assessment. They need to concentrate and listen carefully as others outline their thoughts, powering up their communication skills as they bend their brains around other players' explanations. And original ideas are stored as new connections within the ever expanding networks of their memory.

After the 'same' round, it's time to focus on differences. What are the most interesting differences about the two words you chose?

Again, your child's mental search engine darts around amongst facts, pictures, memories and songs – all the multi-layered RUs that have relevance to the words in the game. They explore complex neural networks as they prepare to deliver their creative results:

'One is living, the other is man-made.'
'The tree helps to beat global warming, the street light helps to cause it.'
'One gives out light, the other takes it in.'

Looking for differences often unearths more similarities too, so encourage players to remember these for later, for example: 'They're both sensitive to the amount of daylight there is.' It also reveals ideas that could be both 'same' and 'different'. For example, both the tree and the street light have 'transportation' systems inside them, but they transport different things (water and electricity). And water can be disastrous for something electrical, but too much water can also be bad for a tree. Quickly the ideas themselves connect and interact, and what may initially have seemed to be a very difficult question can soon stimulate a rich and growing collection of interesting answers.

When everyone has had a turn, work together to choose the three best similarities and the three best differences. Revisit these newly created memories, assessing, sorting and discussing their merits.

Then raise the bar a little. For round two, choose words with no obvious connections at all. See what your brains can do with ideas such as 'speed' and 'onion'; 'river' and 'religion'; 'blue' and 'curry'. Follow the same steps as before. Search for similarities and then differences before discussing everyone's ideas and choosing the best:

'Speed and onions both bring tears to your eyes.'
'You cross a river, and a cross is part of religion.'
'Blue is cold but curry is hot.'

Children enjoy picking the words as well as exploring the ideas, and there can be as much benefit in trying to come up with two unconnected ideas as in thinking up the answers. Although the final assessment stage promotes skills of discussion and debate, this game shows children that thinking creatively isn't really about 'right' or 'wrong' answers. There's a limitless range of interesting ideas, and how easily you find them depends on how well you use your thinking skills.

Improving your child's visualization skills

Games like this can improve your child's ability to 'see' images vividly in their mind's eye. Thinking in pictures is an extremely effective way of exploring and remembering many different kinds of information.

Here are some techniques for strengthening your child's visualization skills at the same time as dealing with tricky moments in family life.

Our brains have a natural urge to create images. Try *not* to think of a blue elephant now, and you'll see just how powerful an urge it is. Your child will quickly picture any images you suggest, and you can use this natural reaction to guide their behaviour.

Give them images instead of abstract instructions: 'There's a white cloth in the sink' is likely to have more impact that 'Help me clean up this mess.' For example:

'That lovely black hairbrush you bought is in your top drawer.'
'I bet you could make that shelf look as tidy as one in a bookshop.'
'The dog's lead is over there by the door. He'd be so excited if he saw you getting it for him.'

Provide your child with clear images to hold in their mind as you explain what you need them to do. Suggest problem-solving strategies to switch on their thinking, rather than commands that they have to decode, remember and obey.

A classic parenting tactic is to offer two acceptable choices: 'This is such a busy road, so are you going to hold hands with Mummy or Daddy?' You can reinforce these choices, and activate your child's visualization skills by offering vivid images to choose between:

'Daddy's big hands or Mummy's red gloves?'
'Are you going to hop upstairs to bed like a frog or trot up like a beautiful pony?'

Tapping into children's imagination is a great way to focus them on the task in hand and remind them about what they've been asked to do. You're also laying the foundations for strong decision-making skills.

There are so many ways that parents can strengthen their children's powers of visualization. Here are just three:

1 **Talk about their dreams.** *What images do they remember? Did they dream in colour? Did the people they saw actually look*

like the real people? Were the places in their dream anything like the actual locations? And if they were very different, how did they know where they were?

2   **Discuss images in advertising.** *What pictures can your child remember from TV commercials? Look at magazine adverts and find the clues that tell you about the product. Why has the advertiser chosen a particular picture? When you hear radio advertisements, talk to your child about the images that appear in their mind. Are they suggested by sound effects, voices, music – or have they simply been reminded of pictures they've seen elsewhere?*

3   **Celebrate images in your home.** *Put up paintings, posters and photographs. Talk about why you chose them and discuss colour, shape, pattern and composition. Look at art collections online and explore a variety of visual styles with your child. There are plenty of great art books for children, and it can be interesting and fun for both of you to learn about famous artists and their particular techniques. Keep talking about what pictures look like and how they make you feel.*

Strengthening your child's senses

Memorable poems suggest powerful visual images, but they also activate the other senses. Skillful story tellers describe sounds, smells, textures and tastes to help bring their words to life. The senses help us to engage with information on a deeper level, and your child can use them to give a major boost to their learning.

Insight
   Challenge your child's 'other' senses by blindfolding them.
   Give them a range of foods to smell and taste and objects
   to touch. Encourage them to use the full extent of their
   vocabulary to describe exactly what they're experiencing.

Whenever you go somewhere new, challenge them to close their eyes and give you evidence about the location through their other

.s. Children of all ages can get a lot out of becoming 'sense ectives', sharpening their abilities to perceive, describe and connect different sensations.

The following activity takes sense connections a step further, probing the way your child's brain makes connections between different kinds of information. It encourages them to express their ideas, but also to consider the thought processes required to generate them.

It's a great way to exercise different thinking styles. Odd-sounding questions are used to stimulate whole-brain thinking and to forge creative links, for example:

'What colour is worried?'
'What sound is strong?'
'What smell is excited?'
'What texture is happy?'

As well as asking the questions, prompt your child to tell you what it feels like trying to think of the answers.

Talk to your child about how it feels when they try to marry together these different ideas. It can be an odd sensation and a real challenge, and like many of the techniques in this book it takes practice. But soon you'll find that very interesting and illuminating ideas can emerge:

'Worried is grey, like the colour of a rainy day, or someone's skin when they're tired.'
'Strong is the sound of a loud drum, or the clank of something being built out of metal.'
'Excited smells like fizzy sherbet sweets, birthday cake candles, Christmas trees.'
'Happy is smooth and warm and squashy.'

Clearly there aren't right or wrong answers in this game, but children tend to provide their own explanations and justifications for the ideas they choose. Even young children can reference particular experiences and memories that explain their thinking. The answers they give often contain many different senses and feelings, and these questions encourage children to find creative ways of communicating their thoughts.

There's a lot for parents to learn here, so be alert to all the clues. You might notice your child using hand movements to convey the texture of a sound, or licking their lips at the thought of a particular taste inspired by a colour or smell. Talk to them about which questions are hardest to answer, and why.

Enjoy unpicking some of the memories they mention, especially those that you share. Use the game to explore the way their brain stores and connects different types of information. Celebrate the brilliant leaps they can make when they break down boundaries and set their thinking free.

SYNAESTHESIA

Some people have no trouble blending senses like this. Synaesthesia (*sin-iss-theez-ee-a*) is a relatively common condition in which the senses overlap and information is given unconventional sensory details. Described by the geneticist Francis Galton in the nineteenth century, it does seem to run in families, and research suggests that it's an important aspect of young babies' thinking. Many of us lose it almost completely as we grow but in some people, synaesthesia is a very important part of their approach to memory and learning.

Solomon Shereshevski, the Russian memory phenomenon studied over many years by the influential psychologist Alexander Luria, exhibited an extreme form of synaesthesia. In his brain, every sound came alive with colours and smells and textures; every word had a specific taste; every memory was multidimensional and packed with vibrant sensory triggers. For him, the problem was remembering too much, too well.

For most of us, synaesthesic thinking can be developed as a powerful way of training the memory to be creative and flexible.

Think about your own sense connections, and talk to your children about theirs. Do numbers come with colours attached? Perhaps they have a particular colour for each day of the week or month of the year? Does their mind produce shapes or textures or sounds for certain bits of information?

Insight

The late Poet Laureate Ted Hughes was convinced of the importance of making unusual sense combinations. He worked with school children to develop their connective thinking, to help them compose powerful poetry but also to build flexible brains.

The techniques explained in this book will help your child get the most out of any inbuilt tendencies towards synaesthesia, as well as helping them to use senses in new ways to activate their creativity and memory.

Improving your child's memory

A key process in memory is linking new pieces of information to things we already know. We can access memories through complex chains of connections: a smell might link to a place, which could remind us of a particular moment in our life and a person we knew – whose birthday, we might suddenly realize, is tomorrow. We're constantly relating one thing to another in our minds, sorting, grouping and linking memories in rich and intricate ways.

THE 'IMAGINE AND DESTROY!' GAME

One useful way of remembering is to connect information with *you*. Your child will enjoy the next activity since it gives them the chance to wreak havoc and destroy some very expensive objects – luckily in the safety of their imagination!

Give them the following list of objects: clock, vase, sandwich, piano, table, telephone, mirror, balloon.

Explain that they're going to take each item in turn and imagine destroying it in the most effective way they can think of. Tell them to let their creativity go wild, engaging as many senses as possible and thinking how they'd feel if they were ruining these things for real.

They could pull all the springs out of the clock, snap the hands and stamp on the dial. Perhaps they throw the vase from the roof or smash it against a wall. They might imagine squashing the sandwich under a car tyre and watching the filling burst out in all directions.

When they've gone through the whole list, give them a quick test. Read the following words to them. For each one they have to say 'yes' if it was on the original list, or 'no' if it wasn't: mirror, sandwich, chair, telephone, football, computer, clock, painting, vase, piano.

If they used their imagination well when they first processed the information, this test should be extremely easy for your child. They'll know immediately and definitively whether or not they imagined destroying each object. Personalizing it in this exaggerated way and adding senses and emotions makes all the information remarkably strong.

Using your brain this energetically is great fun – and that's one of the most important ideas in this whole book. The happiness generated when children take control of their imagination is motivating and empowering. It's also a major reason why the learning strategies themselves work so well.

Most children can't help smiling when they remember the havoc they caused. In class, I find that the children who enjoy this exercise the most are often those who struggle to keep their energy in check. They start to realize that being energetic can actually help them to learn. They can be funny and active and imaginative and a bit silly – and start doing better in school!

'GRANNY WENT TO MARKET'

This classic memory game is another great way to warm up your child's mental connections. It works with any number of players.

The first player says: 'Granny went to market and bought...', and chooses the first item on Granny's shopping list, for example 'a cake'.

The next player takes over, repeating what the first person said before adding their own purchase: 'Granny went to market and bought a cake and... a firework.'

Player three might say: 'Granny went to market and bought a cake, a firework and a cow'... and so it continues, everyone taking a turn to repeat the items that have been chosen so far before adding something of their own to the ever growing list.

You're out if you make a mistake or get stuck, and the game continues until there's just one person left.

You can use 'Granny went to market' as a fun warm up to any kind of learning, boosting concentration, communication, turn-taking and memory. But it really comes into its own when you use it to teach children *how* to remember. It's a powerful way of training them to use their brain brilliantly.

Simply tell them to turn the shopping list into a story. They need to use their powers of imagination and visualization to make each item in the list as vivid as possible; add some extra sense clues; then connect it to whatever came before.

The more unusual, funny, exciting and energetic the story, the more memorable it's likely to be. During the first few turns you can help them get started by working on story ideas aloud:

'I'm imagining the beautiful fruit cake in Granny's basket, smelling like it's just come out of the oven – when suddenly a firework bursts out of the top. There are red and orange sparks and bits of cake flying everywhere. I'm picturing the firework shooting up into the sky, then falling back down to Earth and landing on top of a very shocked black-and-white cow...'

Make it clear that you're not just talking about what happens, you're actively imagining it. Emphasize the connections that hold your story together, the way one object transforms into another: appears from inside it, hugs it, talks to it, fastens on to it, squashes it... There are infinite ways to link Granny's purchases, and you're just choosing the most memorable connections you can. Your story will be different from everyone else's, but they can all work brilliantly.

Insight

Tell your child to imagine they're filming a 'mental movie'. They control the camera, so they can zoom in on particular details or widen the shot to see more of what's happening. They can choose where to position themselves for maximum effect. Their camera could track alongside the action, film from overhead, or even show events from the inside out.

When children learn like this, every rehearsal strengthens the images and links they've invented. Adding new items to the list doesn't have to make it harder to learn. In fact, each new purchase can provide another memorable connection to hold everything together. As long as they keep doing what their brain needs them to do, making the information powerfully memorable, your child should be able to recall the twentieth item on Granny's shopping list as easily as the first.

When it's your turn to reel off the latest list, demonstrate how important questions are to the memory process: 'Something came out of the cake. What was it? Oh yes, a firework. Where did it land? On the back of a cow...'

Asking questions to stimulate memory is a fantastic habit for your child to pick up. It helps them to explore, understand, prioritize and apply new information, as well as to remember it.

> **Insight**
> Sometimes, instead of asking your child, 'What did you learn today?' say, 'What were the best questions you asked?'

Using the power of questions

Tests have shown that simply questioning something can make it easier to remember. Volunteers were given a series of words and asked different sorts of questions about them. Did the word fit into a particular sentence? Was it a member of a word 'family' such as nouns, adjectives or verbs? Did they think it was a positive, negative or neutral word? When the volunteers were tested later, the words they'd answered questions about were the easiest to remember by far.

Try it with your child. Read aloud the following information to them, word for word. Tell them not to answer any questions out loud, just to think about their answers:

'Aeroplane. Candle. Pig. Does "pig" fit into the sentence: "He went to the market and bought a pig"? Boat. Glad. Box. Hungry. What sort of word is hungry? Cliff. Hole. Suddenly. Does the word "suddenly" fit into the sentence: "There was a suddenly cat sitting on the rug"? Holiday. Forest. Yellow. What word rhymes with yellow?'

When you've finished reading, ask your child to tell you as many of the words as they can from memory. See if they do find it easiest to remember 'pig', 'hungry', 'suddenly' and 'yellow' – the words they had to question in some way. Help your child to see just how useful it is to think up questions about the information they need to learn at school.

Here are some other powerful ways to build your child's connected brain.

▶ *Ask them to describe something to you backwards: their school day, the journey to the shops, the plot of their favourite film. Encourage them to explain how each part of the process was connected to the bit that came before.*

▶ *Teach them the game where they have to change one word into another by only altering one letter at a time. So 'boat' can become 'ship' if it goes through the following steps: boat → coat → chat → chap → chip → ship. Can they turn 'warm' into 'cool', or 'fake' to 'real'?*

▶ *Play 'What happened next?' games. You can use:*
  ▷ *historical events: 'What happened after a bakery caught fire in Pudding Lane, London in 1666?'*
  ▷ *family memories: 'Do you remember what Auntie Alice did after she stepped out of the church?'*
  ▷ *stories you read together: 'Can you guess where the pirates are going to take their treasure?'*

Give your child a clear understanding of cause and effect, surprising results and interesting, memorable plots. Build these connections into their brain and equip them to write stories that will revolutionize their learning.

Using 'memory journeys' to connect information

As well as stories, since ancient times people have used 'memory journeys' as a means of connecting and structuring information. Using the imagination, images can be placed at different points in a familiar route and then rediscovered by retracing the mental steps.

To get your child ready to use this powerful strategy you'll need to give them an understanding of different forms of structure and a repertoire of well-known routes. Support this understanding by:

▶ *talking to them about the journeys you take together*
▶ *making sure they're confident with right and left (and later north, south, east and west)*
▶ *showing them what a mile and a kilometre look like*
▶ *challenging each other to estimate distances and journey times*
▶ *practising describing journeys in detail from memory*
▶ *showing your child maps of different kinds, on paper and on screen*
▶ *using jigsaw puzzles, model kits and construction sets to help children build their sense of structure and spatial patterns.*

Insight

As your child learns to tell the time, help them to use it to structure their life. Encourage them to talk about 'before', 'after', 'earlier' and 'later'. Challenge them to describe the pattern of their school day or to write a step-by-step plan for a perfect weekend.

All these activities will help to prepare your child to use the 'memory journeys' technique. It's a simple to use but incredibly powerful way of organizing information to make it memorable. Your child can use it to boost their learning in every school subject, as well as to remember instructions, speeches and ideas – even rules of behaviour.

The Greeks described ways of arranging images around temples and palaces, creating ambitious collections of memorable information. We know that Roman orators were particularly keen on this method for remembering their speeches – and that they taught it to their students.

The basic idea is very simple. You imagine yourself walking around a familiar room, building or town, or travelling along a journey you know well. At key points on your route you leave behind images to jog your memory. When you retrace your steps, the images are there for you to find and use, all held in perfect order. You can walk the route forwards or backwards or jump to any point along the way. Each stopping point can actually hold numerous images, and your journey can give you access to a huge amount of information, all vividly imagined and richly interconnected.

Have a go with your child. Together, design a route based on the place where you live.

Start by making a quick sketch of your home. You need to divide it up into ten 'zones' and decide on a clear route around them. Imagine you were showing someone around your house. What route would you take them on and what would the obvious stopping points be? The zones can be rooms, corridors, staircases – even particular pieces of furniture. Make them as different from each other as possible. Write them onto your sketch and also order them from one – where the route starts – to ten, the final zone.

Now spend a few minutes taking a mental trip along this journey. In your mind's eye, move from zone to zone, visualizing them all as clearly as possible. As always try to bring all your senses into play. Focus on the obvious features as well as the interesting details.

Your route plan might look something like this:

1 *Driveway*
2 *Front door*
3 *Hallway*
4 *Living room*
5 *Kitchen*
6 *Garden*
7 *Staircase*
8 *Child's bedroom*
9 *Bathroom*
10 *Parents' bedroom*

When you're confident with your journey, have a go at filling it with information. Working with your child, try fixing the following ten objects into place: television, ice cream, banana, car, giraffe, fire, guitar, tree, sheep, sandwich.

Position one image in each of your ten zones. Discuss ways to exaggerate the pictures you create to make them powerfully memorable. Use colour, movement, comedy, action – all the factors that activate recall. And encourage your child to think about how they'd feel if these things really were arranged around your home, for example:

'Visualize a large television set standing in the middle of the driveway. Imagine the terrible crash if our car ran it over!'
'How would you feel if you knocked on the front door and found it was made of melting ice cream?'
'In the hallway, picture thousands of bright yellow bananas covering the floor. Think how it would feel to clamber over them to hang up your coat.'

Remind your child to keep asking questions as they build up their imagery: Why is there a car in the living room? How will the giraffe use the cooker? What should we do to put out the huge fire raging in the garden?

By the time you reach the end of your journey you should have stored ten images in the ten separate zones.

To check that it's worked, go back through the journey in your imagination and call out all the images you find. If you struggle at any stage, just leave that bit for later and move on. Try to remember the list backwards. Test each other: one of you asks quick-fire questions, such as 'What came before "giraffe"?' and 'What was the seventh word on the list?' while the other uses the journey system to find the answers.

This approach represents very effective whole-brain learning. You're thinking creatively to design vivid images (right brain) at the same time as creating a logical framework and slotting them all in (left brain). It involves association (the links between images and places); imitation (repeating the journey and rehearsing actions and events within it); exploration (investigating the imagery laid out in such an accessible way) and rote learning (following the system to turn words into a series of linked images). It's a wonderful way to excite children about what they can achieve when they become active and confident learners.

Challenge them to double the number of images. This time they're going to learn a list of ten sports, one in each zone: football, tennis, sailing, golf, basketball, archery, karate, hockey, cycling, skiing.

It really doesn't matter that there are already sheep, bananas and giraffes in there. Those things simply become useful 'hooks' for the new information:

Perhaps the TV set on the driveway is showing an exciting football game. You serve a tennis ball into the soft ice cream door, turn one of the big bananas into a boat to sail down the hallway then drive a golf ball from a tee on the living room sofa...

Use this activity to discuss learning techniques with your child, for example:

▶ *Talk about each other's images and ideas.*
▶ *Suggest questions that will strengthen all the details.*
▶ *Analyse any parts the technique you find difficult.*
▶ *Decide which features you most enjoy.*

Above all, talk to your child about what they think this approach could do for their learning.

With 20 pieces of information stored away, your quizzing can move to the next level:

'*What sport is in the same zone as the guitar?*'
'*Where does archery come on the list of ten sports?*'
'*Which object is in the zone between hockey and skiing?*'

Many children can answer subtle questions like this the very first time they try the journey technique. Even if your child is only starting to use the system effectively, celebrate their achievements and push them to keep going. It's an approach to learning that can play a key role in their studies, helping them to think both creatively and logically and to explore and learn information with real confidence.

They're taking control of their learning, developing thinking skills that will boost their success in a number of other areas.

Building problem-solving skills

To succeed at school your child needs to solve a wide variety of problems every day, from maths questions and design challenges to friendship issues and moral dilemmas. Giving them a strong set of thinking skills provides them with a range of approaches to try:

- ▶ *Careful questioning helps them to clarify issues, challenge assumptions, investigate evidence and evaluate answers.*
- ▶ *Thinking visually lets them see problems from different perspectives.*
- ▶ *Making unusual connections stimulates their imagination to discover new possibilities.*
- ▶ *Laying out the information in a vivid mental landscape, full of senses and emotions, helps your child to enjoy exploring all their ideas.*

You can show your child how to use both logic and creativity; find interesting patterns and generate a range of possible answers.

It's important to start with the right attitude. In school I often talk about 'solution finding', emphasizing the importance of thinking positively; of assuming that the answers can be found.

Insight
While the Apollo 13 astronauts waited in space for answers, NASA mission controller Gene Kranz famously sent his team

off to find the solutions. They weren't 'trying' to solve the life or death problems, investigating to see if there *were* answers; they were *assuming* that the solutions were there, and that they'd simply have to work hard and fast and smart enough to find them.

Challenge your child with the following problems and test some of their key thinking skills.

LEAF PUZZLE

If there are five piles of leaves on the right side of the garden and six piles of leaves on the left side of the garden, and you put all the piles of leaves together in the middle of the garden... how many piles do you have?

This puzzle tempts children to give the first answer they think of: five plus six... *eleven*. But it's not as simple as that (or in fact, more simple).

When they're working out an answer, children tend to guess where the question is leading them. They look for clues in the words and phrases used to frame a problem. They think, 'Why am I being asked this question?' and, 'What sort of question does this seem to be?' They follow reasoning that seems sound and sensible; but if they don't visualize the problem, they can miss answers that are staring them in the face.

Encourage your child to spend a moment picturing the piles of leaves – at the start of the puzzle, and when they're all collected together at the end. Then simply ask them, 'How many piles can you see now?' The answer clearly is, 'One big one.'

OAK TREE PUZZLE

The oak tree in the park is 50 years old and still going strong. It grows at a rate of 3 cm every year. This morning, Billy carved his name in the trunk exactly 1 m above the ground. How high will his name be in ten years' time?

It's another question that offers a tempting way to the solution. But visualization brings new information.

Tell your child to picture the tree and to watch it grow. They need to combine their imagination with their knowledge about the real world. If they find themselves watching the carved name moving up the tree, it's likely that alarm bells will ring as they realize that trees don't grow like that. They can compare their imagined version of the puzzle with what they've actually observed in real life.

Fifty-year-old trees don't grow from their trunks. In ten years' time, the name won't have moved a single millimetre from where it is today.

FATHER AND SON PUZZLE

A father and son were involved in a car accident. They were taken to hospital, and the son was told he needed to have an operation. He was wheeled into the operating theatre but the surgeon took one look at him and said, 'I can't operate on this boy – he's my son.' How come?

Sometimes visualization gets us into difficulties. It tempts us to jump straight to habitual pictures and make assumptions that block our way to the answer.

To solve this problem, tell your child to re-examine the images they saw. How did they picture the surgeon? Have they jumped to any conclusions that aren't supported by the words of the puzzle? It's likely that they assumed the surgeon was a man – but they weren't told that. In fact, the surgeon is a woman, the boy's mother.

So *careful* visualization is essential; and the same degree of care is required when making links and forming patterns. Our instinct to use logic to solve problems can also lead us in the wrong direction.

NAMING PUZZLE

Katie's mum has four children. She's given them the names Monday, Tuesday, Wednesday and… What's her fourth child called?

Will your child avoid falling into the 'pattern' trap? Use this example to show them that sequences need to be followed with caution. The second part of the question offers a very neat pattern, and the natural reaction is to follow it. But the right answer only comes when you keep all the details of the puzzle in mind and see that Katie's mum's fourth child is… Katie!

HAIRDRESSER TEASER

There are only two hairdressers in the village. One has beautiful and stylish hair. The other has lopsided, old-fashioned, tatty hair. I've decided I'm going to get my hair cut by the one with the messy hair. Why would I do that?

In this brain-teaser, visualization gets you started – but there's more to be done to understand what's going on.

It's certainly a good idea to start by imagining the two hairdressers with their very different hairstyles. But these images alone don't explain the puzzle. If anything they make it seem even more confusing. So, widen your view, gather more information. How did their hair get like that? Picture them both having haircuts and examine the images very carefully. Who must be cutting the hair, if there are only two hairdressers in the village…? *Now* which one are you going to trust to cut your hair?

Try the next puzzle on your child. Can they picture the events carefully and explore all the possibilities until one 'clicks'?

TOWER BLOCK CONUNDRUM

Mr Smith lives on the 20th floor of a tower block. Every morning he gets into the lift, goes down to the ground floor and heads off on his way to work. Every evening he parks his car, gets into the lift, goes up to the 18th floor... but then walks up the last two flights of stairs to get to his front door. Why?

It's a classic case of having to examine the images you create. Watching the story play out in your mind gives you a general version of events to work from. But this time, the most helpful tactic is actually to *narrow* your viewpoint; to focus on details.

Nothing of much use comes from imagining what the man's job might be or what sort of car he might drive, so focus on key moments within the events described. Watch him leaving his flat. Watch him entering the lift. Watch him pressing the buttons. Examine that moment, when he decides which floor to select. What might be significant about the button he reaches for?

The accepted answer is that the man is very short, and can't reach all the buttons. On his way out, selecting the ground floor is no problem. But when he comes back he can only reach up as far as button number 18.

There are other possible answers, and questions like this are great for provoking discussion and debate. They help your child to see how useful it is to have a range of problem-solving strategies. It's impossible to know in advance which one will work best, so they just need the confidence to try different angles, to look very carefully at patterns and possibilities, and then to put it all together to form a version of events that fits.

Keep challenging your child with brain-teasers like this. You'll strengthen their ability to use both the creative and the logical side of their thinking. They'll get used to examining all their ideas as they go along. They'll be training themselves to keep going until they've found a brilliant answer.

Encouraging philosophical thinking skills

It's also important to test children's thinking skills with more open questions. Sometimes there really is no right answer at all, just plenty of scope for generating clever thoughts and ideas. See how well your child can offer ways of interpreting the following questions, using their thinking skills flexibly and heading off in different directions. Value all their ideas, gently discuss and debate their theories, and give them the confidence to evolve philosophies of their own.

- *Can you touch the wind?*
- *Could your imaginary friend have an imaginary friend?*
- *Can you be sad and happy at the same time?*
- *If you read a magazine in a shop without buying it, have you stolen it?*
- *Can animals commit crimes?*
- *Is the hole in the doughnut part of the doughnut?*
- *Does anyone really own a piece of music?*
- *Can you be friends with someone you don't like?*

These questions are great for encouraging children's individuality of thought. Younger children in particular may start by offering simple 'yes' or 'no' answers, but carefully chosen follow-up questions will prompt them to probe more deeply:

- *So is there a difference between touching and feeling?*
- *But isn't the hole different all the time depending on where you take the doughnut?*
- *What if a person doesn't understand they've done wrong? Should they still get into trouble?*

It's a wonderful moment when a child realizes that the answer could well be 'yes' *and* 'no', and that it's up to them to decide which view they're going to champion. It can be extremely liberating to realize that a well-argued view is valid, whatever anyone else thinks. They can discover great pleasure in putting their thinking skills to the test just to see what happens.

THINKING ABOUT THINKING

Use these questions at mealtimes or during family gatherings. Encourage your child to speak their mind confidently as well as to listen to other ideas and philosophies. It's a very powerful way to nurture respect and tolerance. By engaging with other people's thought processes as well as their own, your child is also giving a powerful boost to their metacognition: that all-important 'thinking about thinking'.

- ▶ *How do we know things?*
- ▶ *What viewpoint are we looking from?*
- ▶ *How can two contradictory ideas produce brilliant new answers?*
- ▶ *Can memory help?*
- ▶ *Why is it logical, possible or interesting to suggest any particular idea?*
- ▶ *Why do you think this, and I think that?*

The ancient Greeks encouraged their students to reflect on the thought processes they were using. The ability to analyse thinking skills was highly prized. In the Middle Ages, privileged children were taught philosophy and critical thinking. Today, your child can be given a real interest in the work of their brain, and the satisfaction of using it brilliantly. With the right support from you they can seize all the opportunities to turn themselves into better thinkers and learners.

10 THINGS TO REMEMBER

1 *Now that gathering information is easy, processing it is what makes all the difference.*

2 *Show your child what 'whole-brain' learning feels like, combining creativity and logic in an exciting and energetic approach.*

3 *Play games that challenge the brain to make new and interesting connections.*

4 *Take every opportunity to boost children's visualization skills, using examples from advertising, TV and art, as well as using clear images yourself in communicating with them.*

5 *Encourage your child to explore and connect their senses in new ways.*

6 *Teach them to use imaginative stories to activate their learning.*

7 *Use games, construction activities and conversations about time to develop organized and structured thinking.*

8 *Encourage inquisitiveness and careful questions to help strengthen memories.*

9 *Teach your child the age-old 'memory journey' system for learning anything and everything.*

10 *Use problem-solving challenges, including philosophical questions, to practise combining different thinking skills.*

Part two

In school: helping children meet all the challenges of primary education

6

Words and numbers

In this chapter you will learn:
- *the core thinking skills behind confidence in literacy and numeracy*
- *activities for boosting your child's speaking and listening*
- *how to help your child learn to read and write*
- *how children's numeracy skills develop, and how to strengthen them at home*
- *a simple system for remembering numbers and learning times tables.*

English and maths – literacy and numeracy – are at the heart of primary education. As well as receiving the most discrete teaching time, the knowledge and skills they involve are woven into every lesson. Your child's abilities in history, RE and art, for example, will be influenced significantly by their language skills. Their experience of science, design and music will depend heavily on the way their brain copes with maths. In fact, the key skills your child develops in the two main subjects will be fundamental to their whole educational success, and to the way their thinking and learning are set up.

The knowledge your child gains depends a great deal on the topics they're taught. In Literacy it's important and interesting to know about fairy tales, Elizabethan theatre or Japanese haikus. In Numeracy lessons there are huge benefits in knowing the names of shapes, the theories about prime numbers and the rules for plotting graphs. But it's the core skills your child learns during these lessons – in particular the essential literacy and numeracy *thinking* skills – that will have the greatest impact on their long-term success.

It doesn't really matter if your child leaves school without ever studying a science fiction story or a Carroll diagram, or even if they don't know how to use a semicolon or any of the different ways of calculating averages. The important thing is that they have the ability, the interest and the confidence to do so when the opportunity arises.

Obviously you want your child to enjoy rich and wide ranging teaching. But a truly literate child can quickly learn about any form of communication and start practising and using it effectively. They have a foundation level of key skills and knowledge to build on. Teach them about sonnets and they can understand how language is being used and quickly start writing versions of their own.

A numerate child can easily pick up new concepts and techniques, because the core understanding is there. Show them modal averages and they have a context in which to understand them, as well as the key maths skills to practise the calculations themselves.

Most importantly, they have the structures of thought in place to make it all possible. Their brain has been built to support what literacy and numeracy really mean.

We call it Literacy because it's about more than any particular language. Essentially it's the ability to use the written and spoken word flexibly for a wide range of purposes. A literate child uses reading and listening skills to help them understand and interpret; writing and speaking skills to analyse their own thoughts as well as to communicate them to others; and a wide range of thinking skills to generate ideas from their senses and memories. They can apply different forms of language to brilliant effect.

Numeracy is the ability to employ both logic and creativity to solve familiar and unfamiliar problems. A numerate child uses numbers, shapes and other concepts to help organize, explain, predict and understand. They find patterns that help them follow useful rules. All their thinking skills play a role in their investigations and applications.

Insight

The foundations are being laid even before birth. We know that children can recognize patterns of sound heard before they were born – sounds that are the building blocks of language. They also seem to gain a head start in ordering and counting if they're played simple 'beep' sequences while still in the womb.

Literacy and numeracy develop organically, and the influences of both environment and experience are huge. Parents have a fantastic opportunity to prepare their children and support them at every stage.

How well tuned is your child's brain for literacy and numeracy? Are the key mental structures in place to support their development? What can you do to equip them with all the thinking skills they're going to need?

This chapter explains some of the practical things you can do to help your child get the most out of Literacy and Numeracy. Whenever you start, you can support their success, showing them that confidence in these areas brings both practical benefits and deep, lasting enjoyment.

Literacy

In school, Literacy is broken down into three key areas: speaking and listening, reading and writing. There are many overlaps between them, but these are the main ways in which your child's literacy ability and confidence will develop, and by which they will be judged.

Primary children typically receive an hour's focused literacy teaching every day; but of course their language skills are being tested and developed all day long, in school and out. While schools teach *about* language, parents provide essential opportunities to *acquire* language and to practise and enrich it. It can be an extremely powerful combination.

Speaking and listening

In primary school, speaking and listening involves:

▶ *speaking clearly and confidently to different people for a range of purposes: story-telling, reading aloud, presenting and describing experiences*
▶ *sustaining concentration to listen and remember*
▶ *showing interest and asking appropriate questions*
▶ *taking turns to speak, discussing and debating*
▶ *in drama, using language and movement to express emotion and explore characters, and responding to the performances of others*
▶ *recognizing how other people use language in different ways.*

All the activities in this book support these key speaking and listening skills.

By talking and listening to your children you provide them with the most influential model to copy.

By strengthening their concentration, activating their imagination, preparing them to work with others and giving them the self-esteem to shine, you provide the perfect foundation for your child to build on in school.

By giving them a safe environment in which to challenge their communication skills and develop their confidence, you help them to use all of their thinking and learning skills to be great speakers and listeners. You can further support this development in many ways:

▶ *Keep giving them different audiences to communicate with: in person, on the telephone and by video chat.*
▶ *Encourage them to record their own voice and to listen to themselves in different contexts. Remember that many mobile phones are also digital recorders.*
▶ *Discuss current affairs, testing their ability to argue their views and to listen to yours.*
▶ *Suggest interesting souvenirs, photographs or nature discoveries that they could show and talk about in class.*

Reading

What does it mean to be able to read? Essentially it's about decoding shapes on a page or screen to reveal increasingly subtle forms of meaning. We learn first to gather information from print, and then to understand how and why something has been written in a particular way. We use what we read to improve our own written and spoken communication, and we achieve a speed and fluency that makes reading a pleasure itself. It lets us tap into a rich world of interest and imagination.

In primary school, reading involves:

▶ *learning to read with accuracy and fluency, for understanding and enjoyment*
▶ *reading a wide range of texts, both fiction and non-fiction*
  ▷ *fiction includes stories, poems, plays; works with familiar settings and those based in imaginary worlds; stories by significant modern and classic authors; texts from a range of cultures and times*

> ▷ *non-fiction includes texts in print and on screen;*
>   *CD ROMs, emails, internet pages; newspapers and*
>   *magazines; brochures and leaflets; diaries, biographies*
>   *and autobiographies; dictionaries, encyclopedias and*
>   *other reference materials*
> ► *reading effectively to find specific information, judge between*
>   *fact and opinion and consider an argument critically*
> ► *connecting different parts of a text; finding meaning beyond*
>   *the literal; using information gained from other texts*
> ► *understanding how writers achieve their effects through word*
>   *choice, sentence structure and overall construction of the text.*

Reading reveals the brain's breathtaking power. Remove all the 'internal' vowels from a sentence and we can still read it:

> *Vwls are essntl whn we are lrnng to rd, bt thy are mch lss imprtnt whn we are strng rdrs. Rmvng thm prsnts fw prblms. (Vowels are essential when we are learning to read, but they are much less important when we are strong readers. Removing them presents few problems).*

We can still read a sentence if many of the letters are jumbled up:

> *Aoccdrnig to a reschearer at Cambrigde Uinervtisy, it deosn't mttaer in waht oredr the ltteers in a wrod are. The olny iprmoatnt tihng is taht the frist and lsat ltteer be in the rghit pclae. (According to a researcher at Cambridge University, it doesn't matter in what order the letters in a word are. The only important thing is that the first and last letter be in the right place.)*

We can even make a good attempt to read when we can only see the top half of every word. Cover up the bottom half of a line of text – try it now with a line from this book – and you'll demonstrate how little symbolic information your literate brain really needs to be able to read.

Fluent readers use many different strategies simultaneously to turn marks into meaning – which is one of the reasons why there are so many things you can do to help your child become a confident reader. Developing a range of tactics is key to their success.

The reading process actually starts with listening. Your child needs plenty of experience hearing the important sounds and patterns of language. The clear and exaggerated way we talk to babies is perfect for acclimatizing them to the sounds that make meaning. Nursery rhymes and songs get their brains ready for the rhythms of phrases and sentences.

By they time they're around one year old, children can recognize all the 'phonemes' that make up the English language.

Insight

Although there are only 26 letters, there are 44 different phonemes, the smallest 'chunks' of recognizable sound. These are central to the phonics teaching children receive in school, so they need to be used to hearing them from an early age.

Make sure your young child can also *see* these phonemes being formed. Speak in a way that lets them watch how your lips and tongue form the sounds. If too much of their early experience involves cartoons and puppets on television and DVDs, it may limit their ability to understand how the individual parts of a language are formed and put together.

When can a child be said to start reading? It could well be the moment they realize that there's a link between the language they can hear and the strange marks that they see. So the earlier they can take this step, the better. Let young babies see, touch and smell real books. Make it clear where the stories you're reading come from. As your child begins looking at the pages with you, point to each word as you read it. This is the magical concept for them to grasp: that these sounds and rhythms, full of interest and entertainment, are lying there on the page, waiting to be decoded and explored.

Show young children how to hold a book and turn the pages. Of course it's second nature to us now, but we all had to learn which way round to hold a book, which direction to turn the pages and how the symbols go from left to right and top to bottom on each page.

Encourage your child to play the role of reader. Give them a familiar book to hold and let them 'read' it to you, turning the pages just like a real reader. They'll be using their memory at the same time as finding early clues in the pictures and words.

As your child progresses to different sorts of text – from picture books and simple stories to chapter books, poems, non-fiction – keep demonstrating the appropriate practical approach. Show them when it's important to read from beginning to end and when a text can be explored in different ways. Young children are often fascinated by the endpapers of a book, the contents page and the index. Encourage this interest as part of their education into how books work, showing them the range of skills required to read them well.

As well as using phonics – blending sounds together to make words – schools will also teach children to read by using the meaning of whole sentences, and by making the most of any picture or layout clues available. As fluent readers we do this without thinking, and we can encourage children to use these three key strategies with confidence.

LETTERS AND SOUNDS

Long before they start school, your child needs to learn about letters from you:

▶ *Show them letters in a variety of colours, not just black on white.*

▶ *Give them letters made out of wood or plastic so that they can feel their shapes. Can they recognize them with their eyes closed?*

▶ *Let them write letters in a tray of sand or a plate of custard. If you write a letter with your finger on their back, can they tell you what it is?*

The alphabet

Help your child to learn alphabetical order. A classic way to do this is to use the familiar tune of 'Twinkle, twinkle, little star' to sing the letters. Both my children learnt using the following version:

A B C D E F G
H I J K L-M-N-O-P
Q R S, T U V,
W X, Y and Z,
Now I know my ABC
Next time won't you sing with me?

Alphabet posters with memorable colours and illustrations are another useful way of embedding the information. But the best way to become completely familiar with the alphabet is to use it. Buy your child a dictionary appropriate for their age and get them used to finding words in it. Let them look for friends and family in the telephone directory. Show them how indexes and glossaries work and encourage them to search for information that interests and excites them.

Phonics

Although there are only 26 letters in the English language, they can be used to make 44 different sounds or 'phonemes' – as illustrated below.

Vowel phonemes	Example words
a	bat
e	leg, head
i	big, wanted
o	fog, want
u	bug, love
ae	day, train, late, station
ee	feet, meat, belief, these
ie	tried, might, by, fine, mind
oe	throw, toad, cone, told
ue	soon, blue, flew, tune

(Contd)

oo	book, could, put
ar	far, past (regional pronunciation)
ur	turn, first, term, work, heard
au	paw, tall, warn, haul, born, door
er	circus, mister, wooden
ow	down, about
oi	coin, toy
air	pair, bear, mare
ear	rear, here, beer
ure	pure, tourist

Consonant phonemes	Example words
b	boy
d	dog
f	fire, photograph
g	girl
h	house
j	jam, gym, large
k	cat, quite, fix, christen
l	leg
m	mouse, lamb
n	nut, knight, gnaw
ng	thing, sink
p	puppet
r	room, write
s	scarf, house, circle, science
t	table
v	van
w	wet
y	yes
z	zoo, please, his
th	that
th	thin
ch	chip, catch
sh	shop, mission, chef
zh	pleasure

This list gives an insight into the complexities of the English language. The same sound can be created in a number of different ways, and a letter or group of letters can make a variety of different sounds.

Being able to read means understanding how letters and sounds work in combination. You also need a large collection of irregular words that you just *know*. The English language includes many words that simply don't follow the rules.

Schools tend to teach phonics alongside letter names. So your child will learn that the letter 'c' is pronounced like 'see', and that the sound it actually makes is 'cuh' – and later 's', as in 'circle'. You can help them by doing both at home, helping them to understand the relationships between letters and sounds. Using the letter names – 'c', 'a', 't' – will be important for developing spelling skills; but sounding out the phonemes – 'cuh', 'ah', 't' – will be most useful for helping them learn to read.

Think up pictures and actions to match the phonemes. The obvious one is 's'; hiss it to sound like a snake as you wiggle your hand in a snaking s-shape. You could mime knocking on a door for 'd', making the sound repeatedly as you continue knocking: 'duh… duh…duh…'.

Some schools use complete systems in which each phoneme is given a particular 'character'. If your child is being taught in this way, it makes sense to find out how the system works and to strengthen it at home. But if not, have fun with your child matching some of the sounds to memorable ideas.

For 'p' you could imagine prodding a balloon with a needle: 'puh… puh…puh…' until it pops.

To practise 'r' you could pretend to be a roaring lion, bending your wrist and reaching forward with your 'claws' in the shape of the letter r: 'Rrrrroar!'

Your child's teacher will explore the intricacies of phonics with them, building up their repertoire of sounds and spellings. You can encourage the key listening and vocalizing skills, incorporate pictures, sounds and movements, and enrich their learning by switching on more of their brain.

Teachers will also show your child important rules about letters: for example, the 'magic e' which changes the sound of the 'a' in 'rat' and 'rate'; or the fact that 'c' followed by 'i' or 'e' tends to be pronounced like an 's'. Help children to use these rules about letters alongside their developing understanding of sounds.

As you read with your child, encourage them to build up tricky words. The early stages of learning to read can be tiring and daunting, so help them to see that each sound discovered is a victory in itself, getting them closer to the answer.

With my son I found it gave a huge boost to his confidence when I praised him for every clue he found. For a word like 'children', I would say: 'Yes! It's a "ch" word. Well done, that's got us started. Right, what's next? Brilliant, it's a "chi" word. Add the next letter: correct, this is a "chil" word...'

If we were working on the word 'caught', we'd have an early victory with the 'c': 'Good, you know it's a "c" word. Try the next bit. Yes, you're right, "a–uh" sounds odd. Can you remember what "au" sounds like. Excellent – it's "aw". You did that in phonics in school didn't you? So this is a "caw" word. Keep going, you're nearly there...'

Don't be afraid to use terms like 'phonics' and 'phonemes' with your child. You'll help to connect home and school and strengthen both sides of their reading development.

Encourage them to spot phonic patterns. Rhyming games are perfect for this. You could say a line, and ask your child to say anything that rhymes, no matter how silly, for example:

Parent:	'I've just come back from the shop.'
Child:	'I wish I'd decided to hop.'
Parent:	'We're going to have chicken for tea.'
Child:	'I'm throwing mine into the sea!'

You could challenge them to think up ten words that rhyme with 'bread' or 'shoe'. Talk to your child about the different ways in which a single sound can be spelt: shoe, loo, through, pew, true...

You could make up rhyming descriptions and nicknames for famous people: 'Simon Cowell wears a towel; 'Puny Rooney'; 'Spears the Ears'.

Prompt your child to look out for words within words. 'Morphemes' are the smallest bits of meaningful language. So a word like 'cardboard' has two morphemes, 'card' and 'board'. You can spot other words in there, like 'car' and 'boar', but they have no impact on the meaning of 'cardboard'. Some morphemes are prefixes, like 'pre-' and 'un-'; some are suffixes like '-ful' and '-ness'; and some are words in their own right: 'work-man-like'. If your child knows that '-ology' means 'the study of', or '-ly' means 'like', then they have powerful clues about whole sets of words. The more morphemes children can recognize, the wider their vocabulary and the more fluent their reading will be.

A key mechanism of memory is organizing and categorizing, so spotting groups of words is a powerful way of storing them. Can your child tell you a certain number of 'light-' or '-box' words? Encourage them to think about what the morpheme means, to access that all-important visualization, and then to explore their vocabulary for words that fit the pattern. It enriches the connections between bits of information while also strengthening the brain's ability to group and sort data in useful ways.

By sounding out words phonetically and using morphemes to help them read, your child will learn an increasing number of words by sight.

The 100 most common words account for 53 per cent of written English. Making sure your child knows these as soon as possible will give a major boost to their reading success. They are:

> *a, about, after, all, am, an, and, are, as, at, away*
> *back, be, because, big, but, by*
> *call, came, can, come, could*
> *did, do, down*
> *for, from*
> *get, go, got*
> *had, has, have, he, her, here, him, his*
> *I, in, into, is, it*
> *last, like, little, live, look*
> *made, make, me, my*
> *new, next, not, now*
> *of, off, old, on, once, one, other, our, out, over*
> *put*
> *saw, said, see, she, so, some*
> *take, that, the, their, them, then, there, they, this, three, time,*
> * to, today, too, two*
> *up, us*
> *very*
> *was, we, were, went, what, when, will, with*
> *you*

Some parents and children enjoy testing key words with flashcards or computer programs, and it's certainly useful to recognize common words instantly. But reading is much more than processing individual words. The more your child can practise these words within real texts, the sooner they start tapping into the second key strategy for reading, using meaning to provide useful clues.

USING MEANING

It's tempting to tell young children not to 'guess' words; but that's actually what fluent readers do all the time. They make predictions based on what they expect a word to be, using a number of different clues.

The structure of a sentence may suggest the next word. For example, 'I am going to the p____.' Here, the missing final word is almost certainly a noun, rather than an adjective like 'pretty' or a verb like 'playing'. The brain is extremely efficient at narrowing down the possibilities and letting us choose from sensible words.

The meaning of the text can also be very useful: 'Robbie was feeling nervous on his f____ day at school.' A fluent reader will make the most of the meaning here to predict the missing word. It's much more likely to be 'first', or perhaps 'final', than 'fourth' or 'fifth'.

We also use our general knowledge to help us read: 'The goalkeeper pulled on his g____.' If we know that goalkeepers wear gloves then we're likely to try that word first, rather than 'gown' or 'galoshes'.

Children will also use their memory to inform their reading, using recall of particular texts (for example, 'Cinderella's coach turned back into a p____') alongside their growing knowledge of different genres: 'Once upon a ____.'

The more confident children's reading becomes, the more clues they use. Random guessing is ineffective, but predictions based on evidence like this are exactly how reading works, weaving all the clues together and processing the text in a very rich way.

Play 'missing words' games with your child. Start with books they're familiar with and use strips cut from sticky notes to cover individual words. Choose interesting words towards the end of sentences. Challenge your child to read the sentence and tell you the word under the flap. If they guess the wrong word, give them the first letter and let them try again. Point out some of the other clues they might use.

...eir reading develops, use more and more advanced texts. ...can also have fun suggesting the *least* likely words to fill the gaps, and occasionally include words to which there are no clues at all: 'Sasha turned and surprised them all by saying, "I've lost my _____."'

The third key strategy for reading involves what the text *looks* like.

VISUAL CLUES

Parents often worry that their child is guessing words by looking at the pictures. But if they're doing this alongside all the other cues from letters, sounds, sentence structure, meaning and memory, it's another very powerful technique to try.

Give your child wonderful picture books. They'll love to search the details in books by Richard Scarry, or explore all the symbols and picture clues in the works of Anthony Brown.

The way the words themselves look can also be helpful. Help your child to spot capital letters, for example by finding all the 'names' in the book. Texts by Mini Grey and Lauren Child often use different typefaces for particular effects, helping children to spot the important words in a sentence or to see when different characters are talking. This is a great way to heighten your child's awareness of other visible clues like punctuation, line spacing and paragraph structure. Talk to them about any words that are underlined, in bold or italics.

Reading by sound, meaning, structure, memory and appearance represents an approach that's in tune with the way the brain works best. Fluent readers process the text in 'real time' while also exploring their past experiences and imagining future possibilities. Their thinking skills combine in a rich and multi-layered approach to literacy.

Your child only has to learn to read once, so it's well worth the effort. If you feel they're struggling, remember that children progress at different speeds, but also talk to their teacher to check there's no particular problem. The more you understand about how a child reads well, the more specific you can be about any difficulties they have; and, together, find ways to address them.

Children need help from you as well as school if they are going to learn to read. But there's so much more you can do to help them enjoy the full benefits of reading *brilliantly*, such as:

▶ *Let them see you reading, for many different purposes.*
▶ *Provide them with a wide range of texts: fiction and non-fiction; on paper and on screen; owned and loaned.*
▶ *Discuss the books you all read. Encourage their opinions and share your own.*
▶ *Keep reading to your child even when they're fluent. Let them know you love sharing books with them.*
▶ *Sometimes let them read books slightly below or above their current reading level. It's a great way of encouraging awareness of reading skills and that crucial 'metacognition'. Can they tell you why a text is particularly easy or tricky? How does it feel to read a book that's childish or challenging?*

Writing

In primary school, writing involves:

▶ *using writing to communicate; organize and explain; comment and persuade; explore experiences; create imaginary worlds*
▶ *choosing and adapting form, content and style to suit different audiences and purposes*
▶ *developing a wide vocabulary*
▶ *writing increasingly complex sentences and linking them together*
▶ *using punctuation for clarity and a range of effects*
▶ *having a range of good spelling strategies*

▶ *writing neatly and legibly, using different handwriting styles for different purposes*

▶ *being able to plan, draft and improve written work.*

To be good readers, children need to be good thinkers. And to be good writers, it's vital that they use their thinking and reading skills to the full. They need to use their understanding of language, the ideas they borrow from other writers and texts, and all the imaginative energy they can muster.

It's fascinating to watch a child go through the various stages of writing. They begin with mark-making, showing they've understood that meaning can be conveyed in symbols. Their developing understanding of reading inspires them to do some of their own 'writing': wiggly lines, odd-looking little shapes and eventually letter-like symbols. Encourage this by making writing part of the games you play. If they set up a café, get them to take your order. Before you go shopping for real, suggest that they write out their own shopping list. Mark-making is the first stage in understanding the purpose of writing and developing the practical skills to produce it.

HANDWRITING

Keep an eye on the way your child holds pencils and pens. Don't get in the way of their early writing, but do encourage them to use an efficient and comfortable grip as soon as possible. Show them how you hold your pen, and explain why. Praise them whenever they hold their pen like a grown up.

As your child learns about letters, challenge them to write them in the air, in the sand on the beach or by using their finger to trace the shape on your hand. Train them to draw simple shapes as accurately and neatly as they can. Give them dots to join.

As their skills develop and they begin writing on paper, show them the 'entry points' of letters. Their teacher will be able to tell you any particular handwriting rules used at school, and it's important to keep in step with those; but you know enough about letters to practise basic techniques like starting an 'e' from the left of the horizontal line, and making the entry point for 'p' the top of the down stroke.

It's tempting to tell children simply to 'write more neatly', but it's much more effective to be specific and to show them exactly what neat writing looks like. Write down perfect letters and words for them to copy, but also make the most of helpful imagery, for example:

'Your capital T needs to be much taller and straighter, like a tower.'
'Imagine the top part of that 'y' is a pot of yoghurt, and the line in your book is the table it should be resting on.'

Insight

As ever, correct casually. Don't stifle or frustrate them, but do help your child to avoid developing physical habits that will be hard to change. Emphasize that you're helping them write neatly and quickly so that they can capture their brilliant ideas.

SPELLING

The same applies to children's spelling. After mark-making comes the 'semi-phonetic' stage, where their reading skills help them to choose some sensible combinations of letters. Heap praise on your child every time they write something you understand; and when you don't understand ask them – with interest and excitement – to tell you what it says. As their phonic skills develop they will often follow perfect logic to achieve wonderfully creative spellings: 'shoow' for 'shoe', 'peapull' for 'people', 'boks' for 'box'. As this stage, their wrong spellings actually show their improving understanding of language. The more they read the better spelling choices they'll make, as they spot patterns and categories and increase their vocabulary of familiar words. They'll get closer and closer to 'conventional' spelling; and with your help, the progression will be natural and enjoyable.

All the techniques in this book help you to support their developing language, setting up and interweaving their thinking skills in a richly organic way. But there are also some specific strategies to boost their confidence with words.

Insight

Encourage children to take a mental 'photograph' of a word, then to see it as clearly as possible in their mind's eye. Challenge them to focus on how it looks in their mind and to spell it to you backwards.

Suggest that they give words strong colours and exaggerate any important details. The easy-to-miss 'h' in 'white', for example, could become a hard-to-ignore huge white letter rising high above all the rest. The double letters in 'ball' could be highlighted in a particular colour – perhaps the bright red of the child's own favourite ball – and made particularly long or wide in their mind. They could even be turned into the goalposts through which the ball is being kicked.

Encourage your child to use all their developing memory skills to boost their learning of words. Try introducing the following techniques.

▶ *If they spot words within words, they can use them to create memorable 'clues' about spellings. They might see their friends Eva and Elle 'inside' the words 'relevant' and 'jewellery'. If they can't remember whether it's 'different' or 'differant', they could imagine paying* different *amounts of rent to live in different sorts of houses.*

▶ *They could imagine writing a word onto something unusual or appropriate. This brings in more of the senses and emotions and helps to strengthen the memory. Imagine using a sloppy paintbrush to write 'elephant' on the side of a real elephant, or taking a rusty nail and scratching the word 'naughty' into a priceless oak table.*

▶ *Particularly difficult words can be given specific memory prompts. Have fun turning words into mnemonic sentences, such as 'Your anchor could have tangled' ('yacht') or 'Big elephants are useful to Indians for unloading logs' ('beautiful'). Prompt your child to visualize the ideas and help them to design sentences of their own.*

VOCABULARY

As well as spellings, word meanings can be brought to life in the imagination and fixed firmly into memory. Try introducing these skills.

▶ *'Truncated' means cut off; so your child could imagine an elephant with a short trunk or a tree trunk being chopped. A 'goanna' is a type of lizard and it sounds like Joanna – so create a pet goanna called Joanna...*
▶ *Get your child looking at and listening to words, creating memorable links with their meanings, and exploring language with the creativity and spark that brings all their brainpower to life.*
▶ *As well as getting energetic in their imagination, encourage their kinaesthetic learning skills by letting them build key words with straws, construction equipment, leaves or clay.*
▶ *The physical act of writing down a spelling helps build up 'muscle memories', giving your child a strong sense of what it feels like to write particular words – and a growing feel for the language in general. Encourage them to write at the same time as picturing the word and bringing to mind all the creative clues they created, activating their whole brain.*

As always, talk to them about the skills they're learning, prompting them to think about thinking and get involved in their own development and growth.

As your child masters writing, all their thinking skills can be brought into the work they produce. Give them opportunities at home that will excite and enrich their literacy by activating all the key areas of their brain.

Stimulate their visualization and imagination: Can they write a description of their perfect garden? Look at that man on the bus: what's his life story? If our house falls down while we're on holiday, what will we do?

Give them access to the richly imagined worlds in picture books, imaginative posters, and computer games set in vivid virtual landscapes. Get them to talk and write about what they can see, and challenge them to incorporate other senses in their descriptions. What might this place sound like, smell like, feel like? Who might live here? What would they say to introduce themselves?

Help them to weave their experiences and memories into their writing. After a walk in the woods, challenge them to write a poem that captures everything they heard, touched and smelled. Put together scrapbooks combining postcards, tickets and luggage labels as well as written work about a holiday. Buy them a diary where they can record everyday experiences as well as momentous days.

Use physical activities to stimulate ideas. Before they describe the old woman in their story, get them to demonstrate how she might walk across the living room. Encourage them to mime a rollercoaster ride before they write it into their playscript. Help them to tap into kinaesthetic techniques – touching, moving, acting – to inform and energize their writing.

Encourage them to connect their own imagination with the creativity of others, and to link with different media, borrowing ideas from the films they watch and the video games they play.

Challenge them to write for practical purposes as well as for imaginative pleasure. Can they draft some rules for sharing the new computer? What about an instruction book for the neighbour who's going to have their pet rabbit while you're away?

By including writing as a natural part of family life, you encourage your child to grow their confidence and ability in parallel with all the other skills they're developing.

The ideas above involve imagination, logic, memory, communication – all the areas being built into their overall approach to thinking and learning. They all play a huge role in writing; in turn they're all strengthened and extended as your child puts them to use in their work with language – reading, writing and speaking.

Technical terms

As your child's literacy skills mature, encourage them to use powerful memory techniques to learn key vocabulary and ideas.

▶ *An adjective is a 'describing word'. They might imagine a DJ describing all his music tracks before he plays them. Get your child to put on a DJ's voice and describe their favourite tunes.*
▶ *An ellipsis means 'dot, dot, dot'. Your child might imagine their teacher's lips turning into a dotted line, then draw a cartoon face with dots for lips.*
▶ *The word 'simile' looks like the word 'smile'. Challenge your child to think up lots of different similes for a smile: 'Her smile was... like sunshine/like the letter U/like a row of crooked gravestones...'*

Family Literacy

Families that support all these key areas of literacy have a number of things in common. A detailed study by Professor of Education at Illinois University, Dolores Durkin, noted that children who develop literacy skills early tend to have:

▶ *parents who read to them, talk to them and answer their questions*
▶ *access to plenty of real books as well as school reading 'schemes'*
▶ *experience of print in everyday situations*
▶ *families with a love for writing as well as reading.*

A number of other studies have confirmed the importance of deep parental involvement. When families read, write and talk together, visit libraries, and weave literacy into everyday life, they support their children's organic literacy development. They do so in a way that breeds positive feelings and aspirations, and they tap into all the key thinking skills that drive a child's long-term success.

Numeracy

In primary school, Numeracy involves:

- *problem-solving: making connections; breaking problems into simple steps; making creative approaches; estimating and checking*
- *communicating findings in precise, appropriate ways; explaining and persuading*
- *counting and calculating*
- *describing number patterns and sequences*
- *calculating mentally as well as on paper; using a calculator when appropriate*
- *solving abstract and 'real-life' problems and questions involving 2D and 3D shapes*
- *measuring and drawing shapes and angles*
- *interpreting graphs, tables and diagrams.*

The South African scientist and educator Seymour Papert said that a child's home should be mathematically 'literate'. Family life, he said, should reflect an interest in and understanding of maths, allowing it to be discussed and explored during a variety of activities. Maths should be woven naturally into a child's upbringing, helping them form the mental skill set required to be mathematically competent, confident and creative.

As with language, mathematical ability grows organically. A child's environment plays a hugely important role. As a parent, you need to be aware of the natural growth of their thinking to be able to support their developing knowledge and skills in the right ways at the right times. Home life can prepare a child's thinking for the formal work they'll do in school, giving them invaluable opportunities to apply what they learn, strengthen their skills and enrich their understanding.

At just four months old, babies are surprised when the number of objects in front of them changes. You can play simple games to challenge their very early awareness of number.

When you add a brick to the one already there on the mat, mime your exaggerated surprise: 'What's happened? What's different?' When you hide one of them, join your child in the excitement of hunting for it: 'What's changed this time? Where was it... and where could it be now?'

When they're a year old, babies show early signs of understanding what addition and subtraction actually mean. They can spot the gap if one object is removed from a group, and put it back in the right place to restore the total. Count for your child: toys in the play pen, animals at the farm, people around the table. Get them used to the sound of numbers, and to the way you point to each one as you say its number. This helps to establish the idea of 'one-to-one correspondence': that one number refers to one item in the group. Make it very clear that the total number is different when objects are added or removed.

When children begin to talk (around two years) help them to learn number words in context. Emphasize the fact that there are two dolls or three trains, and let them touch and play with the physical things you're describing. Use familiar objects to explore what numbers actually mean:

'What happens when the dolls change places? Are there still two?'
'If you count three trains, then take one away, can you still use the word "three" to describe the trains that are left?'

You're not really teaching, just opening up some intriguing questions to activate your child's interest and stretch their thinking. You're actually engaging them with some big concepts.

Children need to learn that a number is a property of a group of things. Unlike describing words, which can be applied to one thing or to several, numbers apply to sets. You can't point to your teddy and say 'two', even if you own two teddies or this one was second in line last time you counted them. It all depends on how many teddies there are now.

On the other hand, three books on a shelf will still be three books even if they're put in a different order. It's the order of the numbers that stays the same, and those numbers can be used to count anything.

Playing with sets of toys, asking questions in words and mimes, prompting your child to observe and consider patterns and rules; it all helps set up their key mathematical thinking skills.

At three years of age, children can experiment with division, sharing real things like beads or pieces of food. Use words like 'sharing', 'dividing' and 'grouping' to establish some of the key vocabulary. Start with 'One for you, one for me' sharing between two of you, then progress to dividing between larger groups.

Card games are useful for strengthening the concept of division. To divide the whole pack between any number of players, you simply keep dealing them out in 'rounds' until all the cards are gone. You can talk about 'left overs' or even 'remainders' for the extra cards. Encourage your child to look at all the piles: Are they the same size? Is the game fair? If you were to add them all together again, would they look like the pack you started with? Play the game with different numbers of people, showing your child that fewer players means more cards each. Long before they tackle formal division questions, your child can be building key levels of understanding.

Four-year-olds can count to 10 or 20 and play simple number games. Try alternate counting: you say 'One', they say 'Two', you say 'Three', and so on. This is great for promoting concentration and communication as well as for strengthening their counting skills.

Make simple, colourful number lines for your child to help them practise reading the numbers as they say them. Make sure they start at zero. It's a good idea to display some number lines horizontally, which your child reads from left to right, and some vertically, with the numbers going upwards as they increase. Encourage your child to try counting in jumps of two, three, four or five, introducing them to the concept of multiplication.

Introduce differently sized number lines. It's a great way to demonstrate that physical distance isn't as important as the number of steps along the way. Compare the distance between zero and ten on different versions of your number line. Why is one so much greater than the other? On a line with very small gaps between numbers, why is the distance from one to twenty so much less than that between one and five on a wider number line? This is an important concept to grasp. Young children often go through a stage where they believe stretching a line of objects increases its value. So a widely spaced line of five buttons suddenly seems to have more in it than five buttons placed close together. Using a combination of real objects and, gradually, written number lines, helps them discover the truth and strengthen their core understanding of what numbers mean and do.

At five years old your child may be able to count backwards as well as forwards, and you should be able to extend their number lines significantly – perhaps up to 100. At this age the 'cardinal principle' can be established: that the number of the last object counted is the total number of objects in the set. So when they point to their toy cars in turn and say 'One, two, three, four, five, six', the last number tells them how many cars there are altogether.

Let your child see you counting things – and occasionally making mistakes. 'One, two, three, four, six…'. Children love spotting missing parts of a pattern, and this activity helps them to see just how important it is to count in sequence. Sometimes count by pointing to all the items, just not in a clear order from left to right. Show children that the order you count things in doesn't matter, just the order of the numbers you use. Sometimes clearly leave one out. Can your child convince you that your counting isn't right?

Six-year-olds can do simple mental additions. Encourage them to visualize real things as well as to talk in abstract numbers, activating both their creativity and their logical thinking: 'Three bright red cars and one more makes... How many altogether? Three plus one equals?'

Introduce them to subtraction as the 'opposite' of addition. Make the most of their kinaesthetic learning by giving them plenty of physical props to play with as well as suggesting vivid and memorable images: 'Three fluffy little ducks on the pond, then one goes off with the mean fox... How many are left now?'; 'If you're looking out from the top floor of a 20-storey building, and then the lift drops five floors, where are you now?'

EQUALS

An important concept to establish early is what the equals sign means. Too many children are convinced that it's an instruction to *do* something, since that's how it's used in many of the questions they see. They think they simply do the calculation on the left of the equals sign then write the answer on the right. But eventually your child will face questions such as $2 + 3 = 7 - ?$

To help them in the long run, show them that the equals sign means 'is the same as'. The amount on the left is the same as – equal to – whatever is on the right: '2 + 3 is the same as 7 - ... what?' You can use a set of old-fashioned weighing scales as a useful visual model for this. 'Three blocks and four blocks weighs the same as five blocks plus... two/or ten blocks subtract... three.'

Insight

As your child's calculating skills develop, it's a good idea to use many different words for plus ('add', 'more', 'and') and minus ('subtract', 'take away', 'less') but make sure your child masters one at a time. When they're confident about what 'take away' means, and can take one biscuit away and count how many are left, you can then introduce 'subtract'.

NUMBERS

Encourage your child's awareness of numbers in the world around them. Prompt them to count different sorts of things: objects, actions, sounds, events. Play a number version of 'I spy': 'I spy, with my little eye, something... in a pair/in a four/in a set of three.' Challenge them to find the number one somewhere in the shop or street, then the number two, and so on.

MEASURES

Help your child to understand key maths terms like 'more' and 'less', 'larger' and 'smaller', 'greater', 'increase' and 'decrease'. Drop these words into their real life: 'Let's increase the temperature in here shall we?'; 'Watch the water decrease when we pull out the plug.' Use a range of containers to show them that the same amount of something can look quite different. The milk in a thin bottle may be level with the juice in a wide one, so why is there so much more juice when you pour the liquids into same-sized cups? Putting plastic bottles and tubs in the bath is a great way to stimulate hands-on exploration.

SHAPES

Develop your child's awareness of shapes. As always, let them feel and play with a variety of shaped objects as you tell them their names. Let them experiment with the way certain shapes do or do not slot together. Can they guess the next shape in your sequence, and put together repeating patterns of their own? Challenge them to find as many different shapes as they can in picture books and famous works of art. When they're ready, introduce 3D shapes they can recognize: cuboids (shoe boxes), cubes (dice), spheres (balls). Can they identify differently shaped blocks by touch alone?

Using maths every day

Home is the best place to build an understanding of many important maths ideas.

To deal effectively with centimetres, hours, kilograms and millilitres in school, your child will need experience of using them in the real world. They need to understand what a kilometre looks like and what 50 g feels like, otherwise they'll struggle to cope with lots of similar-sounding abstract words.

Point out distances on maps, weights on packets, dimensions on clothes labels. Activate their memory with powerful examples to refer to. A bag of their favourite crisps weighs abound 30 g. The walk to the swimming pool is 1.5 km. An episode of their top TV show lasts 20 minutes.

It's particularly important for your child to have a good sense of time. Start by establishing the concepts 'before' and 'after': 'What did you do before lunch?'; 'What happened straight after Dad came home?' Then start to link key moments in their day with the times at which they happen. You can buy or make a simple clock for them to experiment with. 'What do the hands look like at tea time?'; 'What are you doing when the hour hand's at seven and the minute hand points straight up?' Give them meaningful time problems, about things that matter to them: 'If you're going to play football for another half hour, what time will it be when you come in?'; 'We're leaving at noon and the plane's due to touch down at 2.45 p.m. – so how long is the flight?' Help your child to use both digital and analogue clocks. Their first wristwatch will be important in giving them ownership of time and confidence in using it for their own practical purposes, making possible the abstract calculations they do in school.

Money can be another very useful tool for developing your child's mathematical thinking. Counting their savings, or working out how much more they need to buy a particular toy, can be great ways to motivate their learning. Using money encourages both creative and logical thought: for example, choosing how to spend their pocket money, and working out how much to allocate to what. And money is by far the best way to learn about decimals. When your child tackles questions like 3.09 + 5.7, if they have a strong understanding of money it's much easier to refer to £3.09 + £5.70 to visualize and calculate the amounts involved.

The difference between 2.1 and 2.01 is far clearer when the numbers are related to money.

MATHEMATICAL THINKING

Make the most of natural opportunities to discuss maths – and challenge your child to explain their thinking and persuade you they're right, for example:

'How do you know that 15 sandwiches won't share equally between four people?'
'I think buying three ice creams for £1 ($1.50) is a better deal than two for 70 p ($1). Do you agree?'
'Which is more likely: throwing an odd number or an even number?'

Being able to make detailed, persuasive arguments about maths is one of the key skills developed during primary school. Help your child develop this way of thinking naturally, using it as another way of strengthening their metacognition. It challenges them to use accurate vocabulary, to think creatively and logically, and to analyse the accuracy and usefulness of their mathematical thinking.

Get them talking about *how* they investigate problems. You don't have to know the answers; in fact, it's particularly powerful when you don't, giving your child a chance to make real discoveries, such as:

'I wonder how many different ways we could arrange the chairs around the table?'

'Is there a way to give everyone a different number of chocolates?'
'We've got a 4 l bucket and a 7 l bucket, so can we use them to measure out 1 l of water? What about 2 l, 3 l, 5 l...? Are there any amounts we won't be able to measure out?'

Challenge children to use their full range of thinking skills to pursue the answers and explain them to you. Encourage them to visualize the questions; to use their instincts and to make predictions; to work systematically, using props or written notes to structure their thinking and to check they've explored all the possibilities, especially when they're preparing to give their 'verdict'.

It can be liberating for children to realize that sometimes, maths is about proving that an idea is wrong. It's about testing theories, finding patterns, making discoveries – and not always just arriving at the 'right' answer your teacher expects.

Questions like this give children rich opportunities to use and strengthen their numeracy skills. This mix of creative and logical thought, experiment, analysis, opinion forming, proof finding and checking is what mathematical thinking is all about.

Memory techniques for maths

Memory techniques can play a very important role in maths. Encourage your child to use their creative learning skills to remember the important concepts, rules and vocabulary.

ACUTE/OBTUSE

'Cute' suggests small, so your child can use this clue to remember that acute angles are the smallest group, less than ninety degrees. Ask them to measure and draw an acute angle and then draw a cute little creature inside.

'Obtuse', on the other hand, sounds like 'obese'; which is useful because obtuse angles are bigger than 90 degrees. Can they draw an obtuse angle, then add a few extra lines to show the fat stomach and little arms and legs of an obese person?

CO-ORDINATES

The x axis runs horizontally, and the y axis vertically. It's important to know which is which; so why not think of eggs (x) rolling along the horizontal floor; and someone sitting on top of the vertical axis shouting: 'Why (y)... am I so high...?'

PERIMETER

With a little practice your child can start finding useful memory clues within words themselves. Here, the 'rim' in 'perimeter' reminds them what the word means: the distance all the way around the rim of a shape. By visualizing the word, making the 'rim' bit larger or more brightly coloured, and then imagining measuring the rim of a cup or bottle, they'll fix the information firmly in their mind.

TRANSLATE

It's important that your child has ways of remembering processes in maths.

Translating shapes means sliding them from place to place, so maybe they could change the word 'translate' slightly to 'train's late': 'The train's late... so people have to slide the train quickly along the track to get to the station on time.'

Access to vivid mental pictures gives your child a real head start. They can picture this memorable scene, add sounds and emotions, and create a powerful reminder of what translation means in maths.

You can teach your child a simple system for remembering numbers themselves, both individual digits and longer sequences.

It's a technique that activates creative and logical thinking, transforming abstract digits into vivid images and then linking them together in memorable scenes and stories. It helps children to think carefully about numbers, to find patterns and make connections, and to explore maths in a way that's both highly structured and richly imaginative.

THE NUMBER-SHAPE SYSTEM

This system involves choosing pictures to represent each of the ten digits, 0 to 9. The key image for each digit is based on its shape, making it easy to remember.

0 *is round like a ball*
1 *is as straight as a pencil*
2 *looks like a swan*
3 *on its side resembles hills*
4 *becomes the sail on a yacht*
5 *is a curved hook*
6 *leaning forward looks like a cannon*
7 *is a lamp*
8 *is a snowman*
9 *becomes a lollipop*

Talk to your child about these ten images. They could draw funny and colourful pictures of them to make into a poster for their wall. Encourage them to imagine what it would be like to touch, hear, smell or taste the objects as well as to see them in vivid detail.

To use the system to remember numbers, simply change each digit into the appropriate picture then link the pictures together in a memorable way, such as:

▶ *To remember their friend's house number, 13, your child might imagine using a pencil to draw a picture of some hills onto their front door.*
▶ *If the code for their new combination lock is 7253, the images would be lamp, swan, hook, hills; so they might imagine*

parking their bike under street lamp, on which a large swan is perched. The swan lowers down a sharp metal hook, picks up the bike and flies off over the hills.

▶ You could make sure your child remembers a dental appointment at 4 pm by telling them to imagine that the surgery was being held on a luxury yacht.

▶ Your child is much more likely to remember they've been invited to a birthday party on the 28th if they have a picture in their mind of swans attacking a snowman on top of the birthday cake!

The pictures are easily turned back into numbers, providing clear and lasting clues about the original information:

▶ Using a pencil to draw hills gives you 1 and 3. You drew on your friend's front door, so they must live at number 13.

▶ The lamp post with the swan on top, his hook and the hills he flew over, give you 7, 2, 5 and 3: the code for the lock on your bike, parked underneath the light itself.

NUMBER BONDS

Help your child learn the all important 'number bonds to ten'; the pairs of numbers that add together to make exactly ten.

Since 'ten out of ten' is often seen as 'top marks', you could invent a competition in which the following actions all achieved a perfect score:

▶ drawing a picture of a lollipop (1 and 9)
▶ feeding ice cream to swans (2 and 8)
▶ taking country walks with torches (3 and 7)
▶ shooting cannons on ships (4 and 6)
▶ holding a sharp hook in each hand (5 and 5).

The pictures connect as pairs, so it doesn't matter which way round the numbers appear. Using them as memory aids will help your child learn them off by heart, at the same time as stimulating all their key thinking skills.

The best mathematicians use imagination and creativity as much as logic to solve problems and apply their understanding. A technique like this switches on and challenges creativity, and links it directly to maths. It also helps children to become active learners as they make abstract information concrete, vivid and memorable. It increases their confidence to make effective choices about how they use their brains to boost their own success.

When children are confident about using this basic system they can expand it, using a range of ideas connected with the original ten images.

0   *anything to do with balls and sports: golf ball, tennis player, goalposts*
1   *pen, pencils, paints – and any other creative equipment, as well as characters such as artists and sculptors*
2   *birds, planes, kites*
3   *not just hills but anything found in the countryside: trees, flowers, rabbits*
4   *a range of boats and ships, plus anchors, sailors, fish*
5   *a crane, an elevator, a litter picker, or anything else that hooks, fastens or lifts*
6   *any kind of weaponry: gun, catapult, crossbow*
7   *desk lamps, torches, lasers – even the biggest light source of all, the Sun*
8   *not just a snowman but anything to do with the ice and cold: snow, sledge, polar bear, Santa Claus*
9   *choose any kind of sweet food you like: cakes, biscuits, toffees*

Each original image becomes just the heading for a huge list of possible ideas. As long as you choose something with a clear link to the 'key' image, your creative pictures will always guide you back to the original information. Extending the system like this gives much more scope for creativity, and for including powerful senses and feelings.

Why not challenge your child to learn a long list of numbers? It will give them huge confidence to see that they can memorize ten or 20 digits, perfecting a system for numbers that they can use in school and out. I've witnessed what a huge impact this can have on children's self-belief about maths. The technique is fun and energetic and it gives them a sense of control over numbers that they may never have felt before. Impressing others with your skills can be the perfect motivation to find other ways to improve.

All they need to do is turn digits into pictures and weave them into a story. The funnier, stranger, more energetic, messy, noisy and smelly they can make it, the more likely it is to work brilliantly.

Collaborate with them on their first attempt – at least to get them started.

If the sequence was 5, 8, 9, 3, 2, 4, 0, 5… the memory story might go like this: You are in a speeding lift, alongside a snowman licking a very cold strawberry lollipop. The lift is taking you to the top of a high mountain to do some birdwatching. But a luxury boat crashes noisily on the top of the mountain, spilling golf balls down the slopes. Can your child collect them all with a litter picker…?

TIMES TABLES

The point of multiplication tables – 'times tables' – is that children know them instantly. Numeracy in general involves finding patterns and using logic and creativity to make careful calculations; but times-table facts need to be known off by heart. The information they contain is hugely helpful in many areas of maths and your child will be at a serious advantage if they can recall the key multiplications without having to think.

To get to the stage where this happens, several strategies are important – and they're all things that parents can work on at home.

Understanding
Your child needs to know what times tables mean. The more practical examples you can give them of multiplication, the more

they'll understand what's going on. Show them that two potatoes each for five people is what '2 × 5' means – and prove it's the same as '5 × 2'. Get them used to multiplication meaning 'times', 'lots of', 'groups of' – even just the word 'of' itself ('three of four').

Patterns

There's an obvious pattern to the 10-times table: you just put a zero on the end of your number: 1 × 10 = 10, 2 × 10 = 20... Your child will also learn *why* this works; but for times tables, they just need to have this useful rule to use quickly.

Encourage them to spot the other patterns. The 11-times table works on an obvious rule. In the 9-times table, the digits in every answer add up to 9: 9, 18, 27, 36...

Skills

Your child can use techniques like doubling and halving to get them to an answer quickly. If they know that 3 × 6 makes 18, then 6 × 6 must be double that, 36; 10 × 5 = 50, so 5 × 5 must be half of that, 25. They can use facts they know instantly to help them with slightly trickier questions: 10 × 8 = 80, so 12 × 8 must be 80 plus 2 × 8... 96.

Memory aids

The number-shape system is a great way of 'plugging gaps' in a child's times-table knowledge. We all have multiplication facts we find hard, even after years of practice, so it makes sense to invent personal reminders to help trigger the answers.

Encourage your child to combine this technique with any other learning strategy that might help. They can create clues based on rhymes or real-world associations as well as using the number-shape system itself:

> *To remember 7 × 8, they might think of a lamp (7) shining on a snowman (8) until it melts, leaving behind nothing but a pair of 'filthy socks' – 56!*
> *If you lived at number 49 you could imagine two lamps (7 and 7) fixed on either side of your front door – because 7 × 7 = 49.*

Eat a lolly (9) on a hill (3) while watching birds (2) fly towards the sun (7), to remember 9 × 3 = 27.

Help your child to create just one or two lasting triggers for the times tables they've always found tricky.

Repetition
Once your child has the understanding to make the most of their times tables, they can use all the other strategies above as they repeat and practise their multiplication facts. While they chant or sing the tables, or have you test them at speed with flashcards or computer games, they can use these techniques to get to each answer quickly. Writing out their tables may sound old-fashioned, but for once it's a good way of embedding the facts and activating muscle memory. All kinds of practice are vital to weave together these different approaches to learning into the confident, instant recall that will make all the difference in school.

10 THINGS TO REMEMBER

1   Make the most of conversations, games and family activities to nurture your child's speaking and listening skills.

2   Encourage them to read using a range of prompts: letters and sounds, meaning, memory and all the visual clues available.

3   Give children a range of 'whole-brain' spelling strategies.

4   Play games to stimulate ideas for characters, settings and stories.

5   Make sure that reading and writing – for pleasure and purpose – are key features of your family life.

6   From an early age, play games that strengthen counting, calculating and comparing.

7   Find ways to apply maths to real situations, particularly concepts of time and other measures, money, data-handling and problem-solving.

8   Teach your child techniques for learning key maths vocabulary and encourage them to use it to explain their thinking.

9   Show them how the number-shape system makes numbers easier to remember.

10   Help your child master their times tables by creating memorable images and scenes.

7

Knowledge and skills

In this chapter you will learn:
- *what the other primary school subjects involve*
- *ways of boosting your child's brilliance in every area of the curriculum*
- *strategies to excite children about each subject, helping them to see its relevance and importance for them*
- *how every subject can strengthen your child's memory and learning skills.*

While Literacy and Numeracy are the subjects given most time and importance in primary school, there are many other areas in which your child can learn to shine. The modern primary school is an incredibly busy and vibrant place, with a timetable packed to bursting with opportunities and challenges.

Along with Literacy and Numeracy, two other subjects complete the 'core' group: Science and ICT (information and communication technology). These are both woven into the fabric of the week and often taught through topics as well as being incorporated into other lessons. Your child might carry out an experiment into temperature change as part of a numeracy lesson about data handling, or turn their literacy work on fairy tales into a computerized animation. Teachers are becoming increasingly creative in connecting subjects and making the most of the time available. ICT in particular is being taught as part of other lessons rather than as a subject in itself, and science is also spreading beyond a particular 'slot' in the timetable.

Modern primary teaching supports more meaningful learning and allows your child to apply their skills and knowledge in practical and memorable ways. At the same time it means they must be ready to make the most of these rich opportunities, approaching each school day with energy and enthusiasm. Their thinking skills need to be at their creative, connective best.

Some schools still have separate lessons for geography, history, art, DT (design and technology) and music, but many also build these into themed topics. And even if there is no single topic for a term or half-term, teachers are likely to connect subjects when they can. Your child may develop their art skills by drawing the fruit they're studying in science, or recreating famous paintings from a particular period being covered in History. The model of a shelter they build may refer to a scene from a key text in Literacy, while their work on sounds in Music could stem from a Geography focus on extreme weather.

MFL (modern foreign languages) teaching is playing an increasing role in primary school life. Your child may learn French, German, Spanish, Italian – even Chinese. Their school may teach separate lessons in foreign languages, include them in topics, or offer them as after-school clubs.

PE (physical education) features in every primary timetable. Children should take part in at least two sessions a week, indoors and out, at school and also away at the local swimming pool or on residential trips.

Religious education (RE) features in all primary schools, but it takes a number of different forms – and parents can even choose to remove their children from RE teaching altogether. Schools are encouraged to teach children about different faiths as well as developing the skills necessary for exploring and communicating their own. In some schools, because of their particular faith background, RE takes a very central place in the curriculum.

As well as these key subject areas, children are taught ways of learning about themselves and others in a branch of education known as PSHE (personal, social and health education and citizenship). These sessions may take the form of 'circle time' talks and activities, dropped in at different points in the week to support the children's emotional development; or they can be larger-scale topics, such as 'transition' courses in the lead up to secondary school, or a sex education programme.

These are the contexts in which your child will be challenged to learn and develop in primary school. There are key thinking skills that help in all subjects, as well as specific approaches required to succeed in each one.

This chapter explains how the different subjects are taught in the modern primary school. It offers a range of ideas for supporting and enriching your child's development at home, helping them to get the most out of every day at school and to become confident, skilled and informed learners. It also shows why all the thinking skills explored so far in this book as so important for success in school.

Many of the activities apply to a number of different subjects, so feel free to use them in the best way to help your child. As is the case throughout the book, the ideas can easily be adapted to suit children of different ages.

Science

In primary school, Science involves:

▶ *developing the key skills of 'scientific inquiry', including asking questions, planning experiments and investigations, observing, measuring, making comparisons and drawing conclusions*
▶ *learning about three key areas of science: life processes and living things in their habitats; materials and their properties;*

and physical processes like electricity, forces, light and sound, and those affecting the Earth, Moon and Sun
▶ using a range of scientific equipment, including digital apparatus and computer software
▶ investigating the history of scientific discovery, using a range of sources in books and on screen
▶ developing creative approaches to investigating questions and presenting results
▶ knowing how to carry out experiments safely.

By encouraging your child's natural curiosity and in-built desire to test and experiment, you give them a real head start in science at school. Developing their senses from the day they're born is crucial, as is providing them with opportunities to explore their interests – and to talk to you about what they discover.

Insight

Science is about asking questions. Using good questioning techniques helps your child to pursue theories for themselves rather than simply asking for the answers. It also helps them realize that all scientists are simply trying to find better ways of explaining the world around them, using every source of information they can find. It encourages them to think creatively – which is becoming an increasing feature of science teaching in school.

As well as learning to use equipment and to make accurate observations and measurements, your child will be challenged to present their ideas in creative ways. Their teacher might ask for a poem about seed dispersal, a song about magnetism, or a dance explaining the circulation system. Thinking skills that mix creativity with logic are essential for success in science.

Challenge your child with 'why' questions:

'Why is your shadow longer now than it was two hours ago?'
'Why do we put our wet coats on the radiator?'
'Why is your plant drooping so badly?'

Their initial answers might prompt further questions as you probe deeper into their understanding and challenge them to explain everything they know:

Parent: *'Why does your pulse rate increase when you run?'*
Child: *'Because your heart's beating faster.'*
Parent: *'Yes. So why is it doing that?'*
Child: *'Well, it has to work harder when you're doing exercise.'*
Parent: *'Why's that?'*
Child: *'It has to pump blood around your body faster, so it beats faster.'*
Parent: *'Do you know why your blood has to get around faster?'*
Child: *'Because it takes oxygen to the places that need it.'*
Parent: *'And oxygen helps to...'*
Child: *'...release energy, to replace the energy you're using when you run.'*

Conversations like this are a great way of gauging how much your child knows about particular areas of science. You're encouraging them to use one idea to prompt another and to connect different bits of understanding. You're teaching them to keep going until a question has been answered fully. You're talking to them in an interested, collaborative way, demonstrating the importance of discussion in scientific investigation.

There may well be times when you simply don't know the answer to the next question. When that happens, make the most of it. Show your child how you go about finding solutions – whether that means asking other people for ideas, researching in books or surfing the internet. When you get some possible answers, involve your child in deciding whether they make sense.

SCIENCE VOCABULARY

Questioning like this encourages children to use precise scientific vocabulary. Help them to use their creative memory techniques, working with them to design powerful reminders for all the key science words.

For example, they could imagine a tiny prisoner being held inside a battery pack, to remind them that the scientific term for a battery is a 'cell'.

They might visualize two football pitches: one high up, the other low down. The supporters around the higher pitch are all shouting in squeaky Mickey Mouse voices, while those around the low pitch are singing songs in deep, low tones. So the word for how high or low a note is must be 'pitch'.

Get them used to finding clues in the words themselves, such as, carbohydrates provide fuel, just like a car needs fuel to move; incisors are teeth that cut and snip like scissors.

This sort of visualization forces children to think very carefully about what words mean and why they need to remember them – then to take control of the learning process and make sure the information sticks. The more creativity your child injects into their learning, the more likely they'll be to spot connections, develop imaginative theories and present their findings in interesting ways.

SCIENCE EVERYWHERE

Give your child access to a range of science equipment, from simple bug boxes and magnifiers to microscopes and chemistry kits. Remember that cooking is science and there's a huge amount to be learnt from helping to bake a cake or boil an egg. Every house is full of things to experiment with: old radios, springs, magnets, musical instruments. Let your child help you mend and repair, learning to use tools carefully and safely. Encourage them to make predictions, then to re-evaluate their ideas in the light of what happens. Celebrate when they notice a scientific rule or pattern by themselves and help them explore exactly what's going on.

Keeping a pet is a fantastic long-term science project. Even if you haven't got space for one of your own, friends and family will be delighted if you offer to feed their pet rabbits while they're on holiday or occasionally take their dog for a walk. Children need a wide experience of animals to understand their needs, the ways in which they grow and change, and the similarities to and differences from themselves.

Insight

Gardening is another perfect way of encouraging children's science skills and knowledge. Work with them, talk to them, let them experiment and learn from their mistakes. They'll be using visual, auditory and kinaesthetic learning techniques, building memories based on meaningful first-hand experiences.

Treat all your child's scientific endeavours as positively as you can, encouraging them to draw on them to help with all the science work they do in school. Make sure they access their memories, visualizing their rock collection when answering questions about materials, or picturing their fish tank when they're learning about animals and plants.

Show children that science is everywhere: the way the ball lands in their catching glove; the speed at which their ice cream melts; the design of their new pair of running shoes. Encourage them to keep asking questions and thinking up clever ways of finding answers. Show them that science is interesting and useful, and that they have all the thinking skills to explore and present their understanding brilliantly.

ICT

In primary school, ICT involves:

▶ *finding things out (using CD ROMs, internet sources, video and audio recorders)*
▶ *developing ideas and making things happen (exploring information; programming robots; creating and controlling virtual worlds)*

- *exchanging and sharing information (online, via email, in on-screen presentations)*
- *using ICT skills across the curriculum, for example: videoing gymnastic exercises in PE; creating computer animations in Art; using digital sound editing software in Music lessons*
- *reviewing work and suggesting changes and improvements.*

Modern ICT teaching isn't really about showing children how to use particular software programs or pieces of equipment. It's much more concerned with the idea of 'ICT capability': having the skill, judgement and confidence to learn how to operate *any* equipment and to use it effectively and creatively for a range of purposes.

Rather than requiring an instruction manual, these days most pieces of equipment are designed to be used intuitively. We use drop-down menus, follow on-screen instructions and quickly develop the ability to use any type of phone, camera or music player. Most young children assume that they can learn to use any piece of ICT equipment, applying their experience of one to another and not worrying about making mistakes along the way. This confident spirit is to be encouraged – and guided. You can help your child to make good choices about when and how to use ICT, helping them to reap the huge benefits it offers but also teaching them to avoid the pitfalls and to stay safe.

Make the most of all the ICT equipment you have at home: computers, video and stills cameras, MP3 players, mobile phones. Get them out, check they've got the right batteries, memory cards or tapes, and try to use each one to the full.

It can be an interesting exercise to choose a piece of equipment – your video camera, for example – and work with your child to try to find at least three functions on it that you've never used before. Often we only scratch the surface of what our purchases can do. Perhaps you'll find that the camera takes high-quality still pictures as well as moving ones; that you can use it to film in slow-motion; or that you can add visual effects during filming. Mobile phones can be used as voice recorders. Maybe you've never tried showing video on the screen of your MP3 player? The more practice your child gets experimenting with ICT, the more confident they'll be about using it in clever and creative ways.

Some pieces of equipment may need to be used under supervision, but others will be fine for your child to experiment with on their own. Make sure the 'rules of use' are clear. You may find that you have old gadgets lying around that still work and can be given to your child on a less restrictive basis. Sometimes it's good for them to use a camera or sound recorder that can get a bit scratched or wet. Allow your child to build their own sense of responsibility about looking after all the equipment they use.

Show your child that success in ICT relies on good thinking skills. Simply having the internet in front of you or gaining access to a video camera doesn't have any value in itself. What makes all the difference is how you choose to use it, and the thought processes that go on before, during and after any ICT activity. Set your child some challenges:

▶ *'Can you make a five-minute presentation to remind us of our holiday?'*
▶ *'How can we keep Grandad's memories for ever?'*
▶ *'What's the best way to introduce your new penfriend to our family?'*
▶ *Encourage them to ask some key questions:*
  ▷ *'What exactly am I hoping to achieve?'*
  ▷ *'What's the best equipment to use – and how should it be used in this instance?'*
  ▷ *'What preparation work do I need to do? Whose help will be useful?'*
  ▷ *'Are there other pieces of equipment I could use as well?'*
  ▷ *'What's the best thing to do with the work I've produced?'*
▶ *Before they start, prompt them to use their creative thinking skills to explore all the possibilities, to refine their ideas, and to visualize what they're about to do. Encourage them to imagine the angles they'll be filming from or the sounds they want to capture. They'll be better able to evaluate their success while they're working as well as at the end of the activity.*

▶ *Prompt them to compare their finished product with what they visualized at the start. Talk to them about what they did, be specific about what worked and what didn't and celebrate their ability to suggest improvements.*

KEYBOARD SKILLS

Some schools teach children typing and keyboard skills, while others leave them to work it all out for themselves and develop their own techniques. Although voice recognition software is now widely available, it's likely that keyboards will be the main tools for entering information for some time to come; so it makes sense to check that your child is developing the necessary skills:

▶ *Check that they understand how the keyboard works: that they can use capital letters, find common symbols, move up and down through the text.*
▶ *Set them typing challenges. How quickly can they type out the alphabet, their full name or the first line of their favourite nursery rhyme?*
▶ *How many different fingers can they use to type a sentence of their choice?*
▶ *Can they try to find some common letters with their eyes closed?*

Help your child to realize that pecking at the keys with two fingers is a very limiting approach. Let them see examples of good keyboard skills and encourage them to develop their own efficient and comfortable style.

THE INTERNET

Make sure your child has safe access to the internet. This can be at home, in the local library, museum or café or through computer clubs at family centres or in school itself. The internet is a wonderful source of information and ideas and a powerful tool for communicating and sharing; but of course it can also be a dangerous place, where unsuitable material – and people – may only be a mouse click away. There are many different web safety products on the market that help you control your child's level of access and protect them from dangers online, but you also need to give them clear guidelines to follow.

Here are some of the key rules to give your child:

▶ *Think carefully about internet searches before you set them going. What exactly are you looking for? How can you be as specific as possible from the very start?*
▶ *Make sure you never give out any personal details online without checking with a trusted adult.*
▶ *When you're online, never assume that someone is who they say they are. Even if you can see pictures and hear voices, it always pays to be cautious.*
▶ *If anything appears that confuses, worries or upsets you, simply close the screen, turn off the monitor or just look away – and tell someone trusted straight away.*

Foster your child's ICT confidence while also helping them to keep themselves safe online.

History

In primary school, History involves:

▶ *placing events and objects in chronological order*
▶ *understanding how and why things were different in the past*
▶ *explaining why important changes occurred over time*
▶ *investigating the different ways in which history can be recorded and presented*
▶ *using a range of sources, and learning to make judgements about their value*
▶ *communicating understanding of history in creative ways.*

During their time at primary school, your child will explore a number of different periods of national and world history. As well as building up knowledge and understanding about whatever they happen to study, through their history work they can develop some essential thinking and learning skills.

A child's understanding of time begins with their own experiences and develops as they do, such as:

'What happened before I lay down in my cot?'
'What did we do after lunch yesterday?'
'What can I remember from my year at nursery school?'
*'What do I want to ask Grandma about her childhood in
    the war?'*

Teach them the vocabulary of time by using it in conversations and applying it to their life. However old your child is, use stories to test their memory and understanding of time; ask:

'What happened at the start of the story?'
'What did the Queen do next?'
'Who did she meet before she went underground?'
'How long was she asleep?'
'What was the last thing she said?'

Give your child access to a range of historical sources: books and magazines, videos, CD ROMs, websites, objects, letters, diaries, and the recollections of friends and family. Encourage them to be critical about the value of everything they use and, as always, to ask the right questions:

'Who wrote this?'
'Why did they write it?'
'What suggests this is accurate?'
'Why might it not be trustworthy?'
'How does it compare with other records?'
'How else could we explore what went on?'

Helping your child to understand their own memory gives them a wonderful insight into historical accuracy.

Challenge them to think about an early memory – one in which you were both involved. Encourage them to close their eyes, to visualize the moment and to bring to mind any sights, sounds, smells, tastes or textures associated with this memory. Tell them to let one detail link to another, helping them to go deeper into the moment.

Get them to tell you where it happened and when; how old they were; who else was there. Prompt them to pin down as many details as possible.

When they've finished, tell them your own memories of the moment. Dig out old photographs or videos and talk to other people who were there. Discuss the details you agree on, as well as the things they said that don't seem to fit. Reassure them that everyone's memory works like this, and that personal recollections are notoriously inaccurate. The main features may be true but the details are easily confused with other moments; separate memories blur into one and sometimes quite significant details are simply made up. Memory is creative and connective and offers different versions of the truth. Experiencing this at first-hand will teach your child a very important lesson about the value of different historical sources – even 'eye-witness' reports.

HISTORY VISITS

Family days out can be wonderful opportunities for strengthening history knowledge and skill. There's obvious benefit in visiting castles, stately homes and foreign ruins, but visits to the local park or town centre can be just as illuminating.

Encourage your child to look from different angles. Often the top half of a building retains more evidence of its age, and sometimes the ground beneath your feet holds clues about changes that have occurred.

In obviously 'historic' places, challenge children to find a variety of sources of information. There may be artefacts to touch, guidebooks and maps to read, people to ask. Which ones are the most helpful? Why is it important to have several sources to use together?

In more familiar locations you can talk about the changes that have happened in your child's lifetime, as well as things you remember from when you were young. What clues are we leaving about the way we live? How will future historians learn about us – and what are the most important things for them to know?

TIME CAPSULES

Your child might like to create a time capsule. You can make one at any time, but they're particularly important when you're moving house or carrying out renovations.

Ask your child to choose some objects, documents and photographs that will be useful for future generations to learn from. Talk to them about their choices and suggest some of your own. Narrow the collection down to the ones you both feel are most significant, then bury it in an air- and watertight box in the garden, under the foundations or behind a stone in the attic.

Sometimes capsules can be dug up again after a period of time if you're still living there, providing an interesting snapshot of an earlier life. Others will be left for future generations. This activity will help your child to develop a very rounded understanding of history and their own place in it, along with a practical appreciation of records and artefacts.

REMEMBERING DATES

Encourage your child to use their memory skills to learn historical facts. As well as the key history skills, they need a strong foundation of knowledge to work from.

Teach them an extension of the number-shape system that makes it easy to learn dates. The idea is that each century has a different colour:

> 1300s *all dates in the 1300s are coded green, because*
> *'3' rhymes with 'pea', and a pea is* **green**
> 1400s *'4' rhymes with 'roar' to give the colour of a lion:* **yellow**

1500s	'5' rhymes with 'hive' to give the colour of a wooden beehive: **brown**
1600s	'6' rhymes with 'bricks' suggesting the colour of bricks: **red**
1700s	'7' rhymes with 'heaven' to give the colour of clouds: **white**
1800s	'8' rhymes with 'weight' suggesting the colour of a strong man's weights: **black**
1900s	'9' rhymes with 'fine' to give the colour of the sky on a fine day: **blue**

To remember a particular date, you simply take the second two digits, transform them using the original number-shape system, then code them with the appropriate colour. For example:

▶ *The date of The Gunpowder Plot was 1605; you could help your child to visualize a bright red (16) beach ball (0) being pushed against a sharp hook (5) until it explodes – with a sound like gunpowder!*

▶ *Neil Armstrong landed on the Moon in 1969; what if your child imagined themselves sitting inside a blue (19) cannon (6) sucking a lolly (9) to calm their nerves before being shot up to the Moon?*

The colour codes make it easier to connect dates from the same period, and all the other elements of this technique help to activate the memory while also stimulating creative thinking. It's not necessary to remember every date like this, but it's a great way to learn a few key dates that can help to structure the rest of your child's knowledge. It also gets them thinking about thinking and taking an active role in the way they learn.

Geography

In primary school, Geography involves:

▶ *asking questions about people and places*
▶ *observing and recording carefully and creatively*
▶ *combining first-hand experience with secondary sources*

- *understanding what places are like, how they've developed and why they've changed*
- *recognizing both positive and negative changes in the environment and climate.*

During primary school, children spend a lot of time looking at their local environment but they also study other places in the country and overseas, especially those that contrast with where they live.

Help your child to develop a strong understanding of space and distance. On car journeys, let them look at the distance counter on the dashboard and read the map. Before foreign trips, plot your route in an atlas or around the curved surface of a globe. Encourage them to use the vocabulary of distance and to build an awareness of journey times.

Bring all their thinking skills into play when they visit new places. Can they activate their powers of visualization to imagine the city as it might have looked 100 years ago? What about morphing the coastline into the shape it had before thousands of years of erosion took their toll?

Use foreign films, TV travel programmes, internet resources and books to excite and teach your child about foreign places. They can use their imagination to take themselves there, thinking about all the senses and feelings that might be involved. Prompt them to consider the similarities with their own environment and daily life as well as the differences.

Give your child opportunities to communicate with people from other countries and cultures. Which of your friends might be able to give your child some extra insight into their work on Australia or Poland? Are there any online groups you could help them join to meet children from Iceland or Pakistan? And make sure they give as well as receive. Talking about their own home and routines can be just as important for their geographical development as learning about other people's contrasting lives.

Insight

Encourage your child to make the most of all their travel experiences. Help them to create scrapbooks about the places they've been. Suggest they make books, draw pictures or put together information boards or computer presentations to show in school.

The more memories that children gather of interesting journeys and unusual locations, the better they'll be able to use the 'memory journeys' system to learn any kind of information. Encourage them to visualize the places they've been and the routes they've travelled, and to use these mental structures to hold useful lists. They could learn shopping lists by placing the items around their holiday hotel, or remember a list of friends' names by imagining them at different landmarks on the way to the seaside. As well as improving their spatial awareness and detailed memories of the places they've been, using geography skills like this can give a major boost to your child's learning in general.

Memory techniques will help your child learn key geographical facts. It gives a great boost to their confidence if they know how to learn useful and interesting information for school topics or their own research.

As ever, it's a case of using both the creative right and the logical left side of the brain, and combining the best aspects of different learning styles.

If your child wanted to remember the five largest countries on Earth, here's how you might help them to do it.

Ranked by land mass, those countries are Russia, Canada, China, USA, Brazil.
Imagine… it's rush hour (Russia) and you're stuck in a traffic jam inside a hot car. You open a drinks can (Canada) but instead of cooling drink it's full of bits of broken china (China). To pass the time, you use the china to make a mosaic picture of the American flag (USA), eating Brazil nuts (Brazil) to give you energy to concentrate.

Learning like this is easy, fun and effective. It only takes a few minutes to memorize key facts in precise order, helping your child to build the foundations of a very strong geographical knowledge.

Modern Foreign Languages

In primary school, MFL teaching involves:

▶ *listening carefully and using a range of clues to identify meaning*
▶ *speaking with the correct pronunciation and intonation*
▶ *using a foreign language for a range of real purposes*
▶ *developing techniques for learning words and phrases*
▶ *learning about the lives of people in different cultures*
▶ *working with dictionaries and phrase books in print and on screen.*

As well as their literacy abilities and some of their key geography skills, your child's ability to remember will have a major impact on their foreign language learning.

In primary school, the emphasis is on words and phrases rather than rules of grammar. The sooner your child can remember the new vocabulary they're taught, the sooner they can start using it in conversations and games. This helps them to experience what speaking a new language is like and prepares their brain for all the language learning they'll do in the future. It gives them a core structure of ideas to build on, develops their pronunciation as they practise speaking and listening, and grows their confidence to harness all their thinking skills to help them communicate in a new way.

Language learning in school often starts by looking at the words a child already knows:

in English they play tennis; in French, le tennis; *in German,* das Tennis
in English they can listen to the radio; in French, le radio; *in German,* das Radio

in English, Spanish, Danish, French... a sandwich is still a
   sandwich!

Building a list of familiar words is a good way to make language
learning seem less daunting. Use foreign travel, books, films and
songs to show your child that many words are very easy to guess:

the French word lettre *is obviously a letter*
the German word privat *means private*
the Spanish word hamburguesa *is unlikely to be anything but a*
   hamburger...

There are also plenty of word meanings that can be deduced by
doing a bit of creative thinking about English vocabulary:

Point out that the German word Hund *is similar to the English*
   'hound', and your child should find it easy to remember that
   it means 'dog'.
The French for door is porte. *If your child knows what a 'portal'*
   is, perhaps from computer games or fantasy stories, then this
   information can act as a useful trigger to their memory.

When words in different languages seem to have no connections,
the trick is to invent some. By thinking carefully about what a
foreign word looks like, sounds like or reminds them of, children
can use all their memory skills to connect that idea with the real
meaning of the word. It's a powerful technique because it activates
their imagination, as well as using memorable links to give them a
very clear sense of structure and order. It puts their whole brain to
work on the task of learning foreign words.

Every time your child hears a new foreign word, encourage them to
build a memorable picture in their mind:

The German word for 'hat' is Hut. *They might imagine seeing the*
   hut at the bottom of their garden changing into the shape of
   a hat; going to school wearing a hat shaped like a hut or
   cramming a hut full of every possible kind of hat.

Leiter *means 'ladder'. The German word sounds like 'lighter', so your child could imagine standing on a ladder which feels lighter and lighter... until it blows away on the breeze, carrying them with it.*

In German, the word for 'hole' is Loch. *Perhaps your child pictures a deep hole in their bedroom floor, covered by a door with a very large lock on it to keep everyone out. Or they could imagine dropping their brand new bicycle lock down a hole in the pavement. And what if a huge creature rose out of a hole in their garden – the Loch Ness monster?*

As well as thinking about the 'bridging' word between the two languages (hut, lighter, lock) your child needs to create an unusual, exaggerated, memorable scene that they can visualize very clearly:

The French word soeur *means 'sister'. Maybe the bridging word here could be 'sir'. What if their sister was knighted and made into Sir; or dressed up as a very stern male teacher? Weird – but memorable!*

Main *means 'hand' in French. On paper it looks like the English word 'main', but its pronunciation makes it sounds more like 'man'; so how about imagining using your hand to give your French teacher a 'high five', and saying 'You're my main man!'*

Sud *means 'south' and sounds like 'sued' or the first part of 'Sudan'. Your child might imagine being sued every time they travel south, or watching the south of France transform into the Sudan. Adding a few soap suds to their image would fix it even more firmly into place.*

Creating picture clues like this encourages children to think very carefully about what a foreign word looks like, sounds like and means. They spot connections with their own language and with other new words they've learnt. The 'bridging' words they come up with allow them to create memorable scenes in their imagination and by using these as triggers to start speaking and writing, the memories soon become automatic.

LANGUAGE LABELS

An extension of this system is to start putting stickers on objects around the house. Label items with their foreign names, but also draw pictures to remind children of the bridging links. It's a great way of familiarizing them with new vocabulary and strengthening their creative connections:

If they were learning Spanish you could write the word pan *('bread')*
on a packet of bread, and also draw a cartoon frying pan on
the sticker. Seeing the bread would remind your child about
making fried bread, or using the pan to hit each slice across the
room – or whatever memorable scene they'd designed.

Pastel *is the Spanish word for 'cake'. You might draw some pastel*
crayons around this word on a sticker then put it on top of the
cake tin. Your child could imagine using pastel crayons to
decorate a cake, sticking them into the icing like candles; or
crunching into pastels which had somehow dropped into the
cake mix. The sticker would activate these memorable links
every time they saw it.

Encourage your child to think up their own pictures and links. It helps them to become active learners, interested in new languages and energetic about mastering them. Give them opportunities to use their growing vocabulary. Are there friends, relatives or members of your community who speak the language they're learning? Could you plan a holiday where they could show off some of the words and phrases they know?

Art

In primary school, Art involves:

▶ *exploring and developing ideas, using observation, experience*
and imagination

- *investigating the use of different materials and trying out a wide range of art and craft techniques*
- *evaluating work and suggesting improvements*
- *studying the work of artists and craftspeople from different times and cultures; forming and communicating opinions about art.*

At each stage of a child's artistic development there are important ways that you can offer support.

AROUND TWO YEARS OLD

Children start to give names to their scribbles. Sometimes they'll decide before they draw, sometimes after, but it's always an opportunity to encourage their imagination and build their confidence. Be particularly enthusiastic about details of drawings that match their names, but celebrate all their artistic endeavours. Give them a range of pens, pencils, crayons and paints to experiment with.

THREE YEARS OLD

Children begin more purposeful drawing, setting out to draw objects, people and places. Keep extending the range of materials they have to draw with and on. Encourage them to choose their own best work for you to display. Talk to them about why they prefer some pieces to others.

FOUR YEARS OLD

Children start to draw from logic. They're likely to draw 'a drawing of a house', with four square windows and curling smoke from the chimney, or 'a drawing of the Sun' with straight lines sticking out, rather than what they observe. It's an important stage of development and you should continue celebrating what they do and praising the most successful details but help them to move past this by encouraging more imaginative art. Let them see a range of artistic styles. Talk to them about what different houses look like, or how the Sun could be painted to show how it really looks in the morning or at sunset.

FIVE YEARS OLD AND BEYOND

Children will draw pictures that are more realistic, but still based on the things they know.

▶ *Let them tell you what they've drawn and why.*
▶ *Encourage them to think about the style of a picture as well as the subject.*
▶ *When they draw people, talk to them about what you think the characters are doing, saying, thinking and feeling.*
▶ *Point out interesting details in pictures and praise accuracy as well as signs of imagination in their art.*
▶ *Find famous artworks with similar subject matter to your child's drawings and discuss their opinions about different materials and styles.*

BY SEVEN YEARS OLD

Children can look closely at life to add detail to their art. Give them a variety of objects to study and draw: fruit, flowers, car parts, ornaments. Challenge them to draw family pets, relatives and famous people from pictures and TV. Always discuss their finished work in a positive way, focusing on particularly successful elements and prompting them to say what they're pleased with as well as what they'd improve.

Artist and Children's Laureate Anthony Browne recommends the 'Shape game' for children of all ages. One person draws a random shape then the other person looks at it carefully and adds a few lines to turn it into something identifiable. It's a skill that requires both clear, logical thinking and a great deal of imagination on both sides. It helps children to think about the importance of simple lines and shapes in their drawings, and to find less obvious ways of portraying their ideas.

Another brain-stimulating activity is to try drawing the spaces
between objects rather than the objects themselves. The subject of
a picture emerges in a rather different way, almost from the 'inside
out'. The overall composition is often much more interesting than
when objects are drawn directly. Shadows and reflections appear
naturally to give the picture a much stronger sense of depth.

Show your child pictures and videos featuring the natural art
of Andy Goldsworthy. It can be extremely liberating to work
outdoors, turning stones, leaves and shells into interesting pieces of
art. Talk to them about the patterns they create and the similarities
or differences between their work and the natural world around it.

Sculptors like Giacometti and Henry Moore can provide
wonderful inspiration for children's practical artwork. Encourage
them to look at the skills these artists used, then to incorporate
them into works that are personal to them.

The same goes for artists like Picasso, Monet or Keith Haring.
Talk about the key features of a wide range of artists, the themes
they're interested in, the materials they tend to use – then let
your child take over. Help them gather ideas while developing their
own individual style.

Let your child experiment with photography. Give them a cheap
camera, let them photograph anything they like, then talk to them
about the results: the subjects they chose and the ways in which
they've been captured. Encourage children to surprise you with
angles, details, colours. Show them professional photographs and
get them talking about the ones they find most interesting, funny,
strange or moving.

Visit art galleries, exhibitions and artists' studios. Show your children art books, buy them postcards and prints and give them access to art collections online. Talk about your likes and dislikes and prompt them to form opinions of their own.

Design and Technology

In primary school, DT involves:

- *developing ideas, on paper and using computers*
- *working with tools and materials to make quality products; making choices about equipment and components; working safely, alone and with others*
- *evaluating and improving practical work*
- *investigating how familiar products are designed and made.*

All these skills can be practised and developed at home. You don't have to provide expensive materials or turn your living room into a workshop. Do what you can to give your child practical opportunities to plan and make – but just talking about design ideas and construction skills has a huge impact on your child's attainment in DT.

Talk to children about your own design tastes. Why did you buy that particular toaster, fridge, jumper or car? Focus on how well something performs a task, as well as how it makes you feel. Talk about materials, shapes, colours, textures. Challenge your child to find things around your home built in the same 'style'. Blindfold them and see if they can explore interesting objects by touch alone.

Set your child intriguing design challenges, such as:

- *invent a new type of football boot*
- *design your dream bedroom*

- ▶ *find a better way to open tin cans*
- ▶ *plan the perfect picnic*

Challenges like this prompt children to:

- ▶ *combine logic and creativity*
- ▶ *include practical, aesthetic and emotional benefits*
- ▶ *look carefully at how things are done now in order to suggest alternatives*
- ▶ *ask themselves a series of questions as they explore various possibilities before choosing the best.*

Let them present their ideas to you, give them constructive feedback, and ask for their own evaluation.

Whenever possible, let your child put their final plan into action. When they're old enough they can build their dream sandwich, customize a T-shirt or work with you to construct a go-kart out of wooden planks and reclaimed wheels. Always push them to use all their thinking skills and bring the ideas to life in their mind. Let them see what happens when paper plans are made real, and give them the confidence to make improvements, learn from mistakes, and arrive at the end of the process with quality results.

Give your child experience of using a range of materials: paper, wood, cardboard, textiles, clay. Buy them models to build from logical written instructions, and construction kits to let them explore their imaginative ideas.

Seize every opportunity to let your child see how things are made. Before you throw out an old vacuum cleaner, help them to dismantle it and explore how it works. When you're tinkering with the car, show them safe ways to watch and help. Encourage them to mix left-brained practical reality with right-brained imagination as they formulate their own exciting designs.

Music

In primary school, Music involves:

▶ *learning to use instruments, including the voice, to rehearse and perform*

▶ *choosing sounds and creating musical patterns; evaluating and improving*

▶ *listening to music and analysing features like pitch, rhythm and the 'texture' of sound*

▶ *exploring personal responses to music*

▶ *working with a range of music, live and recorded, from different times and cultures*

▶ *using electronic equipment to capture, change and combine sounds.*

Research suggests that babies are born with perfect pitch. When they're relaxed, listening carefully and able to use their voices without stress or embarrassment, young children can reproduce sounds accurately and sing in a wonderfully pure and natural way. They remember tunes and rhythms with remarkable ease, and the songs they hear and sing play a key role in building their thinking skills, giving children an early chance to delight others and to experience a deep sense of familiarity and fun.

Sing songs to your young child. Teach them nursery rhymes and folk songs, and sometimes make up new versions with their name in. Show them that even the oldest musical ideas can be used for new purposes. Clap and tap rhythms with them; hum and whistle tunes they'll recognize; take them to singing groups to let them make music with others.

Give them access to a range of musical instruments. Young children love to bang saucepan lids and shake boxes. As they grow, buy them cheap instruments like whistles, maracas, tambourines, xylophones and harmonicas. Encourage them to play along with recorded tunes as well as to compose their own. How many different sounds can they make? Talk to them about high and low, loud and soft. Challenge them to make a sound that says 'angry', 'sleepy' or 'magical'.

Let children hear and respond to a wide range of music, in a variety of styles and from many different periods and cultures. Encourage them to have opinions about everything they hear as well as to find their favourite sort of music. Borrow music from friends or hire it from the library. Take every opportunity to let them experience live performance. Talk to them about how music makes them feel.

Use music to stimulate their imagination. Play them a piece of evocative instrumental music and ask them to close their eyes, switch on their imagination, and let the sounds take shape in their mind. Rather than trying to guess what the composer intended or working out what the music is 'about', they're discovering the ideas it suggests to them. Encourage them to think of all the images, colours, shapes and textures it brings to mind. Does it conjure up characters, scenes or events? See if they can add a logical structure to their imaginative ideas and tell you the story of the music.

Help your child to learn to play an instrument well. You might teach them yourself, get help from a friend or relative or pay for a professional teacher. Many schools run instrument hire schemes as well as music lessons, in school time or as after-school clubs.

- ▶ *Get hold of tuition books, videos and online resources.*
- ▶ *Keep your child inspired by letting them hear their instrument being played by the very best musicians.*
- ▶ *Work with them to structure a practice schedule you're both happy with, and take every opportunity to let them perform for you.*
- ▶ *Record them playing and broadcast their work to family and friends.*

▶ *Celebrate their success at every stage of the learning process and do everything you can to make it purposeful, exciting and fun.*

Physical Education

In primary school, PE involves:

▶ *developing a range of physical skills; improving control and co-ordination*
▶ *combining skills and actions; creating movement sequences*
▶ *exploring tactics in a variety of sports and games and learning the importance of rules*
▶ *evaluating and improving physical performance*
▶ *understanding how to stay fit and healthy.*

In primary school children take part in athletics training, dance activities, gymnastics, swimming lessons, 'adventurous' activities such as climbing or sailing and a range of team sports: 'striking and fielding' games like cricket and softball; net games like tennis and volleyball; 'invasion' games such as football and hockey.

When you tickle your baby, or play 'Pat-a-cake', or help them to hold a spoon or throw teddies in your direction you're building early skills that will play an important role in their sporting success. At every stage of their development you can support and stretch their body awareness, hand–eye co-ordination, dexterity and accuracy.

From a very early age children can respond to music, moving their bodies to match rhythms and moods. Babies often enjoy passing things back and forth, learning about gripping, moving and letting go. Challenge them to watch objects as they move, extending their range of vision as you invent games that spark their early competitive streak: How quickly can they point to the ball? Can they 'win' a beanbag by guessing which hand it landed in?

All the key sporting skills can be nurtured through everyday games and activities: throwing and catching in the garden; kicking a ball along the hallway; dancing to songs on the radio; climbing in the park. Encourage your child to try the widest possible range of activities, and to make them a natural part of everyday life, taking every opportunity to practise balancing, skipping, jumping and climbing.

Show children how easy it is to invent a game with even the most basic equipment. Turn counters into tiddlywinks. Play table hockey using drinks mats. Use a beanbag and walking stick to invent your own goal-scoring game against the back door. Challenge your child to make up their own activities, complete with simple scoring systems and rules. Give them plenty of opportunities to win, but also get them used to losing – and still enjoying the game for its fun, excitement, exercise, and all the chances it gives to interact with others.

Insight

Use family life to develop your child's understanding of health and fitness. Talk about the positive and negative effects of different foods and drinks. Discuss the importance of exercise and how it makes them feel. Give them good examples of diet and physical activity to copy.

Let children watch a range of sports, both on screen and in the flesh. Help them to develop their particular interests, but also introduce them to new sports. Talk to them about the sportspeople they see. What are the key abilities, skills and tactics on show? Make comparisons and draw connections between different activities. Ask:

'Which takes more co-ordination: balancing on a beam or operating a Formula 1 racing car?'
'Is the accuracy needed for playing golf the same as for archery?'
'Are there tactics involved in football that can be helpful in volleyball?'

Talk to your child about the benefits of visualization: the way that many famous sportspeople rehearse their skills mentally, running a race in their mind or picturing every detail of the perfect dive. Help them to experiment themselves before a school football match, dance competition or swimming race.

Ask them to close their eyes, picture the place they'll be performing, and put themselves there in their imagination. Talk about the most useful feelings for them to have on the day and get them to imagine those feelings now: excitement, confidence, calmness, focus.
Help them to run through all the important physical and mental preparations: putting on their football boots, checking their javelin, breathing deeply, focusing on the challenge ahead.

Tell your child to imagine the energy pulsing through their body, getting every muscle ready to do its job. Help them to analyse the skills they'll need at every stage of the activity and to rehearse them in their imagination: hearing the starting pistol clearly, leaping to make a perfect serve, getting into a good position going into the final bend. Get them to talk you through the event as if they're doing it now, explaining how their body and mind will need to work to do really well. Train them to use their thinking skills to support all their sporting activities.

An exercise like this strengthens a child's imagination and tunes it in to physical experiences. They'll be better able to remember what actually happens in a sporting event and to replay it afterwards, helping them to evaluate their success and suggest ways to do even better next time.

The remaining areas of primary school teaching, RE and PSHE, are explored in the next chapter. The ways in which your child approaches these subjects have a huge impact on their emotional, moral and spiritual development, in school and beyond. The knowledge and skills they'll need to do well are central to their whole approach to school, to their feelings about themselves and to the success with which they interact with others. The next chapter explains how to support your child in these crucial areas, using all the strategies they develop to help with some of the most important challenges of primary school life.

If your child has difficulties in any particular subject area, encourage them to break the problem down into smaller parts. Focus on what it is exactly that they find hard, and talk to them – and perhaps their teacher, too – to find out what key skills or bits of knowledge they need to feel more confident.

Psychologist Irving Biederman performed a very interesting experiment using expert chicken sexers. These are people who have gained – often as a result of many years of practice and a large amount of handed-down knowledge – the valuable ability to identify the sex of a chicken at a very early stage. After condensing their approach into a set of the key rules, Biederman was able to teach a group of college students everything they needed to carry out the task to a professional level. By being specific and systematic, in a very short time they'd learnt what would normally take years of experience and study.

With the right attitude, the important thinking and learning skills in place, and the necessary support from their teacher and from you, your child can learn the simple rules to any activity. Getting to the heart of a subject helps them to understand it, which in turn helps them to remember it and apply what they've learnt. And the more subjects they grasp, the more connections they can make. When that happens, a child is doing exactly what the modern primary school tries to do: enriching knowledge and skills by linking different areas of learning. It means that your child can return home with a wealth of interconnected ideas to share with you. They can find interest in any subject, and they're constantly improving their ability to explore, learn and apply. They reflect on what – and *how* – they're learning, and they're energetic about adding new ideas and abilities to those they already own.

Comparing two people with the same experiences and attitude, the influential psychologist William James wrote that 'the one who thinks over his experiences most and weaves them into systematic relations with each other will be the one with the best memory.'

10 THINGS TO REMEMBER

1 Encourage your child to explore the world around them, discussing their ideas to challenge and enrich their scientific thinking.

2 Show them new ways to extend their ICT capability and to use all forms of technology effectively and safely.

3 Make the most of opportunities to interest your child in history, helping them to research, explore and remember information about the past.

4 Children can combine real travel experiences with imagined journeys to investigate the geography of places and people.

5 Teach them to make creative connections between words in different languages.

6 Support your child's developing artistic talents, giving them the confidence to try new strategies and techniques.

7 Find opportunities for them to plan and construct in a variety of ways, combining creativity and practicality.

8 Celebrate children's natural musicality, weaving performing and listening into everyday family life.

9 Use physical activity to support your child's learning, and visualization to boost their sporting success.

10 Help your child to find connections between different subjects, developing a powerful approach to exploring and learning anything.

8

Rules, roles and responsibilities

In this chapter you will learn:
- *why RE and PSHE have such a major impact on your child's success*
- *how to give children the right attitude to school*
- *how to play your own part in primary school life*
- *strategies to help your child make the best choices about behaviour, thoughts and feelings.*

RE and PSHE

RE and PSHE lessons are important parts of the primary curriculum, developing key areas of knowledge, understanding and skill. They're particularly influential subjects because they teach children about themselves and everyone else they come into contact with. The thinking skills they nurture help with behaviour, friendships, self-esteem and the ability to handle a wide range of emotional challenges.

Both RE and PSHE let children explore their thoughts, feelings and choices. They encourage them to think carefully about themselves as individuals and as members of different communities. They stimulate some of the biggest thoughts of all: Who am I? Where did I come from? Where am I going? On a spiritual, emotional, and a very practical day-to-day level, they have a powerful impact on children's thoughts and actions.

In primary school, RE involves:

- *learning about the beliefs, practices and traditions involved in the main religion of the country or community*
- *understanding the key features of various religious faiths and lifestyles: locally, nationally and internationally; reflecting on similarities as well as differences*
- *investigating how faith can impact on people's personal lives and their relationships with others*
- *developing an awareness of personal beliefs and the ability to express them in different ways*
- *appreciating the role of religion in developing feelings of community and belonging.*

RE connects with many other subject areas: literacy, history, geography, PSHE. There are opportunities to explore art and music, cooking and dance. The important thing is that your child has enough openness, self-awareness and respect for other people's beliefs to let them make the most of this intriguing and challenging subject in school.

All the thinking skills developed in this book are very useful in RE. A flexible imagination gives children the ability to see different points of view. An awareness of feelings and emotions, and the vocabulary to discuss them, lets children tap into the powerful feelings involved in faith. Good questioning strategies help them to analyse evidence and explore their own opinions. They understand how both logic and imagination are involved in shaping someone's spirituality.

Give your child a respectful interest in other people's beliefs. It's important that they feel comfortable sampling traditions and customs without necessarily sharing someone else's faith. As they grow, encourage them to read appropriate stories about different belief systems. Let them take part in local cultural festivals, sampling food, listening to music and meeting children their own age from different faith communities.

Encourage children to represent their own ideas and beliefs in different ways. In school they'll be making posters, composing songs, even creating computer presentations about aspects of faith. From an early age they need to see that the same thinking and learning skills that bring success in other subject areas will help them excel in RE, whatever their own faith happens to be. In many ways, a flexible, whole-brained approach is more important in RE than anywhere else.

In primary school, PSHE involves:

▸ *learning about feelings, emotions and impulses, and developing strategies for managing them*
▸ *understanding and dealing with the feelings of others*
▸ *investigating healthy relationships: the things that form them and the things that can put them under threat*
▸ *coping with change, including the physical and emotional changes involved in growing up*
▸ *making good choices about behaviour; developing assertiveness; dealing with bullying; staying healthy and safe*
▸ *building confidence, resilience and the ability to set aspirational goals*
▸ *exploring effective attitudes and skills for learning*
▸ *considering the rights of others in communities and learning ways of making positive contributions on a local and global level.*

The skills required to do well in PSHE profoundly affect every other area of your child's happiness and success in school. They're skills that need to be developed first at home.

Helping your child prepare for school

It's essential that your child has the right attitude to school and their role in it. As a parent, you'll play a huge part in influencing their thoughts and feelings. Long before they arrive for their first day, your child is developing ideas about what school is for, what it means for *them* and how they should think, speak and act there. Whatever your own experiences of education, there's a great deal you can do to set your child up for success, giving them a positive and practical approach to getting the very best out of primary school life.

Children need to feel that school is the right place for them to be. Before they start, use their achievements at home as evidence that they are ready for school, for example:

*'Wow, you've put all your clothes on by yourself today. You must
    be nearly ready for school!'*
*'I'm going to tell Dad how well you counted those cows in the
    field. That's just the sort of clever maths they do in school.'*

Help your child to see school as a natural extension of the things they already enjoy and are good at. Tell them about the cooking, art and reading they'll do in school. Excite them about the possibilities, give them clear examples to visualize, and relate it all to the things they know and understand. Give them a sense of security by talking about the aspects of school that will be familiar:

'They've got colourful books just like this in school.'
'You'll have a peg like this one in the cloakroom.'
'They play lots of games like this in primary school.'

Remember that your child's brain will be filling up with pictures and theories about school, and that you can help them select the most useful ones.

Insight
Children need to understand what school is for. Give them plenty of your own positive memories from school and describe all the important aspects of life there. Talk about the fun you had with friends; the sports you enjoyed; the trips you went on; the learning you did; your favourite subjects; the times you impressed your teacher.

Children quickly develop very strong ideas about what school is all about. Make sure they're building up a balanced picture, with learning at the centre of all the other fun activities they'll be able to enjoy. Excite them about the different things they'll be exploring and studying. Help them to arrive at school relishing the challenge to learn lots of new things, and expecting to enjoy everything their school has to offer. Use your knowledge of their 'character' as a learner to give very specific examples of how they'll enjoy their learning in school, such as:

'I know you love hearing stories and you'll learn so much from them in class.'
'You're brilliant at solving problems with your construction kit. Just think how much that will help you learn when you get to school.'

Expectations and responsibilities

Children need to know what's expected of them. With all the opportunities come some important responsibilities, and you can help your child to see them as a chance to show how grown-up they are. The challenge to impress everyone with their behaviour, especially in their dealings with others, can be a big part of the excitement about starting school:

'If you discuss your ideas like that with people in your class, the teacher will be so impressed.'
'We need to help you practise sharing toys. That's going to be so important in September.'
'What beautiful sitting at the table. That's exactly what they need boys and girls to do in school.'

Help your child to feel that school is a safe, structured place and do everything you can to equip them to follow its rules. Many primary schools have different versions of the rules to show to different age groups. Find the one that's right for your child and make sure they know what to do, and why.

Schools tend to phrase their rules positively – which makes good sense, since the brain is so quick to create pictures. It's much more helpful for children to have clear pictures of what to do, so that they can copy them and know when they're on track.

Talk to your children about the rules, helping them to visualize these positive images, and be as specific as you can. What will 'being kind' or 'showing respect' actually mean in practice? What will this sort of behaviour look like?

It's also important that you activate children's logical thinking:

'*You need to pick up coats and bags and look after other people's property, because...*'
'*You always walk carefully in the corridors so that...*'

Encourage them to see the rules from different perspectives. Use phrases such as 'Why will a teacher love seeing you doing this?' or 'Imagine what the other children would think if they saw you doing that?' Help them to realize that rules are about everybody – the whole community getting along together – as well as their own safety, happiness and success. The combination of creative pictures and logical reasons will help your child build a very memorable understanding of everything that's expected of them.

TEACHER–PUPIL RELATIONSHIP

Children need to have the right relationship with their teacher. A big part of supporting your child throughout their school life is helping them to work with their teacher. Before they start school, they need to know that it's going to be an unequal relationship. Their teacher is there to keep them safe, help them learn and encourage them to use all their skills and talents to enjoy a happy and successful time in school. But their teacher is also in charge. Their teacher is an important person who will expect attention, respect, top-quality work and behaviour.

As well as celebrating the success they have in academic work, sports or drama, make sure you're always asking your child about the times they behaved well, made good choices and won praise from their teacher for following the rules.

An interesting experiment compared children born 50 years apart. Half a century ago, children offered books wrapped in paper felt excited about what they were being given, trusting the adults who'd chosen the books for them. In stark contrast, the modern children had no confidence at all that the 'mystery' books would be the best ones for them. They felt they would be much better at choosing their own books. Despite being young children, they felt they were just as able to make informed choices as adults in authority.

While we want our children to be confident and secure in their own ideas, it's vital that this is balanced with respect for teachers and schools. There's a great sense of security, for both children and parents, if they can assume that a teacher is making good choices and imposing rules for positive reasons. Of course both children and parents can always ask to have the rules clarified or discuss any issue further if it's causing problems; but doing so in a respectful way is essential for all concerned.

Simple visualization techniques can be helpful. For parents, it might mean spending a moment imagining the classroom from the teacher's point of view. What must it look and feel like to have 32 children looking back at them, 32 complex and different sets of needs to manage, 32 different families to communicate with?

For children it can be useful to prompt this sort of shift of viewpoint, considering the teacher's thoughts and feelings as well as their own:

'What do you think it looked like to the teacher?'
'Why does your teacher ask you to do that?'
*'The teacher thinks that's very important: can you
    imagine why?'*

As always it's extremely powerful to activate both imagination and logic. Your child may still not like the decision that was made, but they'll be boosting their ability to understand it and move on.

FOLLOWING INSTRUCTIONS

Play games with your child to help them practise hearing and carrying out instructions. 'Simon says...' is a good one. One person gives instructions, and the other players follow them – but only when they're preceded by the words 'Simon says', for example: 'Simon says touch your toes... Simon says put your hands on your hips... Jog on the spot.' Anyone who jogged on the spot would be out, or lose a point or swap roles in the game. Build up the pace to encourage quick thinking. Try more complicated instructions such as, 'Simon says don't stop hopping.'

'Do this, do that' is another useful game for sharpening listening, watching and thinking skills. You do a range of actions with your hands, like tapping your shoulders, clapping or folding your arms. Every time the action is accompanied by the words 'Do this', everyone else has to copy. But if you say 'Do *that*', they have to keep doing the previous action.

There is a third game you can try to stimulate your child's memory. They have to copy your hand actions, but they need to do the *previous* thing you did. So they just watch you clap three times. Then while you tap your head, they have to clap three times. While you put your hands on your knees they tap their head... and so on. Older children can even try to do the action two steps behind the leader. It's a great way of honing the concentration skills vital for following instructions from adults in school.

Teachers know how important it is to give instructions in a way that helps children remember and follow them. They try to break them down into simple steps, not to give too many instructions at once, and to use visual prompts to give extra clues. But school life is busy and demanding, and children are often challenged to use all their thinking skills to cope with complex instructions. New research is revealing that many behavioural and learning problems have their roots in poor memory for instructions. And inability to remember can easily be confused with naughtiness and lack of respect.

Remembering instructions involves all the key learning skills explored throughout this book. Developing good strategies also helps children to work as part of a group, to be attentive to other people's needs and to analyse actions and plan tasks; all core skills in the PSHE syllabus.

Children need to hear or see the instructions in the first place. Their listening and reading skills and the powers of concentration they've developed are essential here, along with their confidence to ask about anything they haven't understood.

When you're giving your child instructions, make sure they're listening – and *showing* you they're listening. Encourage them to ask questions about anything that's not clear, getting them into the habit of gathering all the information they need. Reply in ways that help them find the answers themselves, such as:

'Can you guess where I might want you to put those dirty clothes?'
'I bet you can work out what comes after "Take off your shoes"!'

Repeating instructions to themselves, either under their breath or silently in their head, can be very effective for improving children's recall. They can also give themselves physical cues by extending or touching a finger for every part of the instructions. Techniques like this help to make sure they've heard all the instructions and thought about the separate steps required.

After giving instructions to your child, prompt them to repeat them back to you. Can they show you on their fingers how many different instructions they heard?

Encourage your child to create visual prompts for each part of the instructions. This starts with looking for real things that might help. If the teacher asks them to go to their tray or put their green book in a pile, they can simply look at the trays, their book or the place where the pile is going to be. Already the idea is being strengthened in their mind, and they can make it stronger by using their imagination. The trays could be glowing invitingly. The book might by pulled over to the pile by a magnetic force.

If instructions are more abstract or harder to see, children can create trigger images from scratch, for example:

'Read the newspaper report your partner wrote, then tell them three things they did well and one aspect you'd improve.'

Your child might imagine a huge newspaper filling the room. Their friend's photograph could be on the front page, alongside three large green ticks – positive points – and a golden arrow, the suggested 'direction' for improvement. Another example of using trigger images is:

'Please go to the office, ask them for the lunch list, then you and Jake can go to Year 4 to get their orders.'

Perhaps this time your child could make the image of the lunch list memorable by shrinking it. They could use the number-shape system to picture Year 4 as a yacht. What would the sailors like for lunch – and how can their orders possibly fit on such a tiny piece of paper?

Children often start a task well only to lose their way. This technique gives them clues to refer to all the way through.

When you're giving instructions, ask your child about the picture clues they've used – and suggest some of your own, for example:

'Please can you go up to your bedroom and find a shirt and trousers for school. Imagine if you found the shirt flying around the room, and the trousers were on fire!'

'I'd like you to tidy up your teddies and balls. Imagine the teddies have all come to life and they're going to hurt themselves if they trip over those huge bouncy balls.'

These strategies are useful to children of any age. As they grow, so do the instructions they're given – in length and complexity. Getting them into the right habits early on helps them to cope with every set of instructions they're asked to follow.

REMEMBERING RULES

The same techniques can be used to learn lists of behavioural rules. RE teaching often involves examining religious rules and how followers are reminded of them in scriptures, stories, ritual actions and foods. Much PSHE teaching is about formulating good rules to follow in tricky situations. The ability to reflect on and learn any list of rules is a key thinking skill for school.

Perhaps your child needs reminding to tuck their shirt in, to let others join in playground games and to speak quietly in the corridor; three separate 'rules' to follow. You could work with them to design three trigger images and then link them together in a memorable way. What if they imagined the list itself written at the bottom of their shirt, so that they had to tuck it in to keep the information private? But maybe the shirt becomes so impossibly long and wide and heavy that they have to ask friends to come and help – and it becomes a fun game of 'tuck in the giant shirt'. They could keep playing it in the corridor, as long as they all whisper as they work…

FINISHING WORK

A similar thought process will help your child to complete the work they're asked to do in school.

As well as remembering the instructions to a task, they need to have a strong sense of what they're hoping to achieve. Their teacher may model it for them or show them lots of examples, and this can be helpful as they visualize what their own work is going to look like. They should picture their successful end result in as much detail as possible, and also consider the feelings they'll have when it's finished.

They can then invent a quick series of images to remind them what has to happen to get this work done.

Perhaps they've been asked to plan a model of a house, then to use a pencil and ruler to draw it onto cardboard, before cutting it out and building it. After visualizing the finished model in all its glory and imagining strong feelings of pride and satisfaction, they could picture themselves sitting on a distant planet (a reminder to 'plan it') and getting help from the Queen (a real 'ruler') to use a huge, sharp pencil made out of cardboard (the equipment and materials to use).

They could use these memory clues during the project, even if it ran over several days. And at the end, when they looked at their real model house, they could compare it with the one they imagined at the start, check they'd gone through all the important steps and consider any improvements they might like to remember for next time.

TARGETS

This approach will help your child plan their own activities and set their own goals. An important strand of PSHE involves target-setting, so they're at a big advantage if they already have the thinking skills in place to develop their ideas and break them down into achievable, memorable steps.

Help them to invent pictures to represent all their 'steps to success'. Perhaps the next three stages in their plan to be a professional musician are:

▶ **practise my violin every day:** *they could imagine curling up in bed with their violin; it's the first and last thing they see every day, reminding them to practise it every day*

- ▶ **pass my next violin exam:** *curled around the violin strings is a piece of paper, the certificate to say they've passed their exam*
- ▶ **join the school orchestra:** *perhaps they fold the certificate into a paper aeroplane big enough to climb on board and fly to school, landing in the middle of orchestra practice.*

It's a great way to plan carefully, remember the important steps and keep the end goal firmly in mind. Trained thinking skills like these can give children a very practical approach to turning their dreams into realities.

A focused approach to work is so important to your child's success and the way they're regarded in school. Creative thinking and learning skills are a great way to give them the recall and structure they need to follow instructions, while also enjoying themselves and making the most of their active imagination. They can help others to stay on task, avoid distractions, comment on their own success and make the most of every opportunity to improve and grow.

QUESTIONS AND ANSWERS

Prepare your child for the sort of questioning they're likely to face in school. These days teachers vary their approach, asking for 'hands up', talking to particular children directly or telling everyone to display their answer on mini-whiteboards. At home, in your conversations and discussions, vary the way you ask for responses, for example:

'Does anyone know…?'
'Abdul, what's the cleverest way of…?'
'Kristen, you give me your best idea first.'
'Let's all write down our choices.'

FLEXIBLE WORKING

Many primary schools are now very flexible about how children do their work. For some tasks they'll be working on their own.

They'll often discuss their ideas in pairs and do joint projects.
Plenty of activities will involve groups of children, sometimes
of similar ability, sometimes mixed. And there are even times
when the whole class contributes to a single piece of work,
all the children contributing in different ways.

This is why so many of the skills taught in RE and PSHE are
essential to success across the curriculum.

The more your family life mirrors the flexible patterns of work in
school, the better your child will be at adapting. As well as working
with them on homework tasks, projects, games and activities, make
sure you also give them a chance to work with brothers or sisters,
friends and on their own. Talk to them about the different skills
they've used to succeed each time. In PSHE they'll be looking at
communication strategies – team-working, turn-taking, negotiating –
all the skills that a positive family life helps to instil.

Talk to your child about the different skills required by different
working arrangements:

*'Well done for concentrating so hard on your own and coming up
     with all those ideas yourself.'*
'You two talked brilliantly and found a great compromise.'
*'You all took it in turns to talk about your views, then divided up
     the jobs brilliantly.'*

LEARNING FROM EXPERIENCE

For each new task, encourage your child to think about their
previous successes. They can use their imagination to bring
memories clearly to mind and then think carefully about
connections with the task at hand.

In school, your child may find themselves role playing a servant of
Henry VIII one moment, sitting silently in an hour-long maths test
the next and then working with three friends to plan and bake a
cake. They'll feel so much more confident if they spend a moment

considering each task, trawling for useful past experiences, then choosing the knowledge, understanding and key thinking skills that they know will work, for example:

'I've never tried role playing before, especially not in front of the whole class; but I have acted in a play at the youth club. It was really helpful when I used actions to get me into the character. I also need a moment to get a few ideas, and I'll use all the facts I know about Henry to guess what my character might think and feel.'

NEW ROLES

This approach helps children to deal with all the opportunities and responsibilities they're offered as they go through school. It gives them the confidence to challenge themselves, and all the skills necessary to do a good job.

Whether your child is given the role of class librarian, pen monitor or house prefect, they'll have a set of responsibilities to remember. These can be broken down into manageable steps, explored in the imagination and given powerful memory triggers.

Being a prefect might involve:

▶ *collecting a class from the playground*
▶ *keeping the cloakroom tidy*
▶ *delivering the register to the school office*
▶ *running playground games.*

You could give your child a mental checklist by turning these four tasks into a memorable story. Make sure it has a clear starting point – perhaps the metal prefect's badge they're so proud of, for example:

The badge has turned into a powerful magnet, pulling the whole class of children towards them ('collect them from the

*playground'). The magnetism helps them guide all the children
into the cloakroom. But there's a terrible mess inside; coats
and bags piled so high that no one can get through. As if
by magic, the badge transforms into a large shovel, perfect
for scooping the mess out of the way ('tidy the cloakroom').
When the final coat is picked up, it reveals the register lying
there on the floor. The shovel can be used to carry the register
to its rightful home ('deliver the register to the office').
But something odd is happening in the office. All the staff
members are playing games: hopscotch, skipping, football or
tag ('organize playground games').*

Exploring ideas like this helps children to think carefully about
their responsibilities, talk about them, add or change details as
necessary, and refer to their mental checklist to make sure they're
doing everything they should.

Younger children may only have one or two tasks to remember,
but older children will be given increasingly complex roles to
master. These responsibilities will often involve working with
adults: helping lunchtime supervisors; sorting envelopes with
members of the PTA; showing visitors around the school. As
your child grows, all the techniques explored in this book will
help them to operate well with people of all ages: modifying
their communication, responding appropriately to questions and
instructions, managing their behaviour and using all their talents
to contribute to a range of tasks.

Communicating with your child's school

Parents play an important role in preparing children to deal with
adults, through the ways in which they themselves model good
communication and mature behaviour. This is particularly true of
the way in which you interact with your child's school. Here are
the key rules.

SHOW RESPECT

Treat every member of the school with courtesy and consideration: the head teacher, class teachers, office staff, caretaker. Make sure your child sees you speaking positively and politely.

COMMUNICATE CLEARLY

Teachers aren't mind-readers and they'll always benefit from clearly worded letters and phone calls and focused face-to-face chats. Take time to think about exactly what you want to say. Before meetings, make notes if necessary to help you stick to the specific points you want to raise.

CHOOSE YOUR BATTLES

Save your energy for the times when you really do need a meeting with a teacher or head teacher. Think about the best way of tackling a problem, and set out wanting to find answers to it, offering any solutions you can think of.

Insight

Try to leave a meeting or phone conversation on a positive note, with a clear way forward. Agree a plan for monitoring improvements and communicating in future.

INVOLVE YOUR CHILD

Make sure you talk to your child before raising any concerns at school – and that means proper, focused talking and listening, when everyone's calm. Remember that children do not always tell the full story and that their perspective will only be one of several. But do show them that you want to do everything you can to make things better, because their happiness and success matter to you. Ask for their suggestions to make them part of the process. Agree the things you will and will not mention to their teacher.

PRAISE AS WELL AS COMPLAIN

Leave a phone message to say thank you for sorting something out, or fire off a quick postcard to say how pleased you are with a piece of work. These things have a huge impact on busy teachers, and on your child's outlook on relationships. Show that being honest and assertive is as much about celebrating success as it is about solving problems.

HELP WHENEVER AND HOWEVER YOU CAN

Your child will often bring home requests for parents to come on school trips, help with cooking, supervise cycle training or make costumes. The PTA committee is likely to need plenty of support running summer fairs, film shows and new parents' nights. The governors are always looking for parents to get involved in running the school itself. You can't do everything and there'll be plenty of times when work, family or other commitments simply prevent you from helping. But take the opportunities when you can. Let your child see you offering support as well as agreeing to requests. Use your particular talents to give something back to the school. You'll help the school to thrive, learn more about how it works and build good relationships with staff and other parents; and crucially, you'll show your child what being part of a community is all about.

CITIZENSHIP

Children benefit from seeing their parents' interest in school life. It reinforces the feeling that school is an important place, worthy of that extra bit of effort. It starts them thinking about the ways in which they themselves can contribute to all the different communities they belong to: school, family, church, sports teams, youth groups, neighbourhood and planet. It backs up all the RE and PSHE teaching about the importance and pleasure of helping others, in school and out.

Right-brained creativity lets your child explore their talents and think of ways they can help. Left-brained logic makes the important community connections and suggests practical ways to put ideas into action. At every stage of their development you can give children the inspiration and the opportunities they need to make a difference.

Show your child how to write a poem called a 'kenning' about their developing abilities and confidence. Make each line an imaginative description of one of their roles. Write lots of ideas on slips of paper, then experiment with different ways of ordering them. Some kennings rhyme, some don't. Make it a fun celebration of everything they can do – and keep adding to it as they grow. Here is an example of a kenning:

Rattle shaker
Sandcastle maker
Brilliant walker
Clever talker
Sum solver
Story writer
Church helper
Friend delighter!
Poster designer
Map reader
Lunchtime carer
Rabbit feeder
...ME!

Dealing with the challenges of school

ASKING FOR HELP

Children with well-developed thinking and learning skills are good at asking for help. Rather than saying they simply don't understand, they can explain exactly what it is they find hard – and perhaps even suggest the solution themselves. Teachers are keen to foster this approach in children of every age and you can encourage your child to be as specific and forward-looking as possible. 'I can't think what Roman soldiers might be eating, so could I get some help from one of the topic books?' is a world away from 'I'm stuck' or, 'What was I supposed to be doing?' Trained thinking skills help children stay on task, build from what they know, take a sensible approach, and – when they reach a particular barrier – get help to overcome it.

CHOICES

Good attitude and behaviour in school comes down to choices. We all make poor choices from time to time, and we can all improve the thought processes we use to come to our decisions. Every day in school your child will be faced with countless choices about what they do and say, and the results will help to determine their happiness and success.

There are lots of things families can do to develop good choice-making. The ability to recognize, analyse and discuss choices is vital. Give your child the following challenge:

Your ship is sinking and you're alone in a small lifeboat, about to row to the desert island on the horizon. Before the ship sinks completely you have time to grab just a few things from the wreckage. You can only fit five of the following items in your boat, so choose carefully. You may be stranded on the desert island for a long time...

> ▷ *carton of baked bean tins*
> ▷ *box of books*
> ▷ *pack of playing cards*
> ▷ *packet of foil-wrapped chocolate biscuits*
> ▷ *box of matches*
> ▷ *axe*
> ▷ *large sheet*
> ▷ *magnet*
> ▷ *water filter*
> ▷ *long piece of rope*

▷ *bucket*
▷ *clockwork radio*
▷ *box of tomato seeds*
▷ *carton of pens*
▷ *clock*

Give your child time to make their choices then discuss the thinking behind them. Can they rank the things they chose in order of importance? If they only had time to grab one thing from the ship, what would it be and why?

A game like this challenges children to use their scientific understanding, their logic and imagination, and their knowledge of themselves. They need to compare the objects and weigh up the pros and cons of each one. They're making choices and thinking very carefully about consequences which may not always be clear. Explaining their thinking aloud is important because it lets them hear the sound of their own thought processes at work. Make sure you have a go at the activity yourself and put forward your own case for the best objects to choose.

The 'Either/or' game

Invent a character and put him at the start of an adventure. For example: you might create an astronaut called Bob Black and have him waiting for the signal to get into his rocket. Then you suggest two options for Bob to choose between: perhaps having a sleep to relax or going for a run around the launch pad. It's up to the next player to choose which option Bob goes for. They describe what happens next, suggest two more choices then pass the decision-making to the next person along:

> *'Bob decides to have a run; but he falls over and breaks his leg.*
> *So, does he call for help and miss his space adventure,*
> *or try to crawl on board and blast off anyway...?'*

And so the game continues, each player setting choices, making decisions and imagining the consequences.

Set you child stimulating either/or choices. Would they rather:

▶ *be able to fly or turn invisible?*
▶ *live in a submarine or a tree house?*
▶ *be a giraffe or a penguin?*
▶ *win £10 ($15) every day or make a new friend every day?*

Insight

Discuss the choices characters make in books, TV programmes and films. Which ones does your child agree with and which would they do differently? As well as the actions people choose, consider the choices they make between different thoughts and attitudes.

In both PSHE and RE lessons children explore the ways they can make choices about feelings, discussing different ways of reacting to experiences. The more flexibly they can use their brain, the better they'll be at imagining different responses.

If it rains all day on Sunday, they could focus on not being able to play football and become miserable. Or they could choose more positive thoughts: all the fun things they get to do indoors; the chance to rest before next week's big game – even how the grass will be greener the next time they play.

When their model-making goes wrong they could get angry, decide they're really bad at building things, worry what people will think, regret all the wasted hours... Or they could think about the things they've learnt for next time; praise themselves for having a go; remember how funny it was when the whole thing collapsed; appreciate the chance they got to work with some new people.

Help your child to see that there are usually many different ways to think about an event. When they have worries, encourage them to choose between the 'silly' ones and the 'sensible' ones. They could write down two lists: the inaccurate, unlikely and unhelpful 'silly' worries ('Nobody at school likes me' or, 'Everyone's laughing about my new glasses'); and the 'sensible' worries that might actually help them make good decisions and avoid problems ('We might not get packed in time for the plane' or, 'What if I don't learn my lines for the school play?'). Help them to use the sensible worries to make positive choices and give them tactics to forget about the silly ones.

Children are very familiar with whiteboards, so the image of writing something down and then rubbing it off can be a good way to 'erase' a worry. The same goes for documents on a computer screen. Tell your child to display a worry on their mental screen, then to imagine clicking the icon that 'minimizes' it or deletes it altogether.

By using imaginative stories and pictures to drive their learning, children get used to choosing different angles and viewpoints. Tap into this as you talk about their feelings. How else could they look at a particular situation or problem?

Use your child's developing memory skills to gain perspective: 'Remember how worried you used to be about swimming?' Use real-life examples to prove that the same event can be seen in many different ways: 'We all watched the same movie, but we've come back with so many different feelings and thoughts!'

EMOTION METERS

Visualization techniques can help children to control their very strongest emotions.

Tell them to imagine a horizontal line labelled with extremes of feeling at either end, for example: 'completely calm' and 'out of control' or 'totally happy' and 'sad as can be'. Then ask your child to use this 'meter' to gauge how they feel about particular things:

Where on the line would they put their feelings about their new school?
What's their state of mind about the residential trip?
Where would they place their feelings about performing in assembly next week?

Pinpointing an emotion is a good start because they can then consider how to move it. Talk to them about ways to shift their feelings towards the positive end of the line:

▶ *Discuss practical approaches: 'Let's organize an extra visit to your new school.'*
▶ *Access memories that might help: 'Remember how much you enjoyed that sleepover at Rachel's.'*
▶ *Suggest ways of thinking that might help to move the feeling, bit by bit, along the line: 'Why not imagine that smile on your teacher's face when you stand up to speak?'*

This exercise can be a great way to help you talk to your child about their worries. It gives them strategies to start controlling their feelings – and to remember each positive adjustment they make.

Feeling in colour
Give your child a strategy for assessing the 'colour' of an emotion, and then using their imagination to change it.

Discuss how different colours can make us feel. Which colours help us relax and feel happy? Which ones put us on edge or make us depressed? Talk to children about the colour of feelings like anger, happiness or calm.

In moments of extreme emotion, show them how shifting the colour of a feeling can make a really big difference. When the world seems very sad and black, they might imagine the colour changing to deep purple, then dark blue, then slightly lighter and brighter. Moments of bright red anger could change to orange, then yellow, gradually helping them to see the world more calmly. Help them to use their powers of visualization to gain some control over even the strongest feelings.

Talking about feelings and ways of dealing with them equips children for the emotional challenges of school: friendships, arguments, fears, change. It helps them to understand why they might be feeling a particular way and to make sensible choices about dealing with it.

PSHE lessons will help your child understand that emotions are a natural part of life, especially as they grow and change. Towards the end of primary school they explore the physical and emotional changes caused by puberty; but all through school they learn to recognize particular feelings in themselves and others.

They'll do a great deal of work about friendships, and this is an area where all of the skills explored in this chapter are particularly important. Making good choices, dealing with worries and handling emotions; these are all vital skills for ensuring that arguments, rivalries and shifting friendship groups never get in the way of learning.

School is a complicated place and there will always be problems to overcome. But having the thinking skills to recognize, discuss and control feelings makes a huge difference to children's happiness and success. When they're distracted or unhappy, the best teaching in the world means very little. But relaxed, resilient, positive and secure, your child will be ready to make the most of their learning.

10 THINGS TO REMEMBER

1   *RE and PSHE lessons stretch thinking skills and challenge children to engage with the biggest questions of all.*

2   *Model a positive and ambitious attitude to school.*

3   *Use family activities to prepare children for the expectations of the classroom.*

4   *Strengthen your child's respect for teachers and other adults in school.*

5   *Help your child to use logic and creativity to set goals and complete quality pieces of work.*

6   *Train children to deal with different types of questioning and a variety of working arrangements.*

7   *Both imaginative and creative thinking skills help children take on new roles and fulfil their responsibilities.*

8   *Make the most of opportunities to help in school, developing relationships with staff and proving your interest and support.*

9   *Give your child plenty of practice at making choices, using their flexible thinking skills to explore all the possibilities.*

10   *Give children the confidence to explore thoughts and feelings creatively, to make sure that nothing gets in the way of their learning and happiness.*

Part three

Out of school: adapting home life to support your child's educational success

9

Healthy families, healthy minds

In this chapter you will learn:
- *how to nourish and fuel your child's developing brain*
- *the importance of good sleep, and how to encourage it*
- *strategies for using physical exercise to boost thinking skills*
- *games to develop children's confidence and resilience*
- *strategies for making homework effective, rewarding and stress-free.*

Although school presents children with rich opportunities for learning, the vast majority of their childhood is actually spent at home. The quality of family life is crucial to every child's development. At its best, it prepares them for all the challenges they face in primary school, setting them up for success and supporting them in everything they do.

The EPPE research group (Effective Provision of Pre-School Education) at London's Institute of Education studied children who did particularly well in school. They found key similarities between their home lives and listed what they felt were the important characteristics of supportive families.

The most successful children in their study had:

- ▶ *regular bedtimes*
- ▶ *rules about watching TV*
- ▶ *opportunities to play with friends, in and out of the home*

- ▶ *family outings*
- ▶ *visits to libraries, museums and parks*
- ▶ *family mealtimes*
- ▶ *access to art at home*
- ▶ *opportunities to sing*
- ▶ *responsibilities around the house*
- ▶ *chances to read, and to have books read to them.*

To do really well in school, children need a number of things from their family life. It has to give them structure and security, imposing rules on key aspects of their experience – like sleep and television. It must also offer freedom: physically, to explore new places; creatively to enjoy books, art, music. And alongside all the opportunities to think and learn, family life is about collaborating with others: playing, travelling and talking with people of different ages – the ones who know you best and who have the greatest stake in your success.

Every primary school has a 'mission statement', setting out its fundamental ideas and aims. This chapter is about deciding your family's mission statement about learning. What are your values, priorities and aspirations about learning? How best can you adapt your family life to put them all into practice?

A healthy family life boosts children's physical, mental and spiritual growth. It sends them to school in the best shape for learning, and then rehearses, enriches and extends everything they do when they get home.

Love and learning

A safe, secure, stable home with plenty of love and affection is vital to good learning. Experiments with rats have shown clear links between emotional health and mental skill. The rats who performed best in thinking challenges were the ones given plenty of physical affection, along with a stimulating environment in which to grow. Your child needs all the hugs and the warm support of a loving home, along with the stimulation to activate every area of their thinking and learning.

Pre-school specialist Sian Williams worked with UNICEF to define a five-point plan for nurturing children's happiness and success. It emphasized physical affection and the importance of structure and routine; the need to weave reading into family life; plus the huge impact of food and exercise on a child's development. All these factors will be explored in this chapter.

There is no such thing as a 'normal' family – and certainly no family's perfect – but there are very clear similarities between the families that produce the most successful children. The ideas and activities here are designed to help you make the most of your family life, the resources you have and the time you spend together, to achieve a healthy balance of all the things most important to your child.

Nutrition

The Roman writer Juvenal coined the phrase '*mens sana in corpore sano*': 'a healthy mind in a healthy body'. For thousands of years we've known that a link exists between our physical and mental health, but only very recently have we begun to study the precise impact of nutrition on thinking and learning.

It's an extremely complicated area. Our diet not only helps to build our brain but also controls the way it works, affects its ongoing health, and provides it with the energy it needs to operate. At the same time it contributes to our overall wellbeing, which in turn affects the quality of our thinking... so it's a real challenge trying to untangle all the factors affecting brain development and mental success.

The first studies concentrated on malnourishment and its effects on children's growth. It was quickly clear that the healthy, balanced diet necessary for growing the body is just as important for building the brain. But what are the key elements? In just the last 50 years, scientists have started looking at specific parts of our diet – particularly nutrients and micronutrients – and they've found that these substances do affect the way our 'plastic' brain forms and develops, especially during its times of most rapid growth:

▶ *the third trimester of pregnancy*
▶ *the first few months after birth*
▶ *ages 2–4*
▶ *ages 6–8*
▶ *ages 10–12*
▶ *ages 14–16.*

During these periods, the brain is at its most sensitive to the nutrition it receives. The substances that seem to have a particular impact are fatty acids, vitamins and minerals.

FATTY ACIDS

Fatty acids play a crucial role in assembling the brain. They set up the systems for making neurotransmitters – the brain's chemical communicators – and then help to manufacture the neurotransmitters themselves. They form the parts of brain cells that allow thoughts and impulses to be exchanged, as well as supporting the long-term health of the infinitely complex thinking system they've helped to build.

There are two 'families' of fatty acids, Omega-3 and Omega-6, neither of which can be manufactured by the body and must instead be obtained from food. Both types of fat are found in abundance in the brain and we know that they are essential for good mental function.

Around 97% of the Omega-3 fat in the brain is a substance called DHA (docosahexaeonic acid). A fatty acid known as AA (arachidonic acid) accounts for around half of the Omega-6 fat. In combination, DHA and AA seem to have a particularly powerful impact on brainpower.

A study compared the mental development of two groups of children. The first had been given infant milk formula containing a mix of DHA and AA; these substances were missing from the formula given to the second group. When assessed using standard cognitive tests, the children in the first group did significantly better than those who had not been given the supplements in question – leading the researchers to campaign for all infant formula to be fortified with DHA and AA.

Omega-3 fatty acids have been shown to have wide-ranging benefits for thinking and learning. Supplements have been demonstrated to have a positive effect on babies born prematurely, boys in particular. As well as boosting the speed and connectivity of the brain, we know that they can decrease hostility and anger, removing some of the emotional barriers to a child's learning and overall mental health.

So make sure your child has a good supply of fatty acids in their diet, from which their brain can take as much of each one as it needs.

DHA is found in coldwater fish like salmon, herring, mackerel, tuna and halibut. It's actually the algae these fish eat that gives them such a high DHA content; the algae itself is an alternative, vegetarian source. DHA is also found in 'organ' meats – such as liver – and in smaller amounts in poultry and egg yolks. The body can manufacture DHA by using chemicals found in linseed and flaxseed oils, soybeans and walnuts.

AA is much easier to obtain through the diet, being found in meat, eggs and milk.

MINERALS AND VITAMINS

Iron is known to improve children's cognitive development and concentration. It is found in red meat, fish, pulses and green vegetables.

Zinc is one of the other most abundant minerals in the brain. Sources of zinc include meat, fish, wholegrain bread and soybeans.

As well as being important for growing bones, the calcium found in dairy products, leafy green vegetables and tofu, plays a key role in learning and behaviour. Studies have shown that children with calcium deficiency are less able to concentrate on learning and are much more inclined towards hyperactivity.

Vitamin C is used by the brain to make neurotransmitters. It is found in fruit like oranges and kiwi fruit and vegetables like broccoli and cauliflower.

Vitamin B_{12} is important for maintaining myelin, the tissue that protects brain cells. It's absorbed by eating meat, poultry, dairy products and eggs.

A deficiency of vitamin B_6 is known to be linked to irritability and tiredness. Sources of vitamin B_6 include cod, tuna, spinach, asparagus, bananas and Brussels sprouts.

A lack of folic acid can affect the efficiency of the brain's chemical communications. Folic acid is present in small amounts in many foods, including oranges, broccoli, peas, chickpeas and brown rice.

In a study by Essex University, children's results in tests at the end of primary school rose by as much as 8 per cent when their lunches were enriched with these key brain-building fats, minerals and vitamins. Other studies have shown noticeable improvements in concentration and behaviour linked to these nutrients.

Make sure your child has a diet rich in all of these substances. Take every opportunity to feed them unprocessed food – as close as possible to its natural state – to get the very best out of the nutrients it contains. There are plenty of nutritional supplements on the market, and the brain-boosting claims they make are usually based on fairly common substances like iron and zinc – although many parents do like the reassurance that their child has received a wide range of nutrients. Read the labels carefully to see exactly what each product offers.

CARBOHYDRATES

To work at its best, your child's brain also needs the right kind of fuel. A burst of sugar will give them a temporary lift and potentially a boost in mental performance; however, the best fuel is slow-burning, releasing its sugar into the bloodstream over a longer period. The lower a food's score on the Glycemic Index (GI), the more sustainable its energy is. At breakfast it's particularly important to eat low-GI foods to provide energy which will last all morning. Breakfasts including low-GI foods have been shown to reduce the natural decline in brainpower during the morning.

Take great care to give your child a breakfast that will boost their performance in school. Look for low-GI ingredients, such as oatmeal, porridge and bran; wholemeal bread; grapefruit, apples, cherries and oranges. The amount of sugar in packaged cereals has declined in recent years, but it's important that you read the packet and look at just how much quick-release energy your child is getting. If they're used to very sugary cereals, white bread and spreads, reduce these foods gradually, improving their energy sources bit by bit.

The most important thing is that your child has *something* for breakfast. Tests have shown a significant improvement in mental ability in children who have eaten breakfast compared with those who haven't. The effect is particularly strong an hour after breakfast – when many children are arriving at school, giving first impressions to teachers, and beginning the first lesson of the day.

Most schools allow their children to take in a mid-morning snack, which scientists have shown counteracts the effects of missing breakfast. So at least make sure your child is accessing some energy for their body and brain during the morning; and at best give them a low-GI snack that will top up their fuel and keep them energized until lunchtime.

WATER

Children should also be drinking water throughout the day. Schools have realized the importance of this in recent years and installed water fountains and coolers, as well as expecting every pupil to have their own water bottle. Make sure your child has theirs and find out if they're actually drinking from it. Water is vital to good thinking and learning, helping to combat headaches and drowsiness and boosting concentration.

HARMFUL FOODS

Keep an eye out for any foods that seem to have a negative effect on your child's behaviour or concentration. A recent report listed the following substances as most likely to cause problems, so watch for these in particular and avoid them if your child seems to show a bad reaction.

- *tartrazine (a colouring)*
- *sodium benzoate (a preservative)*
- *cows' milk*
- *chocolate*
- *grapes*
- *wheat*
- *oranges*
- *cows' cheese*
- *hens' eggs*

Many children show no ill-effects whatsoever from eating these foods; but if you suspect your child's diet is having a negative effect on their learning, start by looking at the substances on this list.

When a child's diet supports their overall health and well-being they feel much more like learning. They miss less school through illness and spend more of their time relaxed and alert, able to maintain concentration throughout the busy and varied school day.

Sleep

As well as their diet, a child's sleep patterns play a huge role in their success in school. As soon as possible, get your child into good sleeping habits so that they arrive every morning physically fresh and mentally switched-on, capable of maintaining good energy levels all day.

The amount of sleep we require changes throughout our life, and individuals differ in exactly how much they need. But all children will benefit from having a sleeping routine; a pattern of good habits they follow every night to make sure they get the best quality sleep. The effects of poor sleep are very easy to spot in school.

Children need their parents to make good sleep decisions for them. Your child's night-time routine should be a natural part of family life: no arguments, no distractions, just a clear plan every night to ensure that everyone gets all the sleep they need.

Insight

Avoid computer games late at night. These make it much harder to switch off and relax, often leaving children frustrated and over-stimulated.

Having a light snack at bedtime has been shown to benefit night-long sleep.

Experiment with the benefits of an evening bath, a warm drink, gentle music, a bedtime story – anything that calms your child, relaxes them and eases their brain towards the patterns of sleep.

Make sure their bedroom is helping them get to sleep. Is it dark enough? What is the temperature like? Are there distractions, such as television sets or video games – which they may well be playing when you think they're trying to sleep?

Although children may argue about their need to stay up and their lack of tiredness, they'll recognize the benefits of good sleep and appreciate your help in achieving it.

Of course they'll sleep particularly well if their day has been active, both mentally and physically. All the thinking techniques explored in this book are designed to make them active learners and to use their mental abilities in a very energetic way. The more they use them, the more they'll be ready for a refreshing night's sleep.

Exercise

Children's mental exertions need to be balanced by the right amount of physical activity. They need an active attitude to life, and many opportunities to get physical exercise.

Neuroscientists at the Salk Institute in the US showed that mice encouraged to run performed much better on thinking tests than those kept still for most of the day. Exercise improves the heart's ability to pump oxygen to the brain. It releases chemicals that make us feel good. We know that exercise can leave us energized and alert, as well as giving us opportunities for fun and friendship, the thrill of competition and the chance to test our skills, tactics, endurance and bravery.

Children need to be involved in a range of physical activities that they enjoy. Schools will provide PE teaching and playground games, and children naturally skip and run and dance to explore movement and expend energy. Parents need to find opportunities for trips to the park and swimming pool, times when it's safe to ride bikes, to use skates or scooters, and chances to try a variety of sports and games. Joining a sports team may be a cheap way of getting lots of training, and many councils offer subsidized – or even free – sports for children. Even if your child is receiving paid-for lessons, remember the benefits of walks in the woods and ball games in the park. Encourage them to play in pairs and groups, inside and out, and talk to them about the activities they might like to try. Make exercise a natural part of their life and a key factor in their health and wellbeing.

JUGGLING

Teach your child to juggle. Juggling is a fantastic skill for both mental and physical development. It helps to improve hand–eye co-ordination and body awareness, but it also nurtures some very important thinking skills. Because both hands are used, and the objects juggled cross from one side to the other, it helps to stimulate whole-brain thinking. It's also a great way of showing children the benefit of persisting with training, coping with failures along the way and gradually improving until they've developed a skill that will impress others – and themselves.

Humour and learning

Laughter is good for your child's thinking and learning. It helps their breathing, improves their circulation, lowers stress hormones (like cortisol and adrenaline) and puts children in a very relaxed and creative state. Encourage joke-telling around the meal table. Find funny theatre shows or street performances that will amuse them in new ways. There are many great books of hilarious poems for children – and poetry is particularly important because it helps to develop an awareness of humour itself: the words, rhymes and rhythms that stimulate the smiles and laughter.

Games are a great way to get children smiling and enjoying the humour that comes from fun, interesting, competitive activities. They're especially useful when they also support key thinking skills and subject areas, reinforcing the fact that learning itself is a great source of fun.

Play a word game like 'Dodgy definitions'. Each player in turn uses a dictionary (either a child or adult version) to find an unusual word. They then spend a moment inventing two fake definitions for it. They'll need you to model this first, but even quite young children will quickly get the idea.

Once the 'Dodgy definitions' are ready the player describes them to the rest of the group, along with the real meaning of the word. The others then vote on the one they think is correct.

There are many ways of organizing the game as a competition, depending on the number and age of the players. It's fun to fool others with your definitions as well as to be bamboozled by others. Children find out about word meanings and patterns, boost their communication skills and experience the laughter and fun that can play such an important part in learning.

Another great word game involves the first and last lines of books. Collect a pile of books that your child will be able to read and give each player a piece of paper and a pen or pencil.

The first player chooses a book (or has it chosen for them) then tosses a coin. 'Heads' means the challenge is to write the first line; 'tails', the last line. All the players then have a short amount of time to write down a convincing first or last line.

Modelling this activity once or twice is usually all it takes to show children what to do. Let them see that simplicity is often best and that short sentences will give the other players few clues to go on. Suggest ways of using speech and questions and encourage children to think up offbeat and unusual lines that might just be true.

When everyone's ready, the pieces of paper are collected in. The player in charge of the round then reads them all out aloud, including among them the real first or last line of the book.

The other players vote on the one they think is real. They win points if they guess correctly – or if someone mistakes their line for the genuine article.

It's another great opportunity to find fun with others in a very simple activity. It can turn into a really hilarious experience trying to match writing styles to people you know, looking for clues in words and phrases. It balances lively competition with the pleasure of matching minds with friends and family.

Try a number game like 'Maths bingo'. You'll need paper, pens and counters or tokens. Give each player a piece of paper and get them to draw a simple grid, three squares by three. They then fill in the grid with any nine of the numbers from one to ten, choosing how they want to arrange their bingo card. Older children can use any multiples of 10 between 10 and 100, or the 'hundreds' between 100 and 1000.

When everyone's ready, one player is chosen to be the 'caller' for the first game. They think up maths questions to which the answers are numbers on the players' cards. So, if you were using the numbers 1 to 10, the questions might be:

'What is 6 – 3?'
'What is ½ of 12?'
'What is 20 per cent of 40?'
'What is the number of Cinderella's ugly sisters plus the number of bears Goldilocks met?'

It all depends on the age and ability of the players and the level of creativity they can bring to their question-setting. Without looking at anyone's card, the caller should keep a record of all the answers they use to make sure there's no repetition.

Each time a player spots an answer on their board they can place a counter on it. The first person to claim a line (three counters in a row, horizontally or vertically) wins three points. The first player with all four corners covered receives four points. And the player who's first to put counters on all nine of their grid squares and shout 'Bingo!' claims the full ten points.

Change the caller after every 'Bingo'. You might decide to keep the same numbers, swap cards or make new ones with a different range of answers. Since there are only ten possible numbers, all the players will come close to winning – which only adds to the tension and the need to concentrate.

'Maths bingo' is a powerful way to practise calculation strategies, maths vocabulary and speed of thought. It stretches children's thinking skills, whether they're asking or answering the questions, and combines useful mental maths practice with the fun and excitement of competition.

Another maths game, requiring no equipment at all, is called 'Guess my…'. It can be played anywhere, strengthens any area of maths you choose and is particularly good for developing logical thinking and memory.

You might decide to make it 'Guess my number'. One player simply chooses a number and challenges the others to work it out by asking clever questions – to which the answers can only be 'Yes' or 'No'.

With more than two players you can say that a 'Yes' lets you ask another question but a 'No' means that the next player in line takes over.

If you're playing with just two people, keep a record of the number of questions asked. You can either set a limit ('You've got 20 questions to guess my number') or compare your scores ('You needed 18 questions to guess my number but I win because I got yours in 12').

Player one: *'You've got 20 questions to guess the number I'm thinking of.'*
Player two: *'Is it less than 100?'*
P1: *'Yes.'*
P2: *'Is it less than 50?'*

P1: 'Yes.'

P2: 'Is it a whole number?'

P1: 'Yes.'

P2: 'Is it an even number?'

P1: 'No.'

P2: 'So, it's an odd number less than 50. Is it greater than 10?'

P1: 'Yes'

P2: 'Is it a multiple of 3...?'

Some children will benefit from making notes as they go along, crossing off numbers as they're eliminated. Others will enjoy the challenge of doing it all from memory.

Use the game to practise using key words like 'greater', 'less', 'between', 'odd', 'multiple' and 'factor'. Discuss the questions that got them close to the answer and the ones that didn't really help at all. As well as sharpening their maths skills, use 'Guess my...' to teach your child about game-playing strategy itself, showing them the fun that can come from such a simple battle of wits.

When you've tried 'Guess my number', have a go at playing 'Guess my shape', choosing to use 2D or 3D shapes or a mixture of both. It's a great way to rehearse all the important vocabulary about shapes, using words like 'parallel', 'edges', 'vertices' and 'symmetry'. Encourage your child to visualize shapes as they're thinking about them, and to keep choosing the most effective questions.

P1: 'Let's see who's the first person to guess my shape.'

P2: 'Is it a flat shape?'

P1: 'Yes. So you get another question.'

P2: 'Does it have more than four sides?'

P1: 'No. So now someone else can have a go.'

P3: 'Does it have any pairs of parallel sides?'

P1: 'Yes.'

P3: 'Does it have at least two lines of symmetry...?'

Play 'Guess my...' in the car, walking to school or at any moment when you need a quick, easy and fun family game.

Memory skills and daily life

Use family life to strengthen your child's memory skills. Take every chance you get to discuss memories: the details of particular recollections, but also the experience of retrieving them. Develop your child's awareness of how their memory works and encourage them to explore it in everyday life.

Insight

Revisit important or interesting places. Can your child remember when they lived in a past house, went to their nursery school, first visited the local swimming pool? Ask them about all the sounds, smells and tastes that come back to them. What feelings does a place evoke? Which other memories spring to mind?

Unpack old toys or books you've stored away. My six-year-old daughter spent an hour exploring a box of her baby books that we'd put into the loft. She was delighted to see them again, talked about the familiar characters and stories and also mentioned the textures and smells she recalled. She made connections in her memory to the people who'd read with her and the places where we'd shared these books for the first time. The experience prompted her to remember several favourite books that weren't in the first box we dug out, but were there in the second.

Use songs to stimulate discussion about memory. If you listen to the radio together, at home or in the car, see who can remember what you were doing or where you were driving the last time a particular song came on. Can your child remember the first time they heard a favourite song? When hearing a new song, ask them about the familiar songs or singers it reminds them of.

Occasionally serve your child food that they haven't had for a long time. It might be a flavour that used to be their favourite, an unusual food from a holiday or just something you haven't bought for a couple of years. Food stimulates so many senses and can be a fascinating memory trigger. Ask questions that will probe your child's recall and show them how enjoyable it can be to explore experiences through memory:

'What does this food remind you of?'
'Do you remember where we were when you tried it?'
'Does the smell remind you of anything else from that holiday?'
'What was your life like when you were that age?'

Activities like these sharpen children's memory skills, helping them to tap into a range of senses and follow the interconnected memory pathways in their brain. They also stimulate that ability to think about thinking that can add such a rich layer of interest and fun to all your family talk.

Give your child access to books either just below, or just above, their current level of understanding. Library trips are great for this because children often pick books for much younger children than themselves, or for older readers – even adults. Let them experiment, explore the texts they've chosen and then talk about the experience:

'What is it exactly that you find easy or hard about this book?'
'Is it fun reading books for babies and younger children?'
'How does it feel looking at the grown-up book about trains?'

Help them to think about the reading and thinking skills they've mastered and the ones they still need to develop. Let them compare books and reflect on the particular ways in which their brain is being built.

Thinking games

Play games with your child that stretch both their creativity and their logic. Whether you're waiting for a plane, walking to school or in the car with friends, there are many easy and fun activities that promote vital thinking skills.

FORTUNATELY, UNFORTUNATELY

Take it in turns to tell the next part of a story. To get you started, choose any characters, settings and events you like. After that, the only rule is that each instalment has to start with the word 'fortunately' or 'unfortunately' in turn:

'A man called Bob was walking down the road one beautiful
summer's day. Fortunately... he was wearing a hat to protect
him from the Sun.'
'Unfortunately... a huge seagull landed on his hat and wouldn't
get off.'
'Fortunately... it was a very friendly seagull, and Bob was
delighted to have made a new friend.'
'Unfortunately, the seagull had a very bad habit...'

This game gives very little structure to story-telling, so it builds your child's ability to generate all their own ideas. It helps them to look for logical links, as well as to explore creative flights of fancy, and it can give them a great opportunity to amuse and surprise others with their imagination. It's a good way of strengthening memory skills, since unusual stories like these are at the heart of creative learning. It even builds children's sense of perspective and their real-life resilience, challenging them to imagine the endless ups, downs and ups again of such an unpredictable story.

BEST AND WORST

The idea this time is to have fun exploring the best and worst answers to various problems and situations. Start off by setting the questions for your child and suggesting ideas of your own to spark their imagination. Encourage them to see that there are no absolutely right or wrong answers, just the cleverest and funniest ideas they can imagine. Before long they'll be stretching their thinking to the extremes and producing a variety of suggestions, as well as asking to set the questions themselves.

For example, name the best and worst:

▶ *person to be your teacher*
▶ *theme for a party*
▶ *thing to say to the Queen*
▶ *animal to keep as a pet*
▶ *object to find in the middle of a desert.*

You could use the game to have fun with scientific thinking:

*'What's the best bit of a caterpillar's life? When it can crawl and
stick to things? When it's safe in its cocoon? When it becomes
a butterfly?'*
*'What's the worst material for making teapots? Chocolate?
Custard? Oxygen? Tea leaves?'*

Lots of the best questions strengthen PSHE skills:

*'Who's the best person to share your prison cell? Your mum?
A brilliant story teller? A record-breaking escapologist?'*
*'What's the worst thing to say when someone's feeling poorly?
"I don't believe you"? "I told you not to drink from that
puddle"? "If you die, can I have your games console"?'*

It's even possible to explore maths in this lively and imaginative way.

*'What's the best shape for a new type of egg container? A cube, for
flexible stacking? A sphere, with no sharp corners?'*
*'What's the worst number of children to have in a class? Twenty-seven
because that's an odd number and you wouldn't be able to work
in pairs? Six because someone would be left out of the five-a-side
soccer team? Fifty-two because the teacher might split you up
into four teams of unlucky 13, or make you each her slave for a
week, or cast an evil spell and turn you all into playing-cards...?'*

Encourage your child to explore the extremes of their imagination.
Comedy often comes from exaggeration and you can have lots

of fun pushing these ideas to the limit. Challenge your child's ability to take logical steps in increasingly surreal and hilarious directions.

SUPERHERO SEARCH

This activity is all about inventing superheroes and putting them in funny situations. Your child will love dreaming up superhero names, costumes and special skills, then finding ways to use – and abuse – their new comic-book characters.

Start by suggesting an emergency situation – but not one that superheroes normally tackle. It could be something from their daily life, linked to their hobbies or interests, or themed on a subject at school, for example:

▶ *Grandad's lost his keys again*
▶ *Manchester United are one match away from relegation*
▶ *King Harold needs some help on the battlefield*
▶ *there's a tornado heading for the garden*
▶ *the girls in class have all fallen out again.*

So the aim is to invent the perfect superhero for the job. Work together to come up with all the important details, such as:

▶ *name*
▶ *costume*
▶ *special skills and powers*
▶ *mode of transport*
▶ *sidekick*
▶ *arch enemy*
▶ *weakness*
▶ *catchphrase.*

So how will your superhero get on with the emergency at hand? Talk about what happens when 'Magneto Man' uses his electromagnet arm to steal back Grandad's keys from the evil 'Garage Ghost'. Imagine the amazing 'History Girl' flying back in time to catch the arrow a millimetre away from Harold's eye.

Have fun putting 'The Tickler' into action to make the girls in 4B laugh and forget what they were arguing about.

But what if the messages got mixed up and 'The Tickler' ended up on the beach in 1066? How would 'Magneto Man' help the class sort out their friendship? What could 'History Girl' do with Grandad's keys to save Manchester United from the approaching tornado...?

Show your child the fun that can come from putting characters in unexpected situations. Encourage them to create the most exaggerated, surreal and incongruous scenes. Let them experience the fun of sharing ideas and making people laugh, and give them the imaginative confidence to generate all the comedy and chaos themselves.

CAPTURING IDEAS

Whether it's Archimedes in his bath or Newton under the apple tree, brilliant thinkers often have their breakthrough ideas when they're busy doing something else.

Consider the times when you've had great thoughts while brushing your teeth, jogging round the park or mowing the lawn. Moments of genius can happen anytime, anywhere – particularly when the brain is relaxed and unfocused. Your child may have a wonderful idea about their science homework while they're playing in the bath, or realize the best way to solve a tricky maths question during a kick around in the back garden. They need to cherish these moments and have practical ways of capturing them.

Give your child a wide range of tools for recording their thoughts. As well as notebooks and pieces of paper, show them that they can write on the back of envelopes, in the steam on the bathroom mirror or on sticky notes fastened to their bedroom door.

Insight

Both my children loved being given message boards for their bedroom walls and quickly covered them with ideas, reminders, memories and jokes. Could your child write on a chalkboard in the hallway or with the magnetic letters on the fridge?

Maybe your mobile phone has a voice recorder function, to gather thoughts on the journey home from holiday or while walking in the woods. It probably also has a camera, so get your child to mime their great idea while you photograph their pose.

You're giving them the tools they need to make the most of their thoughts. Even more importantly, you're showing them the value of the brilliant ideas that can pop up in the most unexpected places.

THINKING HATS

Family conversations and discussions are a great way to practise thinking skills. You can experiment with different ways of approaching questions and problems, explore a range of effective strategies – and do some very useful thinking about thinking itself.

Edward de Bono popularized the idea of 'thinking hats', applying different types of thinking in very explicit ways. He defined six key approaches, each with its own colour code:

▶ *White stands for neutral thinking, considering all the facts available.*
▶ *Red involves the feelings: instincts, gut reactions, emotional ideas, intuition.*
▶ *Black is negative judgement, using logic to probe for flaws and problems.*
▶ *Yellow is positive judgement: still thinking logically, but this time identifying benefits and harmony.*
▶ *Green refers to creative thinking, using the imagination to make rich connections and exploring where all the available ideas might lead.*
▶ *Blue is process control: monitoring the whole project; thinking about thinking.*

With enough people involved, you could each wear one of these 'hats' and take a specific approach to the topic under discussion.

If you were discussing where to go for your next extended family holiday, perhaps Mum could be 'White', outlining the facts about dates, times, distances and prices. Dad could be 'Red' and give his gut feeling, while ten-year-old Maya plays 'Black' and looks for problems with the plans. Her brother Tom might be 'Yellow' and point out the positives in the ideas he'd heard. Grandpa could do the creative 'Green' thinking and push everyone to use their imagination, while Auntie Kate could wear 'Blue', making sure that everyone gets a chance to contribute and checking that all approaches are being considered.

Another way to do this is to take each mode of thinking in turn, working together to explore the benefits of each 'hat'.

You could try this out when you were planning some home improvements. First, begin with neutral thinking. Talk together about all the practical details: budget, timescale, space and the help available. Next, switch to emotional thinking and discuss what you want the décor to feel like, the colours you love and the memories you have of other beautiful homes. When you're ready, spend time checking for problems with any of the ideas mentioned. Then focus on the suggestions that fit perfectly and the benefits of doing it a certain way. Think as creatively as possible, looking for interesting ways of combining different ideas and achieving something original. Be clear about each new approach to the problem, maintaining 'process control'; repeat the sequence several times to help you return to key ideas, refining your thinking and shaping the best overall approach.

You might be chatting in the car about your child's next party, talking over the dinner table about their big homework project, or holding a 'family meeting' to solve a particular problem that's come up at school. As with so many of the techniques in this book, this approach helps you tackle the issue at hand as well as training your child's brain to cope with other challenges.

Thinking collaboratively like this helps them to work in groups, makes them keenly aware of the need to combine different perspectives and prepares them to take on any one of the key roles. It also boosts their independent work, giving them a range of strategies to incorporate into their flexible approach to thinking and learning.

Homework

For many families, homework is the most specific way in which they support their children's education. Schools approach homework in many different ways, and the details change as children grow; but whatever form your child's homework takes, it presents a huge opportunity to get involved in their learning and to boost their success.

It pays to find out about the school's homework policy. Prepare yourself for each new school year. Homework might not start until Year 3 or 4. It could be that even Reception children have something to do every night. Or maybe the school has decided against homework altogether. Consider these questions:

What day will homework be set, and when does it have to be returned?
Will there be any longer-term projects alongside the regular tasks?
How will the work be explained: on a sheet, in a particular folder, via email or on the school's website?

Talk about it all with your child and ensure they have a clear understanding of what homework will mean for them. Make it clear that homework is important enough to take seriously from the start.

Work out a system that fits your family life. Again, getting your child's agreement is essential. Discuss the pattern of your week and consider how homework can best slot into it. When would they like to do their homework? What's going to be the best way to avoid last-minute panics? How can you give them the support they need?

Make sure your child has somewhere suitable to work and all the equipment they need.

Think carefully about where your child will work best. Could they use your study or spare room as their 'office'? Maybe the kitchen table could be cleared and all their books laid out there. If they need to use the computer, is it in a place where you'll be able to help if necessary? Give them somewhere to work that's as comfortable, light, airy and calm as possible, free from distractions but close enough to get support if they need it.

When children start a homework task, help them to set a clear goal. Rather than choosing a target based purely on time, focus on what they're going to achieve. They need to know roughly how long it's going to take, but the really important thing is that they have a clear idea about the work they need to do. Ask them to explain it to you briefly and discuss how you'll both know that the target has been achieved. It might be a certain number of multiplication facts learnt, a written activity completed or a particular part of a model made and painted. In school they'll be used to discussing objectives and success criteria and it's important that they approach homework with the same clear vision and expectation of high standards.

Discussing the details of a task will help you to decide how much to help. Some tasks are clearly designed for children to try on their own, to rehearse techniques learnt in school and to show their teacher how much they can do independently. It's fine to offer advice and encouragement but if your child really struggles, their teacher needs to know. Leave a note in their book to show that they tried their best but need some more help.

Other types of homework require more collaboration. An increasing number of schools are choosing tasks that they hope will encourage parental involvement, providing opportunities for children to work with a range of family members. Take the chance to do your bit, but think carefully about what's in it for your child. What skills are they supposed to be developing? Are they meant to draw the castle and then help you build it, find materials for you to put together or build separate parts that you can assemble? If they're interviewing you about your childhood memories, are they meant to be asking questions, turning your answers into a story or just giving you a ready-made questionnaire to fill in? If they've been asked to find out about pandas, are they supposed to be extending knowledge they've gained in school or do they need you to help them learn from scratch?

Make sure you're absolutely clear what your child is supposed to be getting out of every homework activity. It's great to have fun together and rewarding to achieve a joint result, but these are learning opportunities for your child and they need to make the most of them. If you're unclear, never be afraid to ask their teacher for guidance.

Avoid the temptation to do the homework yourself. Homework is a joint exercise between your child, their school and you. It's a way of involving families in learning, showing them what their children are getting up to and inspiring useful discussions and activities. It helps children to further their interests and apply their knowledge and skills in new ways. It also trains them to take charge of their work and deliver quality results when their teacher is not by their side. So keep them on track, provide the appropriate resources and discuss their ideas but let them make the important decisions. Organize the library visit but don't choose all the books. Provide the computer but don't design the layout or change all the spellings. Support your child to produce homework that they can be proud of.

A BALANCED LIFE

Insight
Once in a while, take a 'snapshot' of your child's life. Consider the themes explored in this chapter and throughout the book.

Think about the quality of your child's diet, sleep and exercise. What opportunities do they get to work alone and with others of different ages? What are the key areas of their learning: the knowledge and skills they are developing, and the ways in which they are explored? What is the balance like between work and play? How much time do they spend using computers, television, board games or books? Do you have a chance to chat with them – about daily life, learning, memories or ideas? Is there evidence that they reflect on their own thinking and learning? How much fun did they have today?

Look for balance and find ways to make gradual adjustments. Ensure your child's life has the structure and security to nurture all their key thinking and learning skills. Make the most of everyday activities to support everything they're doing in school, but also drop in surprises and make plenty of time for freedom and fun. Build a family life that gives children the ability, enthusiasm and confidence to take charge of their own learning success.

10 THINGS TO REMEMBER

1 *Make sure your child's diet includes the key brain-building fatty acids, vitamins and minerals, especially during periods of rapid development.*

2 *Encourage them to eat slow-release carbohydrates to provide long-lasting energy and support concentration and good behaviour.*

3 *Children need a healthy breakfast, sensible snacks during the day, and plenty of water to hydrate their brains.*

4 *Be alert to foods that have a negative impact on your child's health and behaviour.*

5 *Give them a clear bedtime routine, remove all distractions and use baths, books and music to help them relax and sleep.*

6 *Make sure your child's mental activity is balanced by a range of physical sports and games.*

7 *Fill your child's life with fun and laughter, playing family games to support all their memory and learning skills.*

8 *Help them to use imagination and visualization to foster a flexible, resilient and confident approach to new challenges.*

9 *Find opportunities to try the 'thinking hats' technique as a whole family, working collaboratively to explore all the different thinking styles.*

10 *Give children the time, space and equipment they need to do their homework, providing targeted support that helps them get the most out of every task they're set.*

10

The end of primary – and beyond

In this chapter you will learn:
- *how your child is assessed and tested in primary school*
- *practical steps to support study, revision and preparation for assessments and tests*
- *how to respond to results and reports*
- *activities to help your child through the transition from primary to secondary school, dealing with all the practical and emotional challenges.*

Tests and assessment: what to expect

Your child is being assessed and tested throughout their primary school career. 'Formative testing' or AFL ('assessment for learning') includes all the ways their teachers monitor their progress and guide their learning accordingly. As well as looking at their work and discussing it with them, modern teachers have a wide range of other assessment techniques at their disposal: recording conversations, videoing drama and exploring computer files. Assessment has taken on a new dimension in primary schools, with the children themselves now expected to assess their own work and take responsibility for their own progress.

Alongside all the formative testing that affects what and how your child learns, 'summative testing' involves making more judgemental assessments of their performance. It uses specific tasks and compares their results with others in the class, against age expectations and even in the context of national or even international statistics. It involves spelling or times-table tests, end of topic or term assessment tasks, or formal tests marked externally and given official recognition. This form of testing is an endlessly controversial topic, subject to a great deal of political involvement and continually changing, but it has become a big part of our education system and it challenges all children to achieve their very best results.

Parents and teachers can also feel the pressure as the tests may be used to compare schools and affect children's future education. Towards the end of primary school they're likely to face tests that will at least affect the classes they're put in at secondary school, if not the choice of school itself. These tests will have a big impact on how others view their abilities and on how they feel about themselves.

Whatever attainment level your child is capable of, you can help them to do their very best in assessments and tests. Whether you agree with the system or not, they need to know how to shine in all the different types of tests they face, achieving their true potential in the short term as well as training themselves for the ever more significant exams they'll take in the future. Equip them with the right skills early and they can become confident test-takers, stay cool under pressure, show off everything they've learnt and gain from every assessment experience.

Motivation and your child

Motivation has been shown to be important in two different ways. It pushes children to devote more time to their preparation for tests and it inspires them to find the very best ways to ensure their success.

To help us survive, our brains naturally prioritize information that's relevant to us. Learning something will automatically be a struggle if your child can't see any benefit in doing so.

Talk to your child about their reasons for doing well. Try to get the balance right from the very start. You want them to do well because you know that they *can*. Failure in the test would only be bad because they wouldn't have demonstrated their talents. The assessment is important as a chance to shine and enjoy all the benefits.

So benefit number one becomes your pride and admiration. Don't burden them with worries about letting you down but give them something positive to aim for. Let them know that you want the very best for them and value their success. As with all their work, praise their effort and commitment. If the test has important ramifications then they need to know that, but don't stress them with fears of failure. Young children in particular need to know that tests really aren't a matter of life and death. What's important is that they do the very best they can.

What about the other benefits? You might make a list of all the positive effects of working hard, which could include:

- *making the most of all the preparation they've put in*
- *impressing their current and future teachers*
- *feeling good about their abilities*
- *getting into the right class or the best school for them*
- *learning useful study and exam skills for the future.*

They might turn their list into a poster, using words and images to remind them of the benefits of success.

They could use their visualization skills and imagine these positive outcomes. What will their teacher say to praise them? How will it feel when they know they've tried their hardest? What will their parents' happy faces look like?

To do well they'll need to extract most of their motivation from the task itself, but it can also help to add in a few additional rewards. We all like to have things to look forward to, so talk to your child about what would help to keep them focused and energetic, even if the going gets a little tough. Their answers might surprise you. Perhaps they'll ask for a day out, a particular computer game, or something less tangible like a new level of responsibility or freedom. Negotiate if necessary and make an agreement that suits you both. Be very clear about what earning this reward will involve: energy, persistence, and doing everything they can to succeed.

It's also a good idea to have some smaller, staged rewards along the way, especially if your child is starting a long preparation or revision process. Again, discuss the details with them and have fun agreeing the plan. You might wrap a small gift for them to open every Friday afternoon after a good week's work or decide that every evening session earns them games-console time, a new flavour of milkshake or tokens towards a cinema trip. Things don't have to cost much to become valuable treats, keeping children motivated to continue and eager to do their best.

Preparing for tests or exams

Check that your child has everything they need to prepare for the test. Their teacher should have communicated all the details clearly; if they haven't, chase them up. When is the test? What form will it take? What topics will be covered? What will the questions be like? You can usually get hold of past papers, either from the school, online or in printed books. There are also plenty of revision guides on the market for every conceivable test.

Insight
Before buying any support materials, talk to your child's teacher to find out which ones are appropriate. Giving your child information pitched at the wrong level or on different topics can easily do more harm than good.

PLANNING

Help your child to organize their time and put together a plan of action. Be realistic, think carefully about clubs and events, social activities and family commitments, and make sure your child has plenty of opportunities to relax and have fun. Make the most of their time by scheduling revision when they're best able to concentrate. Find slots in the week when they'll be fresh and energetic, and draw up a timetable; not a rigid schedule, but a guide to when they should be able to work well. This can also become a record of their success as they tick off each completed session or mark it with a stick-on star.

STUDY SPACES

As with homework, organize a suitable place for your child to do their work. Talk to them about where they study best, but make sure their ideas are realistic and honest. Some children really do work better with background noise and even music playing, but others clearly need silence. If they do want a soundtrack to their learning, the type of music they choose is important. Songs with clear lyrics are much more likely to be distracting than instrumental music, and any speech – if they're listening to the radio or music TV, for example – is most distracting of all. For this reason it's highly unlikely that television will help them to concentrate. Encourage them to use it as a reward when they've finished or to relax between sessions of work. Show them the benefits of a workspace that's calm, tidy, light, comfortable and appealing – with access to everything they need – and where distractions are kept to an absolute minimum.

REVISION SKILLS

Preparation for a test or exam involves strengthening understanding and knowledge, getting used to retrieving it efficiently, and thinking creatively about the best ways to put it to use.

Like any lesson in school, a good session at home begins with a very clear aim. Get your child into the habit of defining exactly what they're going to achieve. It might be 10 minutes spent practising times tables, 15 minutes revising everything they know about green plants, or 20 minutes writing powerful opening paragraphs. By the end of the session, what are they going to know or do better? Focusing on the benefits helps them to start with an energetic and positive approach.

It's a good idea to begin with things that they know. Encourage them to say out loud the most important information they can remember, then to spend a couple of minutes seeing where the ideas lead, for example:

'I know that the heart pumps blood and you need to keep it healthy. When you do exercise it beats faster. There are tubes leading out and in, arteries and… I can't remember the other sort. The heart is here in your chest. Smoking can be bad for your heart…and that's all I can remember.'

Questions play a key role in memory and learning, so it's very useful if your child can now suggest the questions that need answering:

'I've got to find out what the arteries do and what the other tubes are called. And I need to remember why your heartbeat goes up when you exercise.'

The next stage involves filling in gaps in their knowledge. This is where the books and notes they've gathered come into play. They can locate each missing detail, see how it fits in with all the rest of the information, and activate their learning skills to fix it into their memory:

'The arteries carry blood away from the heart. Veins are the other tubes, the ones that take the blood back in.'

The word 'artery' sounds like 'archery'; perhaps they imagine blood-red arrows shooting out of their heart. If they noticed the word 'in' inside 'vein', they'd have a clear memory clue – and could visualize a sign saying 'IN' printed on all the veins carrying blood into the heart.

'When you exercise, your muscles need more oxygen – which gets to them in the blood. So your heart has to beat faster to pump more blood to all the places it's needed.'

Understanding is an important part of remembering, and thinking through ideas like this is a good first step to learning them. But you can do much more to keep the memories strong.

Encourage children to visualize everything they learn. In this case, they might picture the circulation system, exaggerating its size and colour and zooming in on the key details. It might help them to imagine it as a computer animation, arrows and labels appearing to explain exactly what's going on.

Challenge them to activate their kinaesthetic learning skills. They could start jogging on the spot, feeling their muscles working and their heart pumping. They might imagine they're a blood cell and wander round the room, explaining their job and the journey they take.

Make sure they connect new ideas to the things they already know. Get them to think of examples and applications:

'Remember that time you ran all the way home from school and you were panting so hard. Your heart must have been going at top speed!'
'Imagine what's happening in that footballer's heart right now.'

SELF-TESTING

Show children that testing is a key part of learning. The most effective time to do it is when the information is still fairly fresh in their mind. Remind them to test themselves towards the end of their learning session – and perhaps an hour later – strengthening the memories and confirming that they're ready to move on.

Get them into the habit of testing from different 'directions', for example:

'What is an artery?'
'What are the tubes called that take blood out of the heart?'
'What affects how much oxygen muscles need?'
'Why do runners need healthy hearts?'

CONDENSING INFORMATION

Sometimes material needs to be simplified and condensed before it can be put through the process described above.

If your child was revising the seven 'life processes' common to all living things, they might be faced with several textbook pages or sheets of notes. They'd need to start by considering what they knew already and reading the material again; then it would be important to extract the essential details and focus on exactly what they needed to know.

In this case the information could be boiled down to just seven words: movement, respiration, sensitivity, growth, reproduction, excretion, nutrition. Your child would be able to use all their creative learning skills to memorize the seven key facts.

They might imagine moving around their science classroom (movement), breathing heavily (respiration), feeling their lungs become really sensitive (sensitivity) – then realizing that they were growing (growth), turning into not one but two giant versions of themselves, then three then four... (reproduction). They'd have to rush to the toilet in panic (excretion) then sit down for a nice slice of cake to get over the shock (nutrition).

Words, names, numbers, instructions...Your child knows how to learn them all, and they can use their revision sessions to reinforce everything they've studied. They can also add new bits of knowledge. This is a really effective way to boost children's success. They ask questions about a topic, explore it further, memorize the new information then connect it to everything they've already learnt.

JOINED-UP THINKING

If they were revising the names of 2D shapes they might ask themselves what 11- and 12-sided shapes are called. A quick bit of research would give them the answers 'hendecagon' and 'dodecagon', which they could then turn into memorable ideas: perhaps seeing a hen on deck with a gun, and throwing some dough at a duck banging a gong. They'd exaggerate the images, imagine all the senses and feelings involved, mime them – and finally link the new information to their established knowledge.

They could make a connection with other '-gon' shapes like 'polygon', 'hexagon', 'octagon'. They'd probably also realize that the 'dec' in 'dodecagon' means the same when it appears in words like 'decagon' and 'decimal'. Thinking and learning like this stimulates the brain in many directions, creating memories that are interconnected and strong.

PERSONAL LEARNING

Prompt your child to personalize information as much as possible. As always, imagination is the key. What would it feel like to be there at the Battle of Hastings, alongside Neil Armstrong on the Moon, or about to be sacrificed to the Aztec gods? What if they were small enough to be drawn up through the roots of a plant, carried like a seed on the wind, or squeezed through the tiny holes in some filter paper? Get them to imagine themselves 'into' their subject matter, talking it through out loud and acting out the key ideas whenever possible.

CREATIVE NOTE-TAKING

Children can also use paper and pens to strengthen their learning. Rather than simply copying out details or answering test questions, get them drawing memorable cartoons, detailed diagrams or multi-coloured key word lists. Give them a special exercise book or folder to hold their revision notes and encourage them to describe the images they remember when they're testing themselves, for example:

'The French word for apple is "pomme" and I remember drawing an apple tree covered in big fluffy pompoms.'
'Molars are good for chewing and grinding. I did a cartoon of a mole chewing on toffee.'

If their notes are interesting and unusual they'll remember exactly where on the page a particular detail is written, giving them extra visual and spatial memory triggers.

As well as using single images, scenes and longer stories to strengthen their memory, children can make powerful use of the 'journey' system described earlier as they prepare for tests and exams. They can fill familiar rooms, buildings and journeys with images to remind them of facts, people, instructions and ideas.

Their bedroom might store all the facts they know about Tudor buildings. They could use a route around the local shopping centre to hold all the techniques they want to use in an art assessment.

I show children in my class how to remember the skills they need to do well in writing tests, such as, they visualize a parachute hanging over the classroom door and remember to use *paragraphs*; they imagine two people having a noisy conversation on top of the bookcase and remember to include speech whenever it's appropriate; the alphabet spaghetti floating in the sink reminds them to check their spellings...

Train your child to use memory frameworks to hold all the information they need for tests and exams. The details are stored in the form of vivid images, activating their creative thinking and helping them to inject imagination into their answers. At the same time, the organized structures support logical thinking and bring efficiency and order to their test-taking approach. Each 'memory journey' activates whole-brain thinking and boosts children's success – even before they've begun applying the important information it contains.

MENTAL REHEARSAL

In the same way that athletes run races in their imagination before taking to the track for real, your child can prepare for a test by rehearsing it in their mind. It helps them to focus on the practical details as well as rehearsing the tactics that will have most impact on their success.

- ▶ *Get them to imagine they're sitting in the exam room, ready to start the test.*
- ▶ *Emphasize all the positive feelings that will help them to do well.*
- ▶ *Prompt them to think about all the work they've done to prepare themselves and the confidence it should give them.*
- ▶ *Suggest that they use warm, friendly colours to make this scene as relaxed and stress-free as possible.*
- ▶ *Talk them through a successful test. Help your child to see themselves:*
  - ▷ *listening carefully to the instructions*
  - ▷ *skimming through the whole paper before starting to write*
  - ▷ *reading each question carefully*
  - ▷ *looking to see how many marks each question is worth*
  - ▷ *accessing their memory in the most powerful ways*
  - ▷ *using their equipment calmly and effectively*
  - ▷ *staying cool, keeping an eye on the clock and working quickly and carefully to write accurate and imaginative answers to every question*
  - ▷ *leaving enough time to check their work.*

Let your child build up positive 'experiences' of tests before they've even happened. Get them into the right habits and help them to build a rich understanding of what test success involves – and how it feels.

They might even visualize someone marking their work. It's a good idea to remember that a real person will be going through every answer, looking for ways to award marks. Discuss this scenario in the most positive terms. The marker is there to reward good answers and find evidence of knowledge and skill. Ask your child:

'Will the marker be able to read what you have written?'
'Is every answer clearly explained?'
'What will the marker's face look like when they spot another sparkling answer and write down yet another big green tick?'

Insight
When the test is over, discuss how it went and focus on the most positive aspects... then help your child to switch off, relax and celebrate their hard work.

Making the most of the results

When you receive the results, think carefully about what they actually mean. They'll certainly provide evidence about your child's ability in a particular subject, but they're also just a snapshot of their success in one test on one day. Talk to their teacher about how the results will be used and how you can all work together to make the most of them.

Every test a child takes is just another step on their learning journey. The results provide clues about where their particular talents may lie and which areas need more support. Test-taking is a skill in itself which can be improved by using all the strategies explored above, but it takes practice. By their very nature, tests are unpredictable. Help your child to keep setbacks in perspective, to learn from each assessment they undergo and to use the results to guide their future study.

Show children that testing is a useful and challenging part of the lifelong learning process, and make sure they enjoy all the small victories along the way.

School reports

Your child's school will send home a written report at least once a year. This will provide a summary of the work covered in every subject, along with comments about their progress – including an overall assessment of their learning skills, behaviour and attitude to school itself.

Schools approach reports in different ways but the common practice now is to use software programs to speed up the process. Teachers have a range of pre-written statements to choose from, modify and combine with their own original words. Some parts of a report may be the same for every child in class – for example, details of topics studied – and two reports may actually look very similar, with just subtle differences in a few key words. It's important to read your child's report carefully, focusing on the details that say the most about their performance.

As with test results, make sure you keep the information in perspective; but also clarify any points that are unclear. Some aspects of the report may surprise you – for good or bad – but remember that their teacher has had a whole year to get to know them, to compare them with others and to see what they're like when you're not around.

Insight

Teachers should be able to provide evidence for every judgement they make; so if it's not there in the report and you're concerned, follow it up.

Treat the report with respect, use it to shape the way you support your child but remember that much of it will be subjective – the view of just one teacher. If anything surprises you, look for evidence elsewhere. What did previous reports say? What can other adults tell you? What do *you* observe in your child's learning, behaviour or attitude?

If something has changed, or there's a significant difference in opinions, think carefully about why that might be and how you can find out more. The most useful form of assessment is one that moves your child forward and to do that it needs to be detailed, accurate and balanced.

Transition to secondary school

The collaboration between child, parent and school becomes particularly important towards the end of the primary phase. Tests results and reports help to determine what happens next, but there are several other things that ensure a successful transition to secondary school.

Primary teachers work hard to prepare children for the challenges of secondary school. In their final year, PSHE work often concentrates on change and feelings about it. Schools work to reassure children about what's ahead while also giving them tactics to cope with it. It's an approach that needs to be supported at home.

Talk to your child about exactly what's happening to them. Start with the things that *aren't* changing. Make a list of everything that will be as true in their new school as it's always been: the support of family and friends; the opportunities to learn and grow; the need to live and work as part of a school community; the importance of trying their best. Focus on the aspects of their home life, friendships, and out-of-school activities that will continue unchanged.

Then list the things that *are* about to change: school location, journey, lesson times, homework, teachers, friends… Whenever possible focus on the positives, the exciting opportunities. Talk about all the things your child is looking forward to, as well as the things that will be more of a challenge. Helping them form a balanced picture of the next stage in their education is a crucial first step to coping with it.

DEALING WITH WORRIES

Return to the 'emotion meter' exercise described in the previous chapter. Draw a line from 'absolutely terrified' to 'can't wait' and use it to plot your child's feelings about some of the following issues:

- ▶ *leaving their current school*
- ▶ *making new friends*
- ▶ *trying different subjects*
- ▶ *travelling on the school bus*
- ▶ *buying their own lunch*
- ▶ *finding their way around a bigger school*
- ▶ *having more homework.*

As well as reflecting on their current state of mind, discuss how they felt in the past – and consider what their responses might be in the future.

So if they put 'leaving their current school' two-thirds of the way along the line (close to being 'completely happy' about it) ask them whether that was always the case. Would they have been quite so confident a couple of years ago? And can they imagine the feeling moving even further along the line as the time to move schools gets closer?

Perhaps 'travelling on the school bus' gets a much more negative response. It may be close to the 'absolutely terrified' end of the line now; but what would their reaction have been when they were five – when going on *any* form of transport was a thrill? Do they think it's likely to seem less scary when they've done it a few times?

Feelings are fluid. Helping your child to understand that will prepare them to take control and start changing them. All their key thinking skills can help them move their feelings about secondary school towards the positive end of the line.

To gain more confidence about making new friends, they could remember strong friendships they've formed in the past, think logically about other people's worries and imagine how good it will feel to make one new friend, then two, then three...

And as well as thinking in different ways, encourage them to make a list of some of the practical things that might help, such as:

▶ *there'll be at least one 'taster day' for them to meet new classmates*
▶ *their teacher will help them get to know each other*
▶ *they've got three older friends at the school already.*

How could they become more positive about lunchtimes? They could remember the wide range of foods they enjoy; think how lucky they are to choose their own food; imagine the fun of handling money; and perhaps do some practice in advance, buying their own lunch in a café or making more choices in the supermarket.

Use the 'emotion meter' to talk about how they're feeling, as well as to suggest ways of boosting their confidence. At each stage of their education – and particularly at times of big change – your child's emotional stability will play a huge part in their success.

PRACTICAL PREPARATIONS

Information is key. Make sure your child has access to all the details they need about life in their new school: from letters, leaflets, websites and by visiting the school and talking to children who are already there. Do extra research of your own if your child still has questions.

Buy their uniform early and get hold of all the equipment they'll need: books, folders, writing equipment, sports gear and bags. Avoid last-minute panics and help your child feel confident that they have everything they need to fit in and do well.

Plan for the first day, week and term. Discuss how family routines will change to accommodate new travel arrangements, school times and homework expectations. Don't just expect everything to fall into place. Your child needs to see exactly how they're going to be able to cope with their new school life and what their family will do to support them. A clear plan can take away a great deal of uncertainty and stress.

VISUALIZATION

Make the most of your child's trained imagination to boost their confidence. Encourage them to visualize their first day at school, from the time they wake up to the moment they go to bed. Prompt them to consider their feelings as well as their actions, seeing themselves coping with each element of the day in turn. They can build a sense of security and calm by choosing warm, happy colours for the pictures they see and adding other senses that comfort them. Their mental movie camera can choose the most helpful angles: perhaps taking a wide view to see all the other children in the same situation, or zooming in on the best friend, cool new bag or helpful form tutor.

They can use this technique whenever their confidence needs a boost. If they face a new challenge – their first swimming lesson, speaking in assembly, starting a new after-school club – encourage them to 'experience' it beforehand in their imagination. Talk about their feelings and whether there's anything else you could do to help.

After the event, tap into their visualization again as they discuss what went well and what they could learn for next time. Keep reinforcing the fact that feelings are changeable and that their flexible thinking and learning skills will help them cope with every new challenge in school.

ORGANIZATION

Throughout their education, children need to be organized and in control of their possessions, their time and all the tasks they need to complete. Organization becomes particularly important when they move to secondary school. Suddenly they have a much more complicated timetable to negotiate, along with many more teachers to deal with and classrooms to find. Their workload increases, in school and at home, and there are many new opportunities for sport, drama and a range of other extra-curricular activities. The ability to organize themselves is a vital part of their success – so don't leave it too late. As soon at they start primary school, you can be getting them into the right habits and training them to look after themselves.

Developing your child's memory plays an important role. It gives them the confidence to extract all the information they need and to find effective ways of remembering it. They can use timetables and homework diaries creatively, leaving themselves colourful illustrations and memorable notes. They have a repertoire of skills to store all the different types of practical information they're given.

A useful strategy for boosting organization involves turning a familiar place into a 'storeroom' for memories. It's a great way to help children stay in control of their busy lives.

Work with them to choose their own personal storeroom. It needs to be the 'virtual' version of a real place that they see at least a couple of times every day. They might choose the cupboard by the front door, a shop on the way to and from school or the office next to their classroom. Prompt them to visualize it as clearly as possible, exploring how it looks, smells and feels.

Any piece of practical information can then be turned into an image and fixed firmly into your child's personal store. As always, imagination is vital to making the pictures as unusual, exaggerated and memorable as possible.

To remember to hand in a letter about swimming lessons, they could imagine hanging a wet towel on the door of their memory store. If your child needed to remember to bring their violin for orchestra practice, they might picture a famous violinist giving the world premiere of a new piece of music, standing there in the middle of their familiar room. Imagining the floor covered in a sticky mess of flour and eggs would remind them about the cooking ingredients they needed to bring in.

Every time your child passes by the real location – the cupboard, shop, office or wherever – they'll be reminded to check their virtual room and find the clues they left there. They could also get into the habit of going there at fixed points in the day: at breakfast time; during classroom registration; when the bell rings at the end of the day.

When you give them important details to remember, you'll be able to suggest memorable ways of adding them to their growing collection of images:

'Please can you remember to sign up for the nature trip today? How about imagining flowers and butterflies all over the walls of your memory room?'
'Make sure you hand in your French project. What if the Eiffel Tower suddenly appeared right there in the middle of the room?'
'You're going to Ellie's house after school today. Draw a big smiley picture of her on the ceiling to make sure you don't forget!'

'Prospective memory' – remembering to do things in the future – is one of the hardest forms of memory to control, but this technique gives children a much better chance of success. It makes them think carefully about each instruction and prompts them to do something to try to learn it. It gets them into the habit of checking their memory store, keeping it accurate and up to date and using it to remember their own brilliant ideas and exciting plans as much as the practical tasks of everyday life in school.

Learning communities

There's an old saying that it takes a village to bring up a child. All the techniques in this book are about empowering children to shape their own success, using all the help on offer from parents and teachers. But there are many other sources of support: their friends, siblings, extended family and the rich collection of people that make up all the different communities they join.

Be alert to all the opportunities for enriching your child's study by using other people's expertise. If they're particularly interested in a subject or need some extra support, think about the people you know who might be able to help. A simple conversation could be enough to deepen their excitement or answer a specific question. It might be possible to borrow books or equipment or even organize a workplace visit. Just meeting someone else with a passion for a subject can be motivating and empowering.

If your child is exploring a particular topic at school, it's possible that you know people who could share their own knowledge and experiences. Which friend has visited the country, done the job, owned the animal – or studied the topic themselves? Involve your child in requesting help. Perhaps they could make a phone call or send an email, or at least suggest how they'd like this person to help. It could be an interview, a tour, a demonstration, a slideshow. This friendly expert might read their work or even come into school to talk to the rest of their class.

Encourage your child to collaborate as widely and creatively as possible. Let them experiment, but also help them to reflect honestly on how it's going. If their approach is focused and their targets clear, they'll know whether a particular person is helping or hindering their learning.

LEARNING PARTNERS

At its best, working with others can be an enjoyable and energetic way of sharing ideas, exploring information in new ways and testing understanding and recall.

Your children can try learning with school friends, people they know from their neighbourhood or the clubs and teams they're part of – or even children they meet online. As with all electronic communication, monitor this carefully, give them all the tools they need to say safe, liaise with teachers about what would be helpful and appropriate, but do grab the chances when they appear.

Think about organizations that might connect your child with other maths fans, budding writers or scientists in the making. Explore ways to let them communicate with people who could stimulate their interest and deepen their understanding.

Show your child how to take a wide view of their learning and seize every opportunity to tap into the knowledge, skill and wisdom of others.

Through their experiences at home and in school, and by accessing all these other sources of support, your child can take up their place in a large and vibrant community of learners.

10 THINGS TO REMEMBER

1 Children need to be motivated to achieve their full potential in school, so show them all the pleasures and benefits of doing their very best.

2 Teach your child to organize their work and to plan their time and effort carefully.

3 Provide a place where they can think and learn without distractions.

4 Encourage children to use their full range of thinking and learning skills to drive their study and revision, making creative notes, exploring information with their whole brain, and using memory techniques to store and access their knowledge flexibly and efficiently.

5 Train them to rehearse for tests in their imagination, developing a strategic and confident approach to every kind of assessment in school.

6 Read results and reports carefully, keep them in perspective and work with schools to find the best way forward for your child.

7 Visualization techniques can help children to explore and control their feelings about moving on to secondary school.

8 Give them the practical help they need to prepare for the transition, making sure they have all the information and equipment they need and adapting your family life to suit all the requirements of their new school.

9 *Teaching your child the 'memory storeroom' technique prepares them for the increased demands on their organization, time-management and learning skills.*

10 *Take every opportunity to connect your child with people who can help their learning, showing them the benefits of being part of many different learning communities.*

Afterword

The twentieth century Antarctic explorer Ernest Shackleton proved his leadership skills on countless occasions. He was an inspirational figure, commanding huge respect and consistently getting the very best out of all the men in his charge. He inspired and nurtured them to achieve their full potential, making them brilliant in their different ways, often against all the odds.

In *Shackleton's Way*, Margot Morrell and Stephanie Capparell identify eight key elements in his approach to leadership. They represent so many of the key skills necessary for leading children's learning.

1 *Shackleton made sure his men's working environment was as good as it could be: effective for them all but also influenced by individuals' preferences.*
2 *He was a sound believer in the importance of having healthy bodies and healthy minds.*
3 *Shackleton knew that, to work well, people have to be given tasks that are challenging and important.*
4 *He put a great deal of effort into understanding his men, helping them to make the most of their different styles of thinking and working.*
5 *He gave feedback regularly and consistently and used it to support, guide and inspire.*
6 *Shackleton knew the importance of human connections: the interest and attention that would help his men feel valued and want to give their all.*
7 *He chose his rewards carefully, to motivate effort as well as to celebrate success.*
8 *Through it all – in the harshest conditions and toughest challenges – he was endlessly tolerant, able to accept his men for the people they were while still doing everything possible to ensure their success.*

Learn from Ernest Shackleton. Take your leadership responsibilities seriously. Do everything you can to support, nurture, challenge, understand, praise, value, motivate – and finally, accept your child's particular form of brilliance.

Make the most of these magical years, and enjoy all the learning adventures you take together.

Taking it further

Books

Edward de Bono, *Six Thinking Hats* (Penguin, 2000).

Karen Doherty and Georgia Coleridge, *Seven Secrets of Successful Parenting* (Bantam Press, 2008).

Joan Freeman, *How to Raise a Bright Child* (Vermillion, 1996).

Howard Gardner, *Multiple Intelligences: The Theory in Practice* (Basic Books, 1993).

John Gottman and Joan Declaire, *Raising an Emotionally Intelligent Child* (Simon and Schuster, 1998).

Stephen Hastings, *School Smart* (Virgin Books, 2007).

Richard Layard and Judy Dunn, *A Good Childhood* (Penguin, 2009).

Helen Likierman and Valerie Muter, *Top Tips for Starting School* (Vermillion, 2008).

Tessa Livingstone, *A Child of Our Time: Early Learning* (Bantam Press, 2008).

Bill Lucas and Alastair Smith, *Help Your Child to Succeed* (Continuum, 2009).

Sue Palmer, *Detoxing Childhood* (Orion Books, 2007).

Alex Richardson, *They Are What You Feed Them* (HarperThorsons, 2006).

Tim Seldin, *How to Raise an Amazing Child* (Dorling Kindersley, 2007).

Patience Thomson, *101 Ways to Get Your Child to Read* (Barrington Stoke, 2009).

Bernadette Tynan, *Make Your Child Brilliant* (Quadrille, 2008).

Glenda Weil and Doro Marden, *Raise Happy Children* (Hodder Education, 2010).

Dominic Wyse, *How to Help Your Child Read and Write* (Pearson Education, 2007).

Websites

www.allkindsofminds.org
Ideas for using the latest research into learning to boost children's success in school.

www.bbc.co.uk/parenting
News, information and activities relating to every aspect of family life.

www.juniormemorychampionship.com
A national project to develop memory skills in schools, challenging primary children to maximize their learning power.

www.learningskillsfoundation.com
Research, development and promotion of learning skills – and a variety of ways to join the educational debate.

www.campaign-for-learning.org.uk
Removing barriers to education and promoting lifelong learning.

www.literacytrust.co.uk
A campaign to improve public understanding of literacy, offering projects to help anyone improve their skills.

www.parentlineplus.org.uk
Help and advice from a national parenting charity.

www.parentscentre.gov.uk
The latest news about education and family life, and wide-ranging advice to help parents support their children's learning.

Index